Fog Computing

Fog Computing

Concepts, Frameworks, and Applications

Edited by
Ravi Tomar, Avita Katal, Susheela Dahiya,
Niharika Singh, and Tanupriya Choudhury

CRC Press
Taylor & Francis Group
Boca Raton London New York

CRC Press is an imprint of the
Taylor & Francis Group, an **informa** business

A CHAPMAN & HALL BOOK

First edition published 2023
by CRC Press
6000 Broken Sound Parkway NW, Suite 300, Boca Raton, FL 33487–2742

and by CRC Press
4 Park Square, Milton Park, Abingdon, Oxon, OX14 4RN

CRC Press is an imprint of Taylor & Francis Group, LLC

Library of Congress Cataloging-in-Publication Data
Names: Tomar, Ravi, editor. | Katal, Avita, editor. | Dahiya, Susheela, editor. | Singh, Niharika (Professor of computer science), editor. | Choudhury, Tanupriya, editor.
Title: Fog computing : concepts, frameworks, and applications / edited by Ravi Tomar, Avita Katal, Susheela Dahiya, Niharika Singh, Tanupriya Choudhury.
Description: First edition. | Boca Raton : Chapman & Hall/CRC Press, 2022. | Includes bibliographical references and index.
Identifiers: LCCN 2022002014 (print) | LCCN 2022002015 (ebook) | ISBN 9781032036199 (hardback) | ISBN 9781032036205 (paperback) | ISBN 9781003188230 (ebook)
Subjects: LCSH: Cloud computing. | Edge computing. | Mobile computing. | Internet of things.
Classification: LCC QA76.585 .F644 2022 (print) | LCC QA76.585 (ebook) | DDC 004.67/82—dc23/eng/20220416
LC record available at https://lccn.loc.gov/2022002014
LC ebook record available at https://lccn.loc.gov/2022002015

ISBN: 978-1-032-03619-9 (hbk)
ISBN: 978-1-032-03620-5 (pbk)
ISBN: 978-1-003-18823-0 (ebk)

DOI: 10.1201/9781003188230

Typeset in Palatino
by Apex CoVantage, LLC

Contents

v

Preface

This book is intended as a reference material for students, educators, researchers, professionals and developers who are involved or have a keen interest in the domain of fog computing.

Fog computing, a state-of-the-art technology, extends the cloud computing paradigm to the edge of current networks. It reduces the latency in the network, increases business agility and provides less response time. The Internet of Things (IoT) is increasing rapidly, and there is a lot of data being generated by sensors. Before the advent of fog computing, the data being generated by IOT devices used to move to the cloud for processing and computation, which led to the various problems like latency, increase in response time, etc. Fog computing, also known as fogging, is a distributed infrastructure in which the management of some applications and services is done by a smart device at the edge of the network. The fog nodes act as mediator between the cloud server and the hardware so that the processing, analysis and storage of data is efficient. This can be achieved by reducing the traffic in the cloud.

This book provides an overview of the innovative concepts, methodologies and frameworks of fog computing. The book discusses topics such as the basics of fog computing to help readers understand the technology from the ground up, details about the infrastructure and the integration of IoT, fog and cloud computing to help readers in gaining deeper insights into the technology. This book includes chapters for the role of fog computing in the IoT applications, along with the use of software defined networking and machine learning in implementing an efficient fog computing environment. It also discusses the use of communication protocols for secure communication, simulation tools for fog computing and the role of blockchain technology for providing a secured fog computing environment. This book will be a readily accessible source of information for researchers in the area of distributed computing as well as for professionals who want to enhance their security and connectivity knowledge in IoT systems.

This book contains fifteen chapters, which are organized in a proper manner so that a beginner can benefit from this material without any prior knowledge about fog computing. The book also includes the use of emerging technologies like blockchain and machine learning with fog computing.

Chapter 1 is about *Fog Computing: Present and Future*. As the title suggests, this chapter discusses what fog computing is and why it is a necessary paradigm for cloud computing. An overview of three main components of fog computing (i.e. Infrastructure, Platform and Application) is presented in this chapter. This chapter also discusses the real-time uses of fog computing and how it is helping industries efficiently shift to the cloud. This chapter also looks at the opportunities and issues that fog computing presents in both the research and development side and the implementation side.

Chapter 2 discusses *Fog Computing: Foundation and Outline*. The authors found that fog computing performs better compared to the cloud in fulfilling the present need of arising ideal models that require quicker handling and less deferral. The authors also mention, however, that there is no fog without a cloud. The two of them exist together, serving two unique areas and supplementing each other any place required.

The Use of Machine Learning in Fog Computing is discussed in Chapter 3. Machine learning is used extensively in fog computing to provide more efficient models with security mechanisms for detection of different attacks. Machine learning assists in providing efficient processing, computation and management of huge amounts of data that is being generated and analyzed. The most widely deployed supervised learning techniques like linear regression, Support Vector Machine (SVM), decision trees, random forest and regression models in machine learning, along with the challenges and issues are also discussed in this chapter. The authors conclude that despite the issues, machine learning plays a significant role in improvement of performance, accuracy, and security of fog computing applications.

The *Application of Machine Learning in Fog Computing* is presented in Chapter 4. This chapter has aimed to outline the functions and features of fog computing and machine learning and how they can work in confluence to yield a production-ready environment. The chapter discusses various machine learning applications in fog computing, from software aspects like data processing and distribution to hardware aspects like energy consumption and resource allocation processes. The chapter also discusses how machine learning has served to enhance security and privacy in the fog network, as the data procured and produced by the fog and edge devices are sensitive to individual users. The chapter also reviews the open issues and topics of research that provide even more promising applications of fog computing in an increasing variety of sectors.

Chapter 5 presents the *Simulation and Modeling Tools for Fog Computing*. This chapter provides an overview of frameworks and modelling tools that allow the design and testing of fog solutions. Also, a short practical tutorial on installing and configuring fog virtualized testing environments is provided in this chapter. In addition, the current stage of development, challenges and research directions in fog simulation are discussed. This chapter also discusses current fog modelling tools for fog computing and presents the most recent studies found in the literature.

Security and Privacy Issues in Fog Computing are discussed in Chapter 6. The purpose of the presented study is to identify possible security and privacy concerns that are neglected by many IoT devices and their applications. The need of fog computing in real-world applications and related security concerns are also examined. Security and privacy concerns related to user data being transmitted across fog platforms are discussed, along with the security measures that need to be implemented to enhance security across the fog system.

Chapter 7 is about *Leveraging Fog Computing for the Internet of Medical Things*. The introduction to fog computing, the general architecture and features of fog computing are presented in this chapter. This chapter gives detailed information about the services provided by the fog layer like data management, event management, resource efficiency, etc. A new architecture for the Internet of Medical Things with fog computing is proposed, and a discussion about the daily monitoring and healthcare service provisions is also included. In addition, the healthcare use cases of fog computing are also discussed. The chapter concludes with a list of issues that need to be addressed in order to improve Internet of Things applications by extending the functionality of emerging fog computing.

Chapter 8 features *A Single-Point Control System for Consumer Devices Using Edge-Fog Computing*. The research work proposed a Convolutional Neural Network (CNN) model for selecting the device and controlling the consumer device function using a laptop that acts as an edge device. The proposed model uses the camera and microphone of a laptop for selecting a device and its function, unlike earlier work using sensors or other wearable devices. The proposed model uses real time image processing for controlling the range of function that wasn't performed before. The proposed model can be used for complex natural voice recognition functions. We believe that this methodology helps other researchers in the area of single point control systems.

Chapter 9 is about *Fog Computing: A Peek into Communication Security*. Fog networking/computing is known as a decentralized and distributed computing infrastructure in which various endpoints are sending and receiving data and storing them. The various responsibilities are scattered in the most logical and efficient layer in this distributed system, which makes it more effective in terms of the serviceability to the end-user as compared to traditional models like cloud computing. Since it is more robust than the cloud, it has more doors for security loopholes and challenges when it comes to implementation. The algorithms and methods used to handle the security challenges along with their emergence over time are explained in this chapter. The authors conclude that the implementation of security and privacy methods/algorithms is challenging in fog, as different situations might need different solutions for a single application.

Chapter 10 is about *Fog Computing and Machine Learning*. In this chapter, the author talks about fog computing and how it can be paired with machine learning to enhance fog technology and expand its possible uses. Along with the difference between cloud computing and fog computing, the author also talks about machine learning, its pros and cons, implementation strategies and implementation steps. In addition, the applications of machine learning in fog computing, its benefits and challenges, and popular examples of how it is utilized with machine learning are discussed in this chapter.

Chapter 11 presents *Communication Protocols in Fog Computing: A Survey and Challenges*. This chapter provides an introduction to fog computing as well as its overall architecture and benefits. The services provided by fog computing are also discussed in this chapter. The chapter gives detailed information about the various communication protocols like HTTP, MQTT, CoAP, etc. along with the comparison of different protocols based on different parameters. The chapter concludes with the list of research challenges in each protocol.

Chapter 12, *Fog Computing, Today and in the Future with IoT*, discusses fog computing as the best alternative for the Internet of Things to be supported by multiple IoT clients from a competent and comprehensive standpoint.

Integration and Application of Fog, IoT and Edge Computing are the topics discussed in Chapter 13. Herein, the concept of Internet of Things with various architectures that have evolved so far with technologies of IoT, fog and edge computing in the domain of IoT are introduced, and then IoT challenges are illustrated. Edge or fog computing is introduced with its needs and challenges. And further, various applications that have evolved so far in fog, IoT and edge computing are discussed along with the detailed illustration of the deployment models of these applications, along with the required middleware.

Chapter 14 presents *The Role of Block Chain in Fog Computing*. This chapter has approached the data-sharing mechanism using meta-key in which nodes Location of Information (LoI) have encrypted their data under block chain-based fog computing. Information encrypted by owners' public key inhibits the process of key management in block chain. By using encryption data that has been stored in their resolute storage edges, re-encryption techniques are used to secure shared data in an insecure environment. Security analysis of this mechanism exposes traffic-free encryption among the nodes with its specified meta-key architecture. This study explains the roles of security management mechanism and analysis of block chain in fog computing integration. By using key-management technique, this study discusses and clarifies the vision of the integration of block chain in fog computing along with the open issues and future research directions.

Chapter 15 is about *Fog Computing Framework: Mitigating Latency in Supply Chain Management*. The chapter proposes an approach for improving supply chain performance based on fog computing, IoT technology, and cloud computing and mitigating latency issues. The key characteristics of fog computing and a comparison of fog with cloud computing are also discussed in this chapter. This chapter shows how fog is complementary to cloud technology and supports virtualization. A few parallel computing paradigms are also discussed and compared with fog computing. Fog computing applications in warehousing management, with a fog framework to support drone delivery for efficient supply chain management, are also discussed.

The chapters presented here are latest research works in the domain of fog computing. We hope that our efforts are appreciated and the reader benefits from this book.

The Editors

Ravi Tomar
Avita Katal
Susheela Dahiya
Niharika Singh
Tanupriya Choudhury

Author/Editor Biographies

Biographies

Ravi Tomar

Dr. Ravi Tomar is currently working as Associate Professor in the School of Computer Science at the University of Petroleum and Energy Studies, Dehradun, India. He is an experienced academician with a demonstrated history of working in the higher education industry. He is skilled in programming, computer networking, stream processing, Python, Oracle Database, C++, Core Java, J2EE, RPA, and CorDApp. His research interests include wireless sensor networks, image processing, data mining and warehousing, computer networks, big data technologies, and VANET. He has authored over 51 papers in different research areas, filed four Indian patents, edited five books, and authored four books. He has delivered training to corporations nationally and internationally on Confluent Apache Kafka, stream processing, RPA, CordaApp, J2EE, and IoT to clients like KeyBank, Accenture, Union Bank of Philippines, Ernst and Young, and Deloitte. Dr. Tomar is officially recognized as Instructor for Confluent and CordApp. He has conducted various international conferences in India, France, and Nepal. He has been awarded a Young Researcher Award in Computer Science and Engineering by RedInno, India, in 2018 and an Academic Excellence and Research Excellence Award by UPES in 2021.

Avita Katal

Ms. Avita Katal is working as Assistant Professor (SS) in the School of Computer Science, University of Petroleum and Energy Studies, Dehradun, Uttarakhand, India. She has received her B.E. degree from University of Jammu in computer science engineering in 2010 and M. Tech degree from Graphic Era University, Dehradun in 2013. She has a postgraduate certificate in academic practice (PGCAP) and is currently pursuing her Ph.D. in the area of cloud computing from University of Petroleum and Energy Studies, Dehradun, India. Her research interest is in the areas of cloud computing, fog computing, mobile ad hoc networks, blockchain, IoT, and artificial intelligence. She has published various research papers and has also served as a reviewer for renowned conferences and journals. She has a keen interest in improving teaching pedagogies and has participated in various faculty development programs. She is actively involved in all areas of education including research, curriculum development, teacher mentoring, student career preparation, and community work with a genuine interest in students' cognitive and social growth.

Dr. Susheela Dahiya

Dr. Susheela Dahiya is currently working as an assistant professor (Selection Grade) in the School of Computer Science at the University of Petroleum and Energy Studies, Dehradun, Uttarakhand, India. She received her M.Tech (computer science and engineering) in 2008 and her Ph.D. in 2015 from the Indian Institute of Technology Roorkee. She also qualified GATE and NET in computer science. She has more than nine years of academic/research/industry experience. Her research interests include image and video processing, IoT, cyber security, cloud computing, and deep learning. She has authored several research papers in renowned conferences, Scopus, and SCI journals.

Niharika Singh

Dr. Niharika Singh received her doctorate degree in CSE from University of Petroleum and Energy Studies, her master's degree in CSE from University of Petroleum and Energy Studies and her bachelor's degree in ECE from Uttar Pradesh Technical University. She has more than seven years of experience in teaching and research. She is currently working as Assistant Professor in the School of Computer Science, University of Petroleum and Energy Studies (UPES) Dehradun. Her areas of research are artificial intelligence, machine learning, soft computing, and image processing. She has authored many research papers in various conferences and journals.

Tanupriya Choudhury

Dr. Tanupriya Choudhury received his bachelor's degree in CSE from West Bengal University of Technology, Kolkata, India, and his master's degree in CSE from Dr. M.G.R University, Chennai, India. He received his Ph.D. in 2016. He has ten years' experience in teaching as well as in research. Currently he is working as an associate professor in the Department of CSE at UPES Dehradun. Recently he has received a Global Outreach Education Award for Excellence and Best Young Researcher Award in GOECA 2018. His areas of interests include human computing, soft computing, cloud computing, data mining, etc. He has filed 14 patents to date and received 16 copyrights from MHRD for his own software. He has been associated with many conferences in India and abroad. He has authored more than 85 research papers to date. He has delivered invited talks and guest lectures in Jamia Millia Islamia University, Maharaja Agersen College of Delhi University, Duy Tan University Vietnam, etc. He has been associated with many conferences throughout India as TPC member and session chair, etc. He is a lifetime member of IETA, member of IEEE, member of IET (UK), and other renowned technical societies. He is associated with Corporate and he is Technical Adviser of DeetyaSoft Pvt. Ltd. Noida, IVRGURU, and Mydigital360. He holds the post of Secretary in IETA (Indian Engineering Teacher's Association-India) and the Advisor position in INDO-UK Confederation of Science, Technology and Research Ltd, London, UK and the International Association of Professional and Fellow Engineers in Delaware, USA.

Contributors

*indicates corresponding author.

Ajay K. Sharma
Department of Computer Science
National Institute of Technology Delhi
Delhi, India

Dr. Ajay Singh
ABES Engineering College
Ghaziabad, India

*Antonio A. T. R Coutinho
State University of Feira de Santana
Bahia, Brazil

Anurag Mor
School of Computer Science and Engineering
University of Petroleum and Energy
    Studies
Dehradun, India

Ashok Kumar
Department of Computer Science
Government Women Engineering College
Ajmer, Rajasthan

*Avita Katal
School of Computer Science
University of Petroleum and Energy
    Studies
Dehradun, India

Elisangela O. Carneiro
State University of Feira de Santana
Bahia, Brazil

Fabíola Greve
Institute of Computing
Federal University of Bahia
Salvador, Brazil

*Hitesh Kumar Sharma
School of Computer Science
University of Petroleum and Energy Studies
Dehradun, India

*Kabir Jaiswal
School of Computer Science
University of Petroleum and Energy Studies
Dehradun, India

*Karan Verma
Department of Computer Science
National Institute of Technology Delhi
Delhi, India

*Kartik Agarwal
School of Computer Science
University of Petroleum and Energy Studies
Dehradun, India

*Kaustubh Lohani
School of Computer Science
University of Petroleum and Energy Studies
Dehradun, India

Keshav Kaushik
School of Computer Science
University of Petroleum and Energy Studies
Dehradun, India

*Mohammed Ali Shaik
School of Computer Science and
    Artifical Intelligence
SR University
Warangal Telangana, India

*Niharika Singh
School of Computer Science
University of Petroleum and Energy Studies
Dehradun, India

*Parminder Singh Sethi
Dell Technologies
Banglore, India

Prajwal Bhardwaj
School of Computer Science
University of Petroleum and Energy
    Studies, Dehradun
Uttrakhand, India

Prashant Kumar
Department of Computer Science
National Institute of Technology Delhi
Delhi, India

P. Praveen
SR University Warangal
Telangana, India

*Dr. Rahul Gupta
Amity Business School
Amity University
Noida, India

*Ravi Tomar
School of Computer Science
University of Petroleum and Energy Studies
Dehradun, India

*Rohini A
Department of Artificial Intelligence &
    Data Science
Miracle Educational Society Group of
    Institutions
Vizianagaram Andhra Pradesh, India

Roohi Sille
School of Computer Science
University of Petroleum and Energy Studies
Dehradun, India

Samarth Vashisht
Synopsys, Inc.
Bengaluru, India

T. Sampath Kumar
SR University
Warangal Telangana, India

Shlok Mohanty
School of Computer Science
University of Petroleum and Energy Studies
Dehradun, India

Smriti Gaba
Reliance Jio Infocomm Limited
Mumbai, India

*Susheela Dahiya
School of Computer Science
University of Petroleum and Energy Studies
Dehradun, India

Tanupriya Choudhury
School of Computer Science
University of Petroleum and Energy Studies
Dehradun, India

Vitesh Sethi
School of Computer Science
University of Petroleum and Energy Studies
Dehradun, India

1

Fog Computing: Present and Future

Kabir Jaiswal

School of Computer Science
University of Petroleum and Energy Studies
Dehradun, India

Niharika Singh

School of Computer Science
University of Petroleum and Energy Studies
Dehradun, India

CONTENTS

1.1 Introduction to Fog Computing

Cloud computing (also termed "the cloud") has enabled organizations and individuals to drastically shift from brick and mortar data centers (DCs), which are expensive to build and maintain. Although cloud came as a novel way to save infrastructural costs, the burden is high latency, lack of location awareness, and real-time computational needs. Hence cloud had to incur some drastic changes from software capabilities to hardware upgradation. Nevertheless, all of these advances lacked in making the cloud more accessible for applications that required real-time computation as the relay time between the cloud server and the endpoint is exponential, and the number of relays is no less, to say the least, because they had to carry enormous amounts of data to and fro from the cloud server. All of these hindrances gave birth to fog computing. Fog computing implementation is an intermediary between the cloud and the nodes. Fog nodes (end nodes that use fog computing) try to schedule and compute tasks that can be performed on the ground. It was like a cloud but closer to the ground applications; hence came the name *fog*.

DOI: 10.1201/9781003188230-1

TABLE 1.1

Fog Computing Network Architecture

Layer	Function
Transport Layer	Functions include uploading preprocessed data to the cloud.
Security Layer	Helps in encryption and decryption to keep the integrity of the data.
Temporary Storage Layer	Keeps the data stored temporarily for future processing.
Preprocessing Layer	Functions include data pruning and filtering.
Monitoring Layer	Helps keep requests related to services in check.
Physical and Virtualization Layer	Includes virtual and physical sensors and respective networks.

An inclusive definition of fog computing: "Fog computing is a geographically distributed computing architecture with a resource pool consists of one or more ubiquitously connected heterogeneous devices (including edge devices) at the edge of the network and not exclusively seamlessly backed by cloud services, to collaboratively provide elastic computation, storage and communication (and many other new services and tasks) in isolated environments to a large scale of clients in proximity" (Yi et al., 2015a).

Fog computing is a pertinent extension to the already existing cloud computing architecture. The most consequential appendages are:

- Fog computing supports mobility, which is an essential function for many applications that communicate directly with the fog nodes to receive and send information. Fog computing enables the usage of protocols like LISP (Retrieved from www.lispmob.org.), which work directly on the host's location identity.
- Fog computing provides for low latency, service-rich, and geolocational aware network nodes.
- Fog nodes provide a heterogeneous environment (Bonomi et al., 2012) as fog nodes come in different form factors with varied applications.
- Fog provides for real-time processing and helps diminish the need for batch processing at the cloud server level.
- Fog nodes help in the federation of services (Bonomi et al., 2012) and components which are in the network.

These extensions to cloud computing fill the gap between the already existing cloud computing architecture and the loopholes it presented. The fog computing architecture, as given by (Mukherjee et al., 2018), has a six-layer network architecture containing the following layers: transport, security, temporary storage, preprocessing, monitoring, and the physical and virtualization.

Table 1.1 presents an overview of the network architecture of fog computing, but we can also simplify this view using a top-level three-tier architecture, which can be seen in Figure 1.1.

We can infer from Figure 1.1 that the end services are available in millions and do not communicate directly with the cloud. The end nodes first communicate with the fog nodes, which help preprocess data and compute and store data across various fog nodes. The first tier contains smartphones, sensors, and personal computers that send data to the second tier, i.e., fog nodes containing switches, gateways, routers. The third and the last tier hosts the end servers in the DCs.

We have looked at what makes fog computing a compelling opportunity for cloud computing, what are the features and capabilities of fog computing, and the nature of its architectures. In the upcoming section, we will discuss how fog computing evolved to its present-day form.

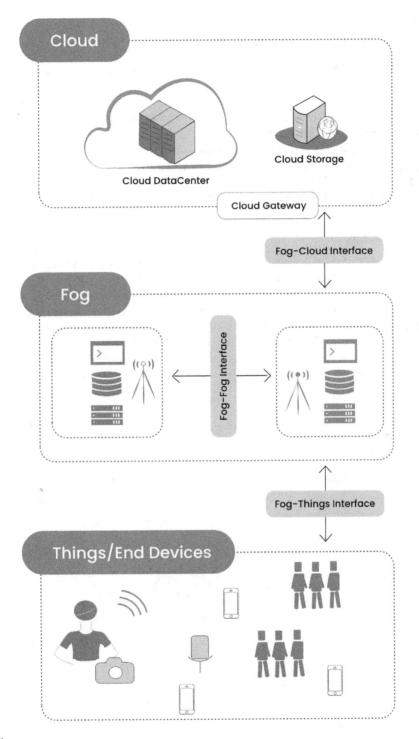

FIGURE 1.1
Three-tier fog architecture.

Source: Based on Mukherjee et al., 2018

1.2 Evolution of Fog Computing

Fog computing was introduced in 2011 to cope with the emerging number of IoT devices and their computational needs. In 2015 Princeton University, in collaboration with industry leaders, formed the OpenFog Consortium to facilitate the developments in fog computing. Since then, myriad surveys and taxonomical developments have been published to define fog's architecture and components.

Naha et al. (2018) give a descriptive approach to a requirement-based taxonomy of fog computing. Figure 1.2 includes three main branches to the taxonomy of fog computing, namely: Infrastructure, Platform, and Application. These main branches of the taxonomy have various factors and stakeholders that build up the fog computing environment.

1.2.1 Infrastructure

Fog computing's infrastructure includes all the sensors, actuators, handheld devices, physical gateways, routers, and servers. As these devices see an exponential increase every year, the network and operational requirements keep increasing. Sensors and actuators are small devices that receive inputs and are programmed to give an output. They work in a unidirectional mode, are generally low bandwidth, and rely upon minuscule amounts of energy consumption. For example, a humidity sensor in an agricultural setting would sense the humidity in the soil and pass this as an input to the corresponding actuator, which will then activate or deactivate the water supply. These sensors and actuators are

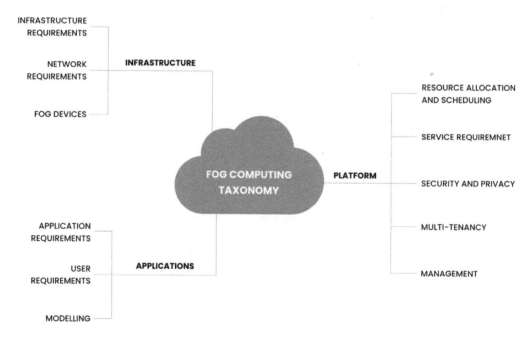

FIGURE 1.2
Taxonomy of fog computing.

Source: Adapted from Naha et al., 2018

just one small portion of what the fog infrastructure hosts; there are also handheld devices like smartphones and smartwatches that host enormous amounts of these atomic sensors and actuators. Therefore, the fog environment must host enough resources to cater to the computational, networking, and storage needs.

We discussed how the physical resources play an excruciating role in fog computing, but enabling these devices to communicate with other components is handled by the network they reside upon. The wireless sensor nodes (WSNs), also known as motes, and the wireless sensor and actuators nodes (WSANs) have been engineered to work in conditions with extremely low bandwidths and minuscule energy consumptions. However, the network is constantly relaying between thousands of these WSNs and WSANs. This creates a bottleneck between the data being sent and received between the fog nodes and the devices. Therefore, it becomes necessary for the existing network architectures to be able to accommodate these devices. Vaquero and Rodero-Merino (2014) suggest that mobile ad-hoc networks (MANET) can be a sustainable option toward creating mesh networks where each device works as a router through which other nodes can communicate. This will also enable deprecating the need for static infrastructural needs, which are expensive and require high computational needs. Devices like near field communication (NFCs) tags, Bluetooth, and Zigbee allow for MANET construction in local area networks.

Another viable solution for onboarding the ideas of a better networking fog node is wireless mesh networks (WMNs), which include several low mobility routers to gain connectivity to the network. While both solutions provide promising approaches to make networking accessible for devices in the fog network, they are far from being the solution to the problem. Extensive research and development are underway for making WMNs and MANET viable for the ever-growing number of devices on the IoT network.

The last dimension of the infrastructure branch in the fog computing taxonomy is fog devices. Fog devices were introduced to aid the existing IoT devices, which have certainly expanded to many applications like airplane landing management systems (Turner, 2016), geolocational systems on ships and yachts, etc. The presence of IoT devices at these planes hinders the possibility of relying on data transmission across the cloud and the devices connected to the cloud directly; hence these fog nodes must perform necessary computations and relay at the edge. This requires coordination between fog management systems, fog devices, and storage units to perform all the required tasks on the ground.

1.2.2 Platform

All fog devices require a platform to perform the task they are designated. This requires a management system or a platform to be handled and executed synchronously and efficiently. The platform has majorly five dimensions: Resource allocation and scheduling, service requirements, security and privacy, multi-tenancy, and management.

Since fog computing relies heavily on spatially closer resources, efficient resource allocation amongst different nodes becomes an essential task to provide seamless operation at the fog plane. Resource scheduling and allocation rely upon a two-fold assessment: the availability of resources that must be kept in check and the efficiency of these available devices. Since each device in the fog network is not specifically a dedicated resource for another node, therefore availability of a multitude of resources becomes paramount to fulfill the functioning of the fog devices. On the other hand, inefficient scheduling can also become an alarming issue resulting in delays and nullifying the complete objective of fog nodes to provide access to clouds at the edge.

The service requirements for fog computing ensure that the user requests are constantly updated on the service results. To ensure the service request's seamless operation, we must consider the fault tolerance and quality of service (QoS). Fault tolerance is an essential part of any actual time application, as there is always a chance for some parts of the systems to stop functioning and hinder the system altogether. Fault tolerance mitigates this risk and provides for solutions when resources become meager, but the maintenance of the service is unquestionable. Processes like point-based restart, job shifting, and task rescheduling are used in cloud architecture to bandage the gap caused by faults in the system.

Quality of service remains important in fog-based systems as it rules the throughput of the systems, its energy consumption, and the total reliability of the system. QoS helps maintain the integrity of the systems by functioning the fault reaction systems, resource consumption systems, etc. While QoS might not be considered necessary in experimental setups, it is of paramount importance in production settings, as failures and errors are bound to happen. If there is an impeccable QoS system that provides operational assurance, the risks can be averted, and reliability can be restored.

Any platform's security and privacy are crucial as the data being generated by the devices at the edge can be personal and task sensitive. All stakeholders in the fog paradigm must be secure, including the network, the user, and the data being generated and relayed. In today's world, almost all personal information is on the brink of being accessed by centralized entities, but since fog is a decentralized system, it serves as an effective means to manipulate and work with data.

Multi-tenancy is another vital domain for fog as there are multiple tenants in a single isolated service. Multi-tenancy becomes crucial as availability amongst the fog nodes is scarce. Therefore multi-tenancy would aid in hosting multiple service requests per fog device in the network. Since fog devices generally tend not to be dedicated networking devices, either container-based or virtualization-based multi-tenancy is applicable.

The last branch of the platform is of the utmost importance, i.e., management. Since fog devices are of different forms and types, the network generally tends to be decentralized, and hence management sometimes becomes a hassle. Fog devices must have self-management or management dependencies in the system for the smooth functioning of the network.

1.2.3 Application

Application is at the core of fog computing, as it fulfills the requirements for direction on what actions are needed based on perception and observation of the environment. Application is a multi-dimensional concept that caters to the requirements of the environment (or the application), the user, and its modelling.

Almost all the physical components in the horizontally and vertically scalable fog network co-ordinate and co-exist in heterogeneity. Heterogeneity is a necessary evil; on one hand, it provides the existence of multiple devices, which is imperative with the exponential number of IoT devices being introduced every day in the fog ecosystem. On the other hand, it provides for a considerable challenge to be incorporated into one-mold-fits-all applications that try to achieve operations at the fog level. Beckel et al. (2011) advocate that those different devices need different commands in the IoT platform. The fog platform has three types of devices (Giang et al., 2015): the input/output devices, the computing devices, and lastly, the edge nodes. In certain instances, like the smart routers, all three might be incorporated in a single device, which provides a creative way to solve the heterogeneity problem.

Since the introduction of IoT and smart devices, the number of devices being implanted in the fog plane has been increasing swiftly; hence scalability of the network and the application become intrinsic. The sheer number of devices hinders the complete application for these devices to reside in the cloud alone. This also increases the latency and location awareness of the devices. Therefore, complete anonymity must be modelled into fog devices so that when it comes to scaling an operation like catering multiple tenants, it should automatically adapt to the changes.

Interaction timeliness and mobility go hand in hand to suffice the application requirements. Giang et al. (2015) propose a perception-action (PA) cycle modelled on human interactions. The PA cycle is very closely related to how fog nodes should operate. These interactions embody how the human body tackles specific changes that are chained to appropriate reactions. With the introduction of timed delays, the PA cycle can operate efficiently, as it does not have to cater to tasks that might not have time-related boundaries. The interaction timeliness directly correlates with mobility in the network. Since all the devices in the fog network, including the edge nodes, are not stationary, mobile instead directly proposes that components like computing resources and storage be available and interact promptly.

Part of the application's responsibility is to fulfill the user requirements. User requirements have their dynamics and are subject to change by environmental and locational constraints. Hence it becomes paramount that the fog network considers optimizing its resources based upon the network capabilities and the user behavior. A task assigned by a user might be constrained by cost and timeliness, which must be adhered to by the network.

Lastly, to encapsulate all the discussed dimensions of the application component of fog computing, there needs to be a focus on application modelling. We must look at application modelling from two dimensions as it might depend on the type of data being generated and forwarded for processing. Most IoT devices produce data in streams that need to be manipulated in real time to gain meaningful results. This gives us the ability to either design our model based on streams or use microservices to perform abstraction of functions and libraries.

In this section, we have seen how fog computing came to be. We also gained facts about the different components of fog computing and how they come together to solve the drawbacks of cloud computing. After the discussion about the evolution, we looked at the comprehensive taxonomy of the fog components.

In the next section, we will focus on the present-day state of fog computing: which advancements enable fog computing to work in production settings. We will also discuss some applications that are using fog computing prominently.

1.3 Present State of Fog Computing

From the previous discussion, we have realized that the state-of-the-art cloud computing architecture has a new extension called fog computing. Fog computing helps lower the burden of cloud computing through much-required intermediary progressing on the edge and fog nodes (Kumar et al., 2019).

Fog computing is only a decade-old concept and hence relatively new. Therefore, it presents much room for research and development. The current research areas range from energy consumption algorithms to content storage and distribution algorithms on the logical dimension. However, the research is not limited to just the algorithmic side. Leaps are being made in specific architectures for applications such as smart homes and cities, bioinformatics, intelligent and connected vehicles. These application-specific architectures are supported by research in areas like cloud and fog continuum, resource management, etc.

Ye et al. (2016) talk about resource optimization in cloud computing using service offloading on bus fog nodes present on the bus. This provides for an exciting paradigm when conjuring resource management and energy conservation frameworks. The paper talks about their architecture, as shown in Figure 1.3, which uses a virtualized bus fog server almost like a cloudlet. These virtualized servers provide the much-required computational and storage resources in fog networks with insufficient devices.

Zhanikeev (2015) proposes a new model for cloud-fog federation in container models. These models can be implemented using services like docker (Retrieved from www. docker.com). The architecture is called cloud visitation platform (CVP). CVPs are aware of the local hardware present in virtual machines and container-based models. The CVP breaks down the platform of the fog using application interfaces (APIs) and interfaces. The interface helps access the different stakeholders involved in the fog network, and the APIs

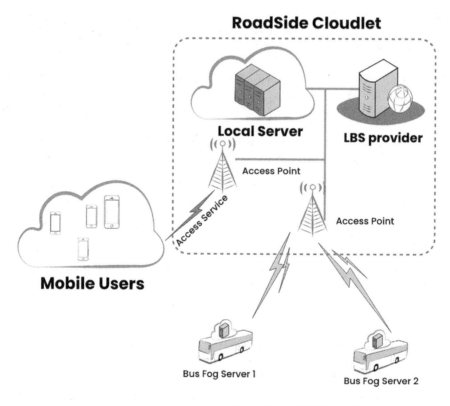

FIGURE 1.3

A scalable fog computing network with service offloading in bus networks.

Source: Adapted from Ye et al., 2016

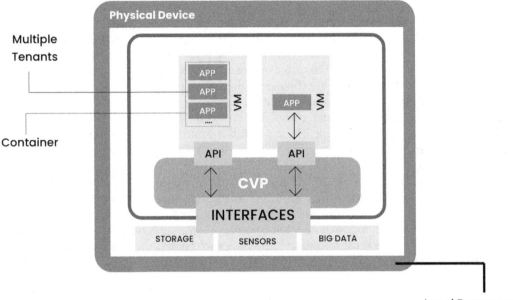

FIGURE 1.4
Architecture of the cloud visitation platform (CVP).

Source: Modified from Zhanikeev, 2015

are used to access the hardware capabilities in a generic way to accommodate for heterogeneity in the fog network. We can look at the architecture of the CVPs in Figure 1.4 to get a deeper understanding of CVPs.

These are a few examples of the research and development that is emerging in the field of fog computing. New research and development provide for better functioning applications with lower computational cost and scalable infrastructure.

1.3.1 Applications of Fog Computing

Applications of fog computing call for the adoption of ongoing research and development to fill the gaps and loops that cloud computing has. Since its introduction, cloud computing has found many different areas with tremendous amounts of effect with optimization, cost-saving, and efficient functioning of the cloud platform.

Fog computing has found applications in healthcare to automobiles, marine sciences, cattle raising, smart cities, etc. While these applications are direct to the user, these are aided by applications like the TinyOS and Paradrop, which help in the functioning of sensors and actuators to the already discussed CVP, which helps aid the cloud-fog federation.

1.3.1.1 Applications of Fog Computing in Agriculture

According to a United States Department of Agriculture report published in February 2020, the average area of each farm in the United States in the year 2019 was 444 acres (Farms and land in Farms, 2019 summary, 2020). This presents a huge challenge for the management and operations of a farm. The logistical requirements to tend the crops and their healthy cultivation are capital- and labor-intensive. This has given rise to intelligent farms. Smart farms use the IoT-fog continuum to perform irrigation, detect plant diseases, and predict yield. While smart farms prove highly applicable, the literature regarding sensor deployment and management is scarce or close to none. There have been relatively new developments in smart farming, but they are still in their infancy.

Malik et al. (2020) discuss an implementation-based approach through a toolkit in their paper. This toolkit helps to render complete farm ecosystems, sensor placements, data collection, and data preprocessing. Their proposed approach uses primarily on-ground devices like sensors, actuators, airborne vehicles, and smart mobile devices, which relay data using the fog paradigm.

Montoya-Munoz and Rendon (2020) propose an innovative approach to machine learning for outlier detection in the data acquired in the farms to implement a smart coffee farm. The greatest challenge in smart farms is reliable data collection to take action. The paper proposes a two-tier model where the data preprocessing is handled by the fog nodes in the smart cloud server for interpolating the inferences based on data that is meant to be used in outlier replacement.

1.3.1.2 Applications of Fog Computing in Healthcare

Healthcare as a sector has found cloud computing an excellent tool for maintaining doctor-patient interactions and post-op and pre-op processes. According to a World Health Organization report (Sabaté, 2003), most patients who have received a diagnosis and prescription lack the will for continuous attention to their prescribed medication, leading to repetitive encounters of diseases and long-hauls in curing the disease.

There are several other problems in the treatment of patients that rely on multiple factors and stakeholders. Therefore, constant monitoring systems are crucial to a patient's recovery and wellbeing.

Stantchev et al. (2015) propose a service-oriented architecture. The architecture harnesses the capabilities of cloud computing and fog computing to enable communications between the nodes. The proposed architecture is a three-tier model that is sensitive to even the slightest changes in the human body. Each aspect in the model triggers a response, which is fed to the next tier as input. The architecture also implements a business process modelling notation (BPMN) structured on the sensor architecture given by the OpSIT project. A BPMN gives standardization to design-based analysis in architecture with multiple resources (Krolczyk et al., 2009). The architectural view in Figure 1.5 gives us insight into how the authors propose to implement the approach in blood pressure management systems.

This case tries to showcase how IoT-fog computing can help with general healthcare. The fog paradigm is not limited to general medicine; it is successfully used to treat and diagnose chronic obstructive pulmonary diseases (COPDs), dementia, and speech-related diseases.

Fratu et al. (2015) has presented a novel case study that deals with the complete cycle of implementation of fog computing. This study talks about the paradigm and how policies and regulations regarding healthcare play an essential role in the adoption of cloud-based healthcare systems in a region.

The study is done in Romania with COPD patients and another set of people with mild dementia (Kyriazakos et al., 2016). The study uses the implementation of the eWALL project (Retrieved from http://ewallproject.eu/), which uses the "wall" as a direct interface

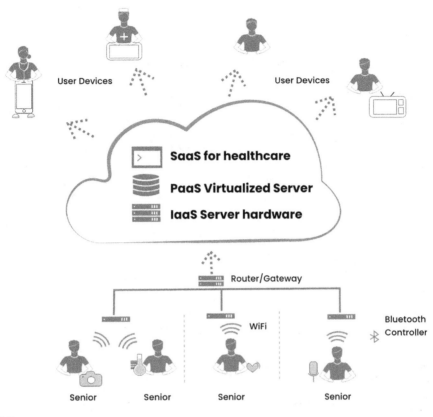

FIGURE 1.5

Architectural view of the proposed framework for service-oriented healthcare systems.

Source: Adapted from Stantchev et al., 2015

between the patient and their body vitals. These vitals can be varied from patient to patient; the wall also provides for advice, the dos and don'ts, etc. The creation of such a device required context-awareness built into the system, sensors, and actuators for patient monitoring and location awareness. This is done using intermediary processing at the fog layer, and then creating data and conducting analysis at the cloud level. The doctor and patient are always in sync, as the data is available on the cloud. This has proven to be immensely influential in continuous monitoring and providing a complete solution as an ambient assisted living (AAL) module.

The patient flow and the eWALL architecture (Figure 1.6 and Figure 1.7) given by the authors demonstrate how the whole system comes together to serve the patient while maintaining an optimized usage of cloud and fog nodes.

Monteiro et al. (2016) present another novel application of fog computing called the fog computing interface (FIT). The paper discusses the data aggregation of speech-related data using a smartwatch for patients diagnosed with Parkinson's disease (PD). According to the Parkinson's Foundation (Retrieved from www.parkinson.org/Understanding-Parkinsons/Statistics), 60,000 people are affected by Parkinson's every year, and currently, one million people with the disease live in the United States. The authors have hypothesized a FIT-based model that enabled remote processing of clinical speech data. This data included sharpness,

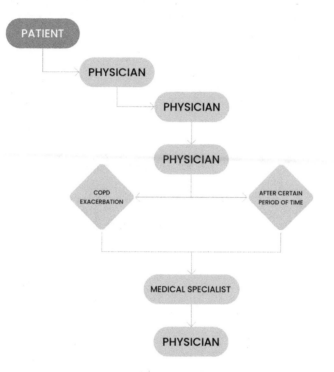

FIGURE 1.6
COPD patient operating procedure.

Source: Adapted from Kyriazakos et al., 2016

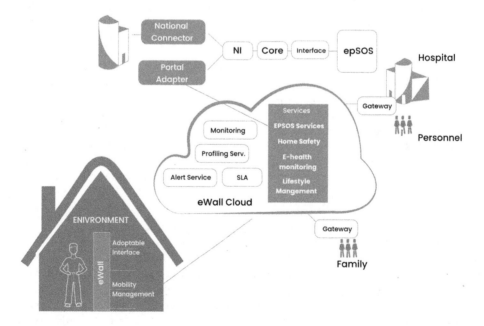

FIGURE 1.7
eWALL architecture.

Source: Adapted from Kyriazakos et al., 2016

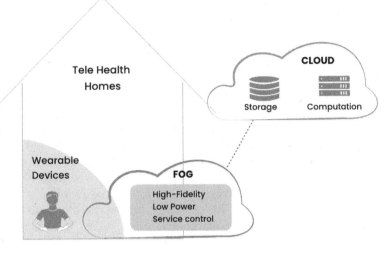

FIGURE 1.8
FIT architecture.

Source: Based on Monteiro et al., 2016

loudness, pitch, etc. The FIT architecture can be seen in Figure 1.8, which describes a home environment conducted with fog nodes and the fog layer that communicates with the cloud. This data on the cloud is shared with the physician for further medical advice.

While many other sectors have leveraged the benefits of cloud computing, they have yet to be viable for practical use in real-time environments. This includes large-scale smart cities, smart vehicles with autonomy, etc. Nevertheless, healthcare and agriculture have genuinely embodied the functionalities of fog computing.

1.4 Future of Fog Computing

In the previous section, what fog computing is, its components, applications, and some of the recent successes were discussed. However, fog computing is relatively new and requires research and development in most of its functioning. Fog computing faces challenges like privacy, security, component and network management, mobility constraints, timeliness and delay management, and energy consumption. These are just a handful of challenges that fog computing faces today. On the hardware and networking side, there are related problems at deployment and accommodations. Hence it becomes imperative that we discuss these problems before looking at the growth opportunities that fog computing presents.

Privacy is a matter of grave concern when it comes to fog computing. Fog is closer to the edge nodes and might store more personal information for processing, giving malicious parties a way to access them with ease. There is also a considerable amount of money to be put up for maintenance of the devices at the edge (Yi et al., 2015a). This leaves most IoT device manufacturers to put privacy protections in the backseat to accommodate more resources for efficient operations of the device itself. However, recent innovations like the HAN protocol are making privacy protection more accessible.

As we have already discussed, the fog network is a heterogeneous network that involves many different devices at many different levels, both horizontally and vertically. The inclusion of all these devices requires authentication and verification at each gateway, which is exceptionally cost-inefficient. Therefore, implementing secure connections between these devices becomes intrinsic. Yi et al. (2015b) propose the use of an intrusion detection system that can serve as a fruitful option in maintaining the network's overall security.

Another need for fog computing is an overall management system, since fog is a decentralized system; therefore, making sure that fog nodes communicate, perform, and function efficiently is imperative. The management system requires monitoring the energy consumptions, as each node is a multi-tenant node and not dedicated (Dastjerdi et al., 2016). The management system also requires the management of the network as various devices are at the network bottleneck and are simultaneously communicating. Lastly, the management of delays and responsiveness is crucial as the whole fog system relies on undercutting the latency delays introduced when working directly with the cloud.

We have discussed the issue and the areas of concern that have the potential for improvement. However, there are areas where fog computing is already being used in production settings and aids in efficient functioning.

Xu et al. (2019) present an exciting avenue where IoT devices are being used. The paper discusses how IoT-based devices aid ocean sensing, water quality monitoring, and coral reef monitoring. The current fog infrastructure supports these applications. These IoT devices are used in such extreme settings to perform intermediary computation and storage at the fog level as relay cost directly with the cloud is simply an inefficient method.

Fog computing is also being used to tend cattle and detect diseases in cattle early on to prevent and cure. Detecting lameness in cattle remains a challenge and often proves to be fatal for them. If lameness is detected prematurely, it can be cured. Machine learning and fog computing are being used to detect these abnormalities in infancy (Taneja et al., 2020) and have proven to work efficiently in real-time settings like farms and herds.

There are several other applications where fog computing is being used to aid predominantly manual or semi-manual tasks. This proves that fog computing truly has the capabilities of future growth and opportunities in various sectors.

1.5 Summary and Conclusion

In this chapter, we discussed what fog computing is and why it is a necessary paradigm for cloud computing. Fog computing has presented opportunities of including devices right from the edge and helping curb the cost and resource needs while transacting directly with the cloud. We discussed the critical components in the Evolution of Fog computing section, which gave us an overview of how fog came into existence. The three main components of fog computing are Infrastructure, Platform, and Application, which can be further branched out. The section Present State of Fog Computing discussed the real-time uses of fog computing and how it is helping industries efficiently shift to the cloud. Lastly, we have looked at the opportunities and issues that fog computing provides in both the research and development side and the implementation side.

Fog computing is at the brink of becoming the standard implementational model amongst all IoT devices. The advantages it has far outweigh the drawbacks it presents. Emerging research will influence the efficient application of millions and billions of devices introduced to the IoT network.

References

Beckel, C., Serfas, H., Zeeb, E., Moritz, G., Golatowski, F., & Timmermann, D. (2011). Requirements for smart home applications and realization with WS4D-PipesBox. In *Emerging Technologies & Factory Automation (ETFA), 16th Conference on Ieee, Sep. 2011* (pp. 1–8). IEEE Publications.

Bonomi, F., Milito, R., Zhu, J., & Addepalli, S. (2012). Fog computing and its role in the internet of things. In *Proceedings of the First Edition of the MCC Workshop on Mobile Cloud Computing (MCC 2012)* (pp. 13–16). New York, NY: Association for Computing Machinery. https://doi.org/10.1145/2342509.2342513.

Dastjerdi, A. V., Gupta, H., Calheiros, R. N., Ghosh, S. K., & Buyya, R. (2016). Fog computing: Principles, architectures, and applications. In *Internet of Things* (pp. 61–75). IEEE Publications.

eWALL Project Homepage. Retrieved from http://ewallproject.eu/ (available on-line).

Farms and Land in Farms 2019 Summary. (February 2020). *3 USDA*. National Agricultural Statistics Service. Retrieved from www.nass.usda.gov/Publications/Todays_Reports/reports/fnlo0220.pdf.

Fratu, O., Pena, C., Craciunescu, R., & Halunga, S. (2015). Fog computing system for monitoring Mild Dementia and COPD patients—Romanian case study. In *2015 12th International Conference on Telecommunication in Modern Satellite, Cable and Broadcasting Services (TELSIKS), 2015* (pp. 123–128). IEEE. https://doi.org/10.1109/TELSKS.2015.7357752.

Giang, N. K., Blackstock, M., Lea, R., & Leung, V. C. M. (October 2015). Developing IoT applications in the fog: A distributed dataflow approach. In *Proceedings of the 5th International Conference Internet Things (IOT)* (pp. 155–162). https://www.semanticscholar.org/paper/Developing-IoT-applications-in-the-Fog%3A-A-Dataflow-Giang-Blackstock/a6954cd8b460a97598072200e26a72f1c49e672d

Krolczyk, A., Stantchev, V., & Senf, C. (2009). Service-oriented approaches for e-government. In *Proceedings of the 11th International Conference on Information Integration and Web-Based Applications and Services* (pp. 441–446) – iiWAS '09. The 11th International Conference. ACM Press. https://doi.org/10.1145/1806338.1806420.

Kumar, V., Laghari, A. A., Karim, S., Shakir, M., & Brohi, A. A. (2019). Comparison of fog computing and cloud computing. *International Journal of Mathematics Science Computer (IJMSC)*, 5(1), 31–41.

Kyriazakos, S., Mihaylov, M., Anggorojati, B., Mihovska, A., Craciunescu, R., Fratu, O., & Prasad, R. (2016). eWALL—An intelligent caring home environment offering personalized context-aware applications based on advanced sensing. *Wireless Personal Communications Journal*, 2016, 1–3.

Malik, A., Rahman, A. U., Qayyum, T., & Ravana, S. D. (2020). Leveraging fog computing for sustainable smart farming using distributed simulation. *IEEE Internet of Things Journal*, 7(4), 1–1. https://doi.org/10.1109/JIOT.2020.2967405.

Monteiro, A., Dubey, H., Mahler, L., Yang, Q., & Mankodiya, K. (2016). Fit: A fog computing device for speech tele-treatments. *IEEE Publications. International Conference on Smart Computing (SMARTCOMP)* (pp. 1–3). Retrieved from www.parkinson.org/Understanding-Parkinsons/Statistics.

Montoya-Munoz, A. I., & Rendon, O. M. C. (2020). An approach based on fog computing for providing reliability in IoT data collection: A case study in a Colombian coffee smart farm. *Applied Sciences*, 10(24), 8904. https://doi.org/10.3390/app10248904.

Mukherjee, M., Shu, L., & Wang, D. (2018). Survey of fog computing: Fundamental, network applications, and research challenges. *IEEE Communications Surveys and Tutorials*, 20(3), 1826–1857, Third Quarter. https://doi.org/10.1109/COMST.2018.2814571

Naha, R. K., Garg, S., Georgakopoulos, D., Jayaraman, P. P., Gao, L., Xiang, Y., & Ranjan, R. (2018). Fog computing: Survey of trends, architectures, requirements, and research directions. *IEEE Access*, 6, 47980–48009. https://doi.org/10.1109/ACCESS.2018.2866491

Sabaté, E. (2003). *Adherence to Long-term Therapies: Evidence for Action*. Geneva: World Health Organization.

Stantchev, V., Barnawi, A., Ghulam, S., Schubert, J., & Tamm, G. (2015). smart items, fog and cloud computing as enablers of servitization in healthcare. *Sensors and Transducers*, 185, 121–128.

Taneja, M., Byabazaire, J., Jalodia, N., Davy, A., Olariu, C., & Malone, P. (2020). Machine learning based fog computing assisted data-driven approach for early lameness detection in dairy cattle. *Computers and Electronics in Agriculture*, 171. Alan, France: Nikita and Davy. https://doi.org/10.1016/j.compag.2020.105286.

Turner, V. (2016). *IDC Link: IBM and Cisco Bridge the IoT Edge and Enterprise* (pp. 1–2). Retrieved from www-01.ibm.com/common/ssi/cgi-bin/ssialias?htmlfid=WWL12359USEN.

Vaquero, L. M., & Rodero-Merino, L. (October 2014). Finding your way in the fog: Towards a comprehensive definition of fog computing. *ACM Sigcomm Computer Communication Review*, 44(5), 27–32. https://doi.org/10.1145/2677046.2677052

Xu, G., Shi, Y., Sun, X., & Shen, W. (2019). Internet of Things in marine environment monitoring: A review. *Sensors*, 19(7), 1711. https://doi.org/10.3390/s19071711.

Ye, D., Wu, M., & Tang, S. (2016). Scalable fog computing with service offloading in bus networks. *IEEE 3rd International Conference on Cyber Security and Cloud Computing (CSCloud)* (pp. 247–251). Beijing, China. https://doi.org/10.1109/CSCloud.2016.34.

Yi, S., Hao, Z., Qin, Z., & Li, Q. (2015a). Fog computing: Platform and applications. *Third IEEE Workshop on Hot Topics in Web Systems and Technologies (HotWeb), 2015* (pp. 73–78). https://doi.org/10.1109/HotWeb.2015.22. Retrieved from www.lispmob.org.

Yi, S., Qin, Z., & Li, Q. (2015b). Security and privacy issues of fog computing: A survey. *International Conference on Wireless Algorithms, Systems, and Applications*. College of William and Mary. https://doi.org/10.1007/978-3-319-21837-3_67

Zhanikeev, M. (2015). A cloud visitation platform to facilitate cloud federation and fog computing. *Computer*, 48(5), 80–83. https://doi.org/10.1109/MC.2015.122. Retrieved from www.docker.com.

2

Fog Computing: Foundation and Outline

Kartik Agarwal

School of Computer Science
University of Petroleum and Energy Studies
Dehradun, India

Roohi Sille

School of Computer Science
University of Petroleum and Energy Studies
Dehradun, India

Niharika Singh

School of Computer Science
University of Petroleum and Energy Studies
Dehradun, India

CONTENTS

Introduction to the Chapter

Data handling, data processing, data storage versatility, and data processing into the cloud are some of the key trends over the tech-decade. Notwithstanding, the cloud alone experiences developing limits, like decreased inactivity, high versatility, high adaptability, and continuous execution, to meeting the impending registering and savvy data/network organizing requests. Henceforth, another worldview called fog computing has arisen to conquer these cutoff points.

Fog stretches out distributed computing and administrations to the edge of the organization, be it for data or network preferences. It gives information, data computing and registering, data-piling, and application assistance to end-clients that can be facilitated at the organization edge. It diminishes system idleness and further develops quality of service in hand with quality of experience, which brings about a prevalent client experience. This chapter is about the presentation and outline of fog computing, correlation between fog computing and distributed computing, fog computing and its contrast to edge computing, a perfunctory touch on the computing history, conceivable fog computing evolution, applications and advantages of fog computing, and possible conclusions and future scope!

2.1 Introduction to Fog Computing

The Internet of Things (IoT) is framing quickly into a thing. There are sensors all over, which also implies a great deal of information being gathered. Most of this information is investigated at brought-together workers and in the cloud. With the ascent of IoT, distributed computing has become another well-known move by significant partners. In any case, at that point, there's fog computing [1].

2.1.1 Distributed Computing/Cloud Computing

To comprehend fog computing, we should initially characterize distributed computing. Distributed computing is an arrangement where PCs, workers, and different gadgets are associated over the Internet. Information can be shared and recovered from this standard organization. With the ascent of IoT, there is a requirement for a quicker and productive information access method. That is the place where fog computing comes in.

2.1.2 Fog Computing

Fog computing is a term begat up at Cisco. Otherwise called "fog networking/computing," it is a design where a few applications are administered at the edge of an organization by a shrewd gadget. The remainder of the applications and administrations are taken care of in the cloud. Figure 2.1 shows the the fog computing paradigm and its relationship with various cloud resources and accessories. Fogging is basically a middle ground between the cloud and the apparatus to permit more proficient information handling, investigation, and capacity. This is accomplished by lessening the measure of information to be shipped to the cloud [2].

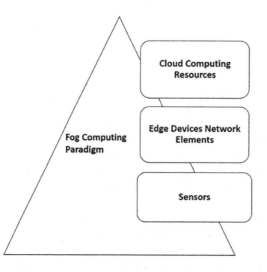

FIGURE 2.1
This portrays the fog computing paradigm and its relationship with various cloud resources and accessories.

Fog computing, or "fogging," is a conveyed foundation where specific application cycles or administrations are overseen at the edge of the organization by a shrewd gadget; however, others are yet overseen in the cloud.

2.2 Literature Review

Fog computing is an arising worldview that is considered the up-and-coming age of cloud computing. Nowadays, the expansion of information and information hubs in the IoT has presented issues for cloud design [3].

Fog computing can resolve such issues by providing versatile assets to end clients at the end point of the organization. This investigation aims to get an outline of reference models, related applications, and difficulties with the haze worldview. To this end, a thorough writing audit systemic literature review, which offers an organized way to deal with better grasp fogging, is conducted. The investigation uncovers a broad scope of utilizations that can profit from fog computing; in any case, they are not entirely executed indeed. The writing just presents calculated models or proposed models. What's more, the examination additionally shows that security and protection are among the incredible difficulties for fog computing.

The development and utilization of fog computing are filling in the field of cloud-based arrangements. Maybe then the necessary administration given by the cloud to the IoT framework has given exponential growth to the cloud architecture alongside [4]. Fog has been utilized in an assortment of administrations. Fog computing moves the capacity and figuring assets nearer to the IoT gadgets. Fog computing emerges when the requirement for guaranteed responsive errands arises in increments in IoT applications. Fog computing is a decentralized framework that is emotional by setting mindful data of the information sources, such as reaction time, area, and assets dispensed by the assistance. Fog computing is given at the edge hub in the organization, either honestly or in the virtual structure. In this survey, the design of fog computing, its different sending models, ongoing IoT applications where fog computing is used, and the benefits of fog computing instead of cloud are uncovered. Aside from the issues in the execution of the fog computing equipment stage, many problems in assistance arrangement and administration arrangement in fog computing are tended toward the finish of this study.

Fog computing has been, as of late, acquainted with overcoming any issues between cloud assets and the organization's edge.[5] Fog empowers low dormancy and area mindfulness, which is considered instrumental for acknowledging IoT, yet it also faces unwavering quality and trustworthiness issues because of node versatility and asset requirements. This chapter centers around the last mentioned and studies the best in class concerning steadfastness and fog computing. Our discoveries show the developing interest in the point yet the general youthfulness of the innovation, with no driving exploration bunch. Two issues have drawn in exceptional interest: ensuring reliable information stockpiling/assortment in frameworks with questionable and untrusted nodes and securing practical errands within sight of changing computing load. Repetition-based procedures, both static and dynamic, overwhelm the designs of such frameworks. Unwavering quality, accessibility, and QoS are the main trustworthiness prerequisites for fog, though angles like wellbeing and security, and their significant interaction, have not been explored inside and out.

Furthermore, fog frameworks are equipped to handle much information locally, work on-premises is entirely convenient, and can be introduced on heterogeneous equipment in order to be a framework that handles heterogeneity smartly. These highlights make the fog stage profoundly appropriate for time and area delicate applications. For instance, Internet of Things (IoT) gadgets are needed to deal with much information rapidly. This broad scope of usefulness-driven applications escalates numerous security issues in regard to communication, virtualization, isolation, organization, malware, and checking—this chapter overviews existing writing on fog computing applications to recognize usual security holes. Comparative advancements like edge computing, cloudlets, and micro-server farms have additionally been incorporated to give an all-encompassing survey measure. Most fog applications are persuaded by the longing for usefulness and end-client prerequisites, while the security perspectives are frequently overlooked or considered a bit of hindsight. This chapter likewise decides the effect of those security issues and potential arrangements, giving future security-applicable bearings to those answerable for planning, creating, and keeping up fog frameworks.

2.3 Timeline of Fog Computing

The history and beginnings of decentralized computing can be followed back to the 1990s [6].

- 1990: Akmani launched the first cloud service for the content delivery network (CDN).
- 1997: Work task named "Agile application-mindful variation for mobility," Nobel et al. showed how various types of uses (Internet browsers, video, and discourse acknowledgment) working over asset-compelled cell phones can reduce load on certain undertakings to incredible workers (substitutes).
- 2001: Here regarding persuasive computing, Satyanarayanan et al. summed up this methodology in their paper "Persuasive Computing: vision and difficulties." In 2001 adaptable and cloud applications utilized, as offered, peer-to-peer (conveyed distributed hash tables) overlay organizations. These self-arranging overlay networks empower effective and deficiency lenient steering, object area, and burden adjusting.
- 2006: The year when Amazon initially advanced its "Elastic Compute Cloud." This opened up a pile of new freedoms as far as calculation, perception, and capacity limit.
- 2009: In 2009, Satyanarayanan et al. presented the term *cloudlet* in their paper "The case for VM-based cloudlets in mobile computing." The report proposed two-level engineering. The principal level is called a *cloud* (high latency), and the next is known as *cloudlets* (lower latency). The last is decentralized and broadly distributed web foundation segments.
- 2012: Cisco presented fog computing for scattered cloud foundations. The point was to advance IoT adaptability, i.e., to deal with enormous IoT gadgets and huge information volumes for ongoing low-dormancy applications [7].
- Today: Cloud and edge computing are present for wide ranging IoT based applications. The answer needs to counterbalance many more extensive prerequisites. We see that, by and large, associations settle on a mix of cloud and edge processing for integrated IoT arrangements.

2.4 Evolution of Fog Computing over the Era

Thought up by Professor Salvatore J. Stolfo, fog computing, otherwise called fogging, is a spread processing framework where application and its administrations are dealt with either at the organization's edge or in a distant server data cloud, yes, the one talked about above!

Fog computing was acquainted with meeting three essential objectives.

1) To improve proficiency and trim the measure of information that needs to be sent for preparing, examination, and capacity
2) To spot the information near the end client
3) To give security and consistency to the information transmission overcloud

Fog computing comprises a control plane and an information plane, where most of the preparation happens in the information plane of a savvy portable or on the edge of the organization in a door gadget [8].

As talked about, in fog computing, a significant part of the handling happens in a neighborhood gadget. This kind of computing makes a virtual stage that organizes, registers, and capacities administrations in cloud server farms and end gadgets. These administrations are critical to both cloud and fog computing.

Fog computing can be treated as an extensively decentralized "cloud" that capacities close to the measure where data is produced and used regularly [9]. This empowers executives, register force, dependability, and recuperation restricted uniquely to those end clients who meet its prerequisite. Presently, since most of the data will be handled by the nearby end client, just customized measures of summed up data can be communicated up to the cloud and down from the cloud to the neighborhood activity. This decreased the weight of cloud transmission capacity, as 80% of information is required inside the neighborhood setting. This further makes fog computing a helpful answer for inactivity, conveying top-notch mixed media application measure information with low deferral and bundle misfortune.

Even though the information in the cloud is encoded, it remains on the way for a long time, and it turns out to be more helpless against security dangers. Here, fog gives the briefest conceivable distance between the customer and the worker, and it decreases the hazards of information security breaks.

2.5 Why Fog Computing for IoT?

There is a blast in the measure of information being produced by computerized gadgets. The conventional model of preparing and putting away all information in the cloud is getting excessively expensive and regularly too delayed to even think about gathering the necessities of the end client. This is persuading a move toward an edge computing approach that works with the preparing of gadget information nearer to the source [10].

Gartner Group proposes: "Around 10% of big business produced information is made and handled external a conventional brought together data center or cloud [11]. Gartner reckons about this figure increasing to 75% by 2022." The change to edge processing may significantly affect an association's IT and OT (information and operational technology) frameworks and how new advanced items are assembled.

To help better comprehend the development of fog computing, we should take a gander at a portion of the advantages.

- A critical thought for fog computing is to defeat organization dormancy. On the off chance that the IoT application requires sub-second reaction time, sitting tight for a solicitation to the cloud may turn into an issue. For example, a security basic control framework working a mechanical machine may have to stop promptly if a human is excessively close. The handling of human acknowledgment by a sensor and the preparation of choice to control a device cannot be deferred by organization collaboration. A postponed reaction time may make genuine mortal mischief or harm the machine. Also, self-ruling vehicles or increased reality applications need a reaction time beneath 20ms. This can't be conveyed by standard correspondence with the cloud. Moving the handling of the sensor information to an edge door is an approach to stay away from network inactivity and accomplish an ideal reaction time [12].

- Cost is likewise a driving component for edge registering. The more significant part of telemetry information produced by sensors and actuators is likely not pertinent for the IoT application [13]. The reality, a temperature sensor that reports a 20°C perusing each second probably won't be fascinating until the sensor reports a 40°C perusing. Fog computing considers the information to be sifted and prepared before it is shipped off the cloud. This decreases the organization's cost of information transmission. It likewise lessens the distributed storage and handling cost of information that isn't pertinent to the application.

- Sending investigation calculations or AI models to an edge passage takes into account the computational preparation to be performed on more modest informational collections [14]. Fog computing will regularly be more computational and productive to handle this sort of information.

- Numerous computerized items should be self-ruling in their activity. This permits them to accomplish the necessary wellbeing, unwavering quality, and client experience needs. Fog computing gives the capacity to have the nearby capacity and neighborhood calculation. In this way, the gadget can keep working regardless of whether it isn't associated with the organization.

- At long last, fog computing can improve the security and protection of an IoT application. Fogging can decrease the number of sensors and actuators associated with the web. This reduces the potential assault vector of safety assaults. Nearby information handling and separating by an edge entryway can likewise decrease the measure of touchy and private data sent through an organization. In this way, it tends to security needs or guidelines for the application.

2.6 Advantages, Applications, and Pros of Fog Computing

Fog stretches out the cloud near the gadget that creates or produces the information. This framework is known as the fog node. The gimmick with network association, stockpiling, and figuring highlights is known as a fog node. Models incorporate switches, regulators, workers, switches, cameras, etc. Fog computing is even called edge computing [15]. Fog computing is additionally supposed to be edge computing/fogging. Fog is a model created for information preparation, application administrations, and focused on client gadgets at the organization's edge instead of in an existing sort called cloud computing. Like cloud computing, fog computing gadgets are dispersed on traversing different spaces, heterogeneous platforms. To beat the weaknesses of distributed computing, fogging was created by Cisco frameworks. Fog computing is safer than distributed computing.

Fog broadens distributed computing and expands the cloud by putting intermediate nodes. Utilizing fog computing decreases the information development when contrasted with shadow, and fog has a superior security level than cloud. The fog even permits the quicker transfer and download of information.

So here, the benefits of fog computing are more likely to comprehend this theme [16].

- It offers better security.
- Fog nodes are versatile in nature. Henceforth they can join and leave the organization whenever.
- It is not difficult to foster haze applications utilizing the correct apparatus that can drive machines to force clients' needs.
- Fog nodes, like tracks, vehicles, and manufacturing plant floors, can endure cruel natural conditions.
- Fog computing offers a decrease in inactivity as information is broken down locally. This is because of less full-circle time and is likewise a smaller measure of information transmission capacity.
- It diminishes the idleness necessity, and thus fast choices can be made—these aid in keeping away from mishaps.
- It measures chosen data regionally as opposed to conveying them to the cloud for preparation.
- This computing offers better protection to the client's information as they are dissected locally instead of sending them to the cloud. The IT group oversees everything and manages the gadgets.

These, amongst many, are just a glimpse of the massive fog computing genre. IT environment in the era would genuinely advise one to use cloud and fog computing and experience the best of computing platforms on themselves.

2.7 Future Scope of Fog Computing

The IoT, as of now, delivers monstrous measures of information. It's an ideal opportunity to begin managing fogging. Are fog and edge computing unavoidable?

What will happen when the cloud isn't sufficient?

This is an advanced issue if at any point there happens to be one. Specialists supposed that 2016 would check the ascent of another framework: fog computing. Fogging includes stretching out distributed computing to the edge of an organization. It assists end gadgets and data centers to cooperate healthily [17].

Fog computing is a solitary response to a few inquiries. Truth be told, the expression "fog computing" is a new production of Cisco and is frequently exchanged with "edge computing." The "edge" just alludes to focusing closer to the point where information is delivered as compared to the data set and brought-together handling places. This implies the edge of an organization or even access-giving gadgets like switches.

Fog computing can likewise resolve issues in mechanical technology. Robots looking at a space gather tremendous measures of information [18]. Sending that information rapidly, notwithstanding, isn't simple. Getting guidelines from the control place basically sits around. Pacific Northwest National Laboratory research researcher, Ryan LaMothe, clarified a portion of the advantages of edge computing to Government Technology.

Fog computing likewise takes into consideration better by and sizeable distant administration. Organizations accountable for oil, gas, or coordination may detect that processing at the edge optimizes time, cash, and sets out up-to-date open doors. The momentum at which information can be examined additionally upends a degree of wellbeing [19]. Any data that may demonstrate a dangerous circumstance ought to be broken down as closer to the edge as expected.

For a few, the fate of the cloud will definitely include fog computing. Princeton, as of now, flaunts their Edge Lab, coordinated by Mung Chiang, prime supporter of the OpenFog Consortium. His research on fog networking suggests four logics that fog computing is essential in this day and age: it puts forward ongoing handling and digital actual framework control, helps applications better satisfy clients' prerequisites, pools nearby assets, and takes into consideration fast development and moderate scaling.

2.8 Conclusion

Fog computing is a more enormous stretching out view with a worldwide aspect to cloud computing and administrations to the organization's nodes [20]. Like cloud, fog supplies details and knowledge, register, stockpiling, and application administrations to end clients. The ingenuity of fog computing lies in a progression of real circumstances like Smart Grid, shrewd traffic signals in vehicular organizations, and programming identified networks.

Cisco presented its fog computing vision in January 2014 to lead cloud computing magnitude to the fog of the organization.

As the outcome, nearer to the rapidly progressing figures of connected gadgets and applications that devour cloud interest and produce successively enormous information measures, the fog was more appropriately introduced, adapted, and evolved.

From the earlier examination, it is evident that fog computing performs better compared to the cloud in fulfilling the present need of arising ideal models that require quicker handling and less deferral. With the presentation of this idea, we can genuinely zero in on the administrations of IoT and its progression.

One reality that I can't escape without referencing is although mist processing and its application look different, it can't supplant cloud and become the solely distributed computing module of things to come. Where a lot of assets are required, autonomous of deferring factor, it very well may be dealt with by conventional distributed computing innovation at a lower cost. It is protected to express that there is no fog without a cloud. The two of them exist together, serving two unique areas and supplementing each other anywhere required.

References

[1]   White Paper, Fog computing, and Internet of Things, Cisco {www.cisco.com/c/dam/en_us/ solutions/trends/iot/docs/computing-overview.pdf}

[2]   Brien Posey, Sharon Shea, Ivy Wigmore, Fog computing (fogging and Fog networking), IOT Agenda {https://internetofthingsagenda.techtarget.com/definition/fog-computing-fogging}

[3]   Deepika, Mrs. Kavita Rathi, 2017, A literature review of Fog computing, *CS Journals IJITKM*, 11(1), 66–71 {http://csjournals.com/IJITKM/PDF%2011-1/13.%20Deepika.pdf}

[4]   Denis V. Gadasin, Andrey V. Shvedov, Alexander V. Ermolovich, The concept "fog computing", *IEEE Explore* {ieee.ieee.org}

[5]   Zeinab Bakshi, Guillermo Rodriguez-Navas, Hans Hansson, Dependable fog computing, *IEEE Explore* {https://ieeexplore.ieee.org/abstract/document/8906732/authors#authors}

[6]   Blesson Varghese, Philipp Leitner, Suprio Ray, Kyle Chard, Adam Barker, Yehia Elkkhatib, Herry Herry, Cheol-Ho Hong, Jeremy Singer, Posco Tso, Eiko Yoneki, Mohamed Faten, Cloud futurology, *Computer* 52(2019), 1–5. {10.1109/MC.2019.2895307}

[7]   S. Gujral, 2018, What is FOG computing and why do we need it? *LinkedIn*. {https://www.linkedin.com/pulse/what-fog-computing-why-do-we-need-sukhvinder-gujral/; https://www.google.com/url?q=https://in.linkedin.com/in/sukhvindergujral?trk%3Dpulse-article_main-author-card&sa=D&source=docs&ust=1646764232996504&usg=AOvVaw2IyWXcTxRQ2LaSgIJhEmpA}

[8]   Saad Khan, Simon Parkinson, Yongrui Qin, 2017, Fog computing security: A review of current applications and security solutions, *Journal of Cloud Computing* 6, Article no: 19 {https://journalofcloudcomputing.springeropen.com/articles/10.1186/s13677-017-0090-3}

[9]   Brandon Butler, Jan 2017, What is fog computing? *Network World* {www.networkworld.com/article/3243111/what-is-fog-computing-connecting-the-cloud-to-things.html}

[10] Ismet Aktas, n.d., Why edge computing for IoT, *Bosch Connected World Blog*. {https://blog.bosch-si.com/bosch-iot-suite/why-edge-computing-for-iot; https://blog.bosch-si.com/author/aktas-ismet/}

[11] G. Lewis, S. Echeverría, S. Simanta, B. Bradshaw, J. Root, 2014, October, Tactical cloudlets: Moving cloud computing to the edge. *2014 IEEE Military Communications Conference*, IEEE, pp. 1440–1446. {https://www.researchgate.net/profile/Grace-Lewis-8}

[12] K. Saranya, Jaya Prakash, Sethu Balaji, Survey on Fog computing and its application benefits in real life, *International Research Journal of Engineering and Technology*, 5(5)(2018) {www.irjet.net/archives/V5/i5/IRJET-V5I5376.pdf}

[13] S. Kosta, A. Aucinas, P. Hui, R. Mortier, X. Zhang, 2012, March, Thinkair: Dynamic resource allocation and parallel execution in the cloud for mobile code offloading. *2012 Proceedings IEEE Infocom*, IEEE, pp. 945–953. {kosta@di.uniroma1.it}

[14] J. K. Zao, et al., 2014, Augmented brain-computer interaction based on fog computing and linked data. *2014 International Conference on Intelligent Environments*, IEEE.

[15] A. Radford, 2019, Edge and Fog Computing: Overview and Benefits – Securus. Secure Communications. {https://securuscomms.co.uk/edge-and-fog-computingoverview-and-benefits/; https://securuscomms.co.uk/author/andyradford/}

[16] Advantages and disadvantages of fog computing, n.d., *Way2Benefits*. {http://way2benefits.com/advantages-and-disadvantages-of-fog-computing/}

[17] Y. Cao, C. Songqing, P. Hou, D. Brown, 2015, FAST: A fog computing assisted distributed analytics system to monitor fall for stroke mitigation, *2015 IEEE International Conference on Networking, Architecture and Storage (NAS)*, IEEE, pp. 2–11.

[18] R. Jain, M. Gupta, A. Nayyar, N. Sharma, 2021, Adoption of Fog Computing in Healthcare 4.0. In: S. Tanwar (ed.). *Fog Computing for Healthcare 4.0 Environments. Signals and Communication Technology*. Cham: Springer. {https://doi.org/10.1007/978-3-030-46197-3_1}

[19] H. Augur, 2016, Is fog computing the future of the cloud?. *Dataconomy*. {https://dataconomy.com/2016/03/fog-computing-future-cloud/}

[20] What is Fog computing? *Webopedia* {www.webopedia.com/definitions/fog-computing/}

3

The Use of Machine Learning in Fog Computing

Smriti Gaba

Reliance Jio Infocomm Limited
Mumbai, India

Susheela Dahiya

School of Computer Science
University of Petroleum and Energy Studies
Dehradun, India

Samarth Vashisht

Synopsys, Inc.
Bengaluru, India

Avita Katal

School of Computer Science
University of Petroleum and Energy Studies
Dehradun, India

CONTENTS

DOI: 10.1201/9781003188230-3

3.1 Introduction

The digital era has witnessed a rise in utilization (Naha et al., 2018) of IoT devices or smart devices generating abounding data including variety and velocity factors. Due to latency and bandwidth issues, the emerging cloud computing technology did not provide efficient processing, storing, and management of the generated data (Assunção et al., 2015). Fog computing came into existence to overcome these challenges, and it acted like a catalyst or in other words it is the missing link between the edge of a device (where data is being generated) and cloud (where data is processed, stored, and analyzed). With its efficient decentralized model, fog computing extended services and features providing secure and accurate responses to time-sensitive applications for decision making, reducing latency issues.

Fog computing, despite being an efficient model for optimization of bandwidth and reduction of latency problems, introduces concerns regarding security of data and lacks in providing efficient resource management services. As the fog computing paradigm is widely being deployed across emerging IoT smart systems, its implementation also causes security and computational issues. Furthermore, since these IoT devices are resource constrained and data communication over sensors also needs to be compressed, machine learning algorithms and techniques are being used to overcome resource allocation issues, providing better security and high performance by processing, compressing data, and optimizing communication in the network layer.

Machine learning (ML) has become an essential part of IoT based systems as the smart devices carry out features like routing, monitoring, processing, and computational operations, and ML provides techniques for data aggregation, resource allocation and management, anomaly detection to enhance security, and many other applications to deliver high performance in fog systems.

Machine learning is an application of artificial intelligence (AI) that gives computers the ability or provides software applications to learn from data and optimize their accuracy over a period without being explicitly programmed. Machine learning is based on an input-output mapping system, or in other words it is basically a running AI system which takes Input A and processes it and maps to Output B as illustrated in Figure 3.1.

For example, consider a scenario of implementing a secure anomaly detection system based on machine learning in a fog system, which includes a labelled dataset of whether or not a specific behaviour or pattern is an attack. It could be observed that Input A would be the pattern or behaviour that will then be sent or processed by a machine learning system that will match the signature of the pattern in the labelled dataset and make a decision as to whether it is considered as attack or not. After processing the decision it maps the result, which is Output B as illustrated in Figure 3.2. This way a simple machine learning technique is deployed to detect suspicious behaviour in a foggy environment, hence improving the security.

The proliferation of data from IoT devices and sensors is transforming the way organizations process and analyze this data. They currently rely on complex clusters for analysis of data, which could lead to slow decisions and reduce the value of data over time due to latency. Therefore, the fog computing approach provides a fast and reliable system. In a foggy environment both high-level and low-level fog nodes are present for processing, managing the heterogeneous

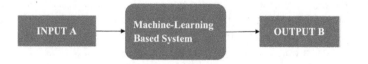

FIGURE 3.1
Machine learning input-output system.

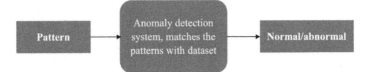

FIGURE 3.2
Machine learning-based anomaly detection system.

data generated by devices and sensors. This improves efficiency and response time, however analyzes of complex data become challenging. To overcome this difficulty, machine learning-based applications can be used by implementing different libraries and frameworks such as Scikit-Learn (Pedregosa Varoquaux et al., 2011) and Weka (Hall et al., 2009).

3.2 Machine Learning Techniques and Applications

Machine learning grants the ability to learn and perform tasks including clustering, decision-making, classification, etc. to a computer system. The system is trained by implementing algorithms and models based on statistical approaches to analyze the proliferating data coming from devices, actuators, and sensors. This collected data must be characterized based on various features, or say data is labelled with its feature and machine learning algorithm is implemented on top of labelled data, which then understands the relation between the characteristic features and the labels. Based on this observation and learnings of the machine learning algorithm during its training period, patterns are identified to make decisions and predict output results.

These learning algorithms serve the purpose of providing highly efficient and optimized performance in accomplishment of a particular task or operation by learning from its experiences. Take, for instance, the case of an intrusion detection system (IDS) where the task is to determine whether the behaviour of the system is normal or abnormal. A machine learning algorithm in this case will understand the input patterns and learn the behaviour of the system based on this input pattern. It is then trained to classify the behaviour changes observed into different groups based on similarities and determine the output result as normal or abnormal. This could also be implemented on the basis of a labelled training dataset by which the system identifies the behaviour of the system on the basis of training of labels, determining the result.

Machine learning algorithms can be classified into three categories:

1. Supervised Learning
2. Unsupervised Learning
3. Reinforcement Learning

These are further subdivided into different categories such as classification, regression, clustering, etc., and algorithms with respect to these categories as illustrated in Figure 3.3 (Granville, 2017) are used in various applications for improving performance of a system to perform computational tasks efficiently and accurately.

3.2.1 Supervised Learning

Supervised Learning is a widely used method where input variables (x) and output variables (y) are mapped using an algorithm that learns the mapping function. The mapping function

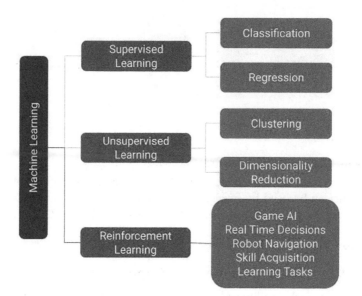

FIGURE 3.3
Machine learning categories and sub-categories.

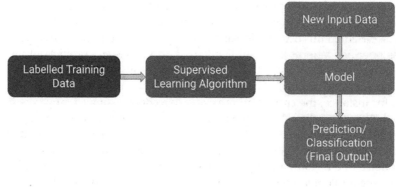

FIGURE 3.4
Supervised learning.

is to be well designed such that when new input data or variable is introduced, the algorithm based on its learnings could predict the output variable. This can be represented as:

$$y = f(x) \tag{3.1}$$

As this model learns from a training dataset, based on this labelled training data the machine predicts the correct output. So, we can say that the training data is probably supervising the learning process of the algorithm, which is why it is called Supervised Learning. A typical Supervised Learning algorithm is shown in Figure 3.4. Supervised Learning is achieved in two phases, i.e., training phase and testing phase. Data collected could be divided into a training dataset, which is the labelled dataset used to train the system, and a testing dataset that handles new data by predicting results based on its learnings (Van Loon, 2018). This model gives accurate results and fast performance, therefore it is widely used for improving efficiency of fog computing systems to achieve higher accuracy and improved decision-making.

Supervised Learning can further be classified into Classification and Regression. A detailed discussion on these two categories is as follows:

(i) **Classification Algorithms:** These algorithms are deployed in systems where the output result is based on categorical specifications such as diagnostics, identity or fraud detection, speech recognition that is achieved by implementation of algorithms like Support Vector Machine (SVM), Decision Tree (DT), Random Forest, K-Nearest Neighbor (KNN) as described:

3.2.1.1 Support Vector Machine (SVM)

SVMs are based on statistical learning for classification of the training dataset by creating a dividing hyperplane in such a way that the distance between the hyperplane and sample data points of classes is maximized. To separate two classes of data points, many dividing hyperplanes can be created in possible ways, however for better performance and classification it is to be considered that the hyperplane must be created where the distance between sample data points of each class is maximum (Al-Dulaimi and Ku-Mahamud, 2019). Support vectors are the data points that help build the SVM, as they are closer to the hyperplane and influence its orientation based on which classification becomes efficient.

Application

SVM is proven to be one of the best machine learning algorithms for intrusion detection, malware detection in a foggy environment. Fog computing-based IoT applications are resource-constrained and face challenges regarding memory storage. SVM is efficient in this scenario as it creates a hyperplane and divides the data points with $O(n2)$ complexity, which efficiently saves space for storage in memory.

Fog solutions deployed for smart grid, smart metering applications have improved performance as the model reduces latency and congestion issues. However, the security of the system is the main concern. Attack detection becomes important for smart grids to prevent any tampering and manipulation of data that could be implemented using SVM algorithms to detect attacks based on classifiers, as proven in the research study.

3.2.1.2 Decision Tree

Methods based on decision trees perform classification of data by sorting according to feature values by using a tree-like model of decisions. This tree is constructed using an algorithm that determines ways to split (Kotsiantis et al., 2007) the dataset based on feature attributes and different conditions. A decision tree generally begins from the root node and branches into possible outcomes that further lead to other additional nodes. This process is iterative, as illustrated in Figure 3.5 (Vardhan, 2020).

Application

While considering the fact that fog computing is a link between cloud and edge device, it is observed that the security issues that apply to cloud computing could be inherited by a fog computing platform (Stojmenovic and Wen, 2014) thus introducing security concerns

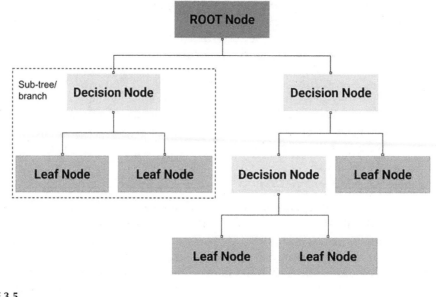

FIGURE 3.5
Decision Trees.

that increase potential surface to distributed denial of service (DDoS) attacks, DoS attacks, Sybil and intruder attacks that are carried by targeting fog node of a fog system to take control over other fog nodes of the network to form a DDoS attack, which degrades the performance of the network and affects availability of resources. To maintain the performance and optimize security of the fog system, Decision Tree-based machine learning algorithms can be used for intrusion detection (Goeschel, 2016), detection of DDoS attack (Alharbi et al., 2017) patterns, and analysis of network traffic for any suspicious activities inside the fog environment.

3.2.1.3 Random Forest

Random Forest-based supervised learning algorithms consist of many constructed individual decision trees, hypothetically creating a forest of trees as the name implies. These trees are trained to vote for a class. Each individual tree splits into a class for prediction, branching out possible outcomes of the condition (Cutler, 2007). The most-voted class will be the output of this classification algorithm.

Application

Random Forest algorithms address security concerns of a fog system by providing solutions such as network intrusion detection application, anomaly detection, and DDoS detection (Zhang and Zulkernine, 2006). IoT devices have low memory and power to handle cryptographic calculations, so they require fog nodes for such computations, an attacker may bypass authentication by impersonation and get unauthorized access to these fog nodes. Random forest algorithm plays a significant role in identification of such unauthorized fog nodes, and IoT devices in the network detect and secure the network.

3.2.1.4 K-Nearest Neighbor (KNN)

The KNN algorithm classifies data by analyzing k, given data points to classify new data points by identifying K-Nearest Neighbors using Euclidean distance as a distance metric. For instance, if there is a system to identify malicious activities, and a new pattern or data point which is unknown enters the system of known data points, then the KNN classifies it as malicious or non-malicious based on the votes of its nearest neighbours.

Application

A KNN algorithm is used for network intrusion detection and anomaly detection in a fog-based system. It classifies fog nodes in a wireless network as normal or abnormal behaviour, which further helps in identification of unauthorized and impersonated fog nodes that must not have access to the network resources, as attackers may try to increase congestion in the network by introducing a DoS attack. According to research, a detailed implementation of an intrusion detection system based on KNN providing efficiency is to be developed and deployed for maintaining security of the system.

(ii) **Regression algorithms:** These algorithms are deployed in a system where a relationship can be defined between the input and output variable. It is widely used for predicting continuous variables or where the output variable is a real value, for example, weather forecasting, population growth prediction with the use of algorithms like linear regression, Random Forest, and Bayesian Regression. A detailed discussion on the most commonly used linear regression follows:

3.2.1.5 Linear Regression

Linear regression is a statistical model that identifies relations between variables and forecasting based on independent variables. It carries out the functional task to predict a dependent value (y) based on an independent variable (x) by defining a linear relation between input variable (x) and output (y) (Tran, 2019).

Application

Linear regression machine learning algorithms can be deployed in fog-based IoT systems to predict trends between sensor data and time for monitoring, controlling the embedded applications that are generating real-time data. This will result in optimized performance and efficiency of the system. During the transmission of real-time data and aggregation of data streams there may be some missing values that can be repaired using linear regression models at real-time, as mentioned in the research study.

3.2.2 Unsupervised Learning

Unsupervised learning is where only input data (x) is present while there is no output data corresponding to it. In this technique the training dataset does not supervise the learnings of the system; instead it has to find insights from the data itself. For instance, if a training dataset containing images of different animals is given as an input to an unsupervised learning algorithm, it is expected to identify the features or attribute characteristics of the images by itself. This will be accomplished by clustering of the image dataset into groups based on similarities between them.

Unsupervised learning can further be categorized into clustering and association. It is used for applications such as discovery of hidden structures, credit card fraud detection using hidden Markov models, and identifying certain patterns on testing dataset. Algorithms like K-means clustering, association rule, and the Markov model are used for unsupervised learning applications. A detailed discussion on the most used K-means clustering follows:

3.2.2.1 K-Means Clustering

K-means clustering technique comes with an objective to allocate each data point of the input dataset to one of the discovered k clusters based on features such that each cluster will have data points with similar features. For instance, if a credit card fraud detection system is to be implemented, it could be given the value of k (number of clusters) and a dataset containing the amount of money spent via credit card as input. The system will process and form k clusters for different ranges of amount spent as low expenditure, normal expenditure, and high expenditure. The system will learn the user behaviour pattern on how the user spends by putting the new data point in a similar cluster; once it encounters abnormal behaviour in the expenditure amount, it would generate an alert for fraud.

Application

The K-means algorithm can be implemented to mitigate security issues in fog-based systems. It can detect abnormal behaviour patterns contributing to anomaly detection application. However, the K-means approach is less effective than supervised learning algorithms in detection of known attacks. Furthermore K-means can be implemented to detect sybil attacks in wireless sensor networks by clustering channel vectors as presented in a study. It can also preserve the privacy of data in fog-based systems where privacy is a concern.

3.2.3 Reinforcement Learning

Reinforcement learning aims to make a sequence of decisions where the output depends on the environment state of current output; the calculated output then becomes new input based on which a new output is calculated. It is based on the approach where it involves an agent that learns to take appropriate actions in an environment of accomplishment of which it is rewarded, so that the agent which has no previous knowledge learns to produce the actions that will generate maximum rewards. RL uses Q-learning, a deep Q network.

Applications

Considering the wireless security issues like jamming attacks that highly impact the bandwidth and efficiency of a fog-based wireless network system, reinforcement learning algorithms are efficient in mitigating such security issues in fog systems. For example, RL provides an application implementing anti-jamming techniques for WACRs (wideband autonomous cognitive radios). The RL-based system learns how to select a sub-band accurately to avoid jamming signals and other interferences to improve efficiency and bandwidth performance of the fog system. Many other research and techniques are proposed for anti-jamming solutions based on different reinforcement learning models.

3.3 Fog Computing with Machine Learning

Fog computing being a decentralized infrastructure provides improved performance, reduces latency, however in a fog-based system there are challenges that introduce resource management, accuracy, and security problems. To overcome these challenges machine learning algorithms are widely adopted. An overview of these challenges and their implemented solutions are discussed as follows:

3.3.1 Resource Management in Fog Computing

In a foggy environment, there are multiple devices, sensors, and actuators connected to each other. These generate huge amounts of data for processing, which requires utilization of resources by each of the devices or sensors that make multiple requests to use these resources. Therefore, resource management becomes a necessity in the fog system. Resource management in fog computing is accomplished by implementing ML algorithms.

In research (Lu et al., 2018), implementation of ML techniques in cloud servers is achieved, which processes data related to music by recognizing it and assigning an automatic score; this is carried out to achieve efficient allocation and management of resources. Deep learning and machine learning methods are also used to solve the problem of big data, in which they adopted efficient algorithms that shift the burden of computational operation from central server to fog nodes (Li et al., 2018). In a similar manner a study was proposed (Pérez et al., 2018) to solve backhaul connectivity issues such that during connectivity outage situations data can be preserved, avoiding any data loss.

Most fog-based systems (including network applications) involve services that utilize resource allocation for virtualized network operations as in the fog-based SDN solution, which delivers efficient results. However, it comes with the challenge of resource allocation, as virtualized networks make simultaneous requests for utilization of multiple resources. This problem is resolved by implementing machine learning algorithms based on cognitive techniques to provide higher energy efficiency and resource management (Chen and Leung, 2018).

Fog-based IoT solutions also involve processing of critical real-time data such as in the healthcare system which requires time-sensitive decisions and faster response. However, there are scenarios where latency issues in decision response could result in life-critical conditions. Therefore, to overcome the latency problems and to achieve efficiency, accuracy in time-sensitive applications based on the fog computing paradigm. ML algorithms including SVM, Decision Trees, and other supervised learning techniques are adopted.

The concept of smart fog was introduced, which reduces latency issues, improves decision making, and provides efficient resource management. In this scenario, machine learning in combination with the Markov model for the network is selected, forming a directional mesh network (DMN). The DMN framework extends services that analyze time-sensitive data near its source using various ML algorithms. This way the fog device makes smart decisions using these ML techniques and decides in what conditions data is to be stored in the cloud. This is accomplished by considering the proper allocation of resources with ML. Unsupervised ML techniques like clustering and spectral clustering are adopted to accomplish decision-making and efficient resource management in a foggy environment.

A study proposed provisioning of resources in multimedia fog computing by introducing an algorithm for prediction of resources that are available in fog-based systems (Hong et al., 2017). The algorithm is based on implementation of different ML algorithms that predict results efficiently and accurately. A study has also been proposed for a similar purpose that is focused on the communication problems between the fog nodes and end devices by introducing MQTT protocol that is widely used as a standard message-queuing protocol based on publish/subscribe mechanisms for communication in these resource-constrained devices (Peralta et al., 2017).

Primarily, supervised learning techniques like SVM, Random Forest, linear regression, Decision Tree are used widely for resource provisioning, prediction of delay, and latency concerns in fog computing.

3.3.2 Accuracy in Fog Computing

Fog computing-based systems or IoT applications use real-time functionalities and are time-sensitive as well. In case of such scenarios, it is important that the real-time data is reflected timely with accuracy. ML algorithms are implemented in these fog applications to deal with inaccuracy. Various implementations and studies are proposed to overcome inaccuracy:

(i) Authors propose a method including the implementation of hypothesis transfer learning (HTL), which is a distributed popular framework to perform analysis of data moving through IoT devices and fog gateways in a network by shifting large amounts of data to various data collectors where partial learning is performed. This method is efficient in improving the processing of huge amounts of data that are being generated in a fog network or environment. Supervised ML technique SVM is adopted to accomplish accuracy in this model approach.

(ii) Network overhead and latency problems in communication traffic are solved by the use of supervised ML techniques that predict the network traffic using high-performance computing and UbeHealth (Muhammed et al., 2018) framework. The output-predicted results are used by the network layers for performing decision-making on routing decisions, optimizing the speed of data, and achieving accuracy in fog-based network applications like healthcare, smart cities, detecting obstacles, and others.

(iii) Data processing accuracy is also achieved by implementing supervised machine learning techniques based on classification. The self-learning algorithm uses classification of data to improve results of data processing by reducing the volume of data required to process in the fog network and solves communication problems.

(iv) Bagula et al. (2018) propose machine learning techniques that provide accuracy in recognition of patients' conditions in a smart healthcare system using supervised learning algorithms such as linear regression, logistic regression, and classification using neural networks to handle heterogeneous data so that accuracy can be achieved in these multi-layered fog architectures of a healthcare system. Accuracy of results and timely decisions are the most critical aspects of this category of fog systems.

3.3.3 Security in Fog Computing

The fog computing model enables a wide range of services and benefits including reduced latency, decreased bandwidth, real-time time-sensitive decisions, and many more. However, the deployment of fog devices and the involvement of cloud and edge models incorporate many security and privacy threats (Khan et al., 2017). Fog introduces fog nodes and other new concepts, which increases security and privacy concerns that need to be addressed in order to enhance security (Yi et al., 2015). Therefore, to address these security issues various ML techniques are integrated with the fog application system.

Studies proposed different approaches for adopting various machine learning techniques to protect privacy of data using a linear regression algorithm that provides support to heterogeneous and complex data by providing data aggregation models (Yang et al., 2018) and privacy protection mechanisms. Using the K-Nearest Neighbor algorithm, prediction of disease (Malathi et al., 2019) with efficient privacy protection of patient's records in a healthcare system can be achieved.

ML techniques provide a secure mechanism to protect against DoS attacks, ransomware attacks (Homayoun et al., 2019), malware, and phishing attacks. Such attacks can be detected by implementing a ML algorithm like convolutional neural networks (CNN) for ransomware or fraud detection, SVM supervised learning for anomaly detection, artificial neural network based on feedforward technique for phishing detection, and multilayer perceptron for intrusion detection applications in fog-based systems.

3.4 Challenges in Fog Computing with ML

The use of ML in fog computing can lead to a few concerns like privacy, protection of data during communication, and heterogeneous data handing. A detailed discussion on these challenges is given in the following:

(i) Machine learning techniques that serve functionalities to improve efficiency and maintain security of a system may be misused by an attacker for breaking cryptographic and security implementations such as bypassing CAPTCHA using convolutional neural networks that process CAPTCHA images and are trained with a dataset of CAPTCHAs, learn to recognize the letters and numbers in image using different OpenCV modules, then bypass the CAPTCHA system. Attackers may also implement such techniques to build a system that is self-learning and learns the techniques like RNN to decrypt encrypted data and communication, causing privacy concerns.

(ii) ML algorithms that provide privacy protection mechanisms can leak private data, as they are vulnerable to attacks. ML techniques based on a distributed mechanism can also be easily bypassed, and private datasets being used as training sets of models are leaked. Attackers may build a system based on ML techniques that could detect and recognize the methods used in ML algorithms implemented for detection of attacks and then, based on its learning, it can discover a backdoor or entry point to bypass the detection application.

(iii) Fog computing applications face difficulties in managing and processing huge amounts of data for which ML techniques are integrated with the system to provide performance efficiency, accuracy in decision-making, and resource allocation. These techniques also solve network latency and communication issues (La et al., 2018) for time-sensitive applications along with providing accuracy in computation and processing of tasks. However, the proliferating number of sensors, data generated from them, complexity and heterogeneity of data introduce new challenges that require further implementation of IoT architectures based on cloud (Peralta et al., 2017).

3.5 Conclusion

Machine learning is an emerging field that is used extensively in different areas including fog computing and IoT applications to provide more efficient models that are secure with security mechanisms for detection of different attacks and provide efficient processing, computation, and management of huge amounts of data that are being generated and analyzed. Machine learning techniques enable resource-constrained devices to predict and manage allocation of resources in such a way that limited computation is required with reduction of latency and communication issues in a distributed fog network. In fog computing, supervised learning techniques including linear regression, SVM, Decision Trees, Random Forest, and Forest-Other classification, regression models are most widely deployed in applications. However, the implementation also comes with new challenges and issues that are considerably important, thus it needs to be further investigated. Despite the issues, machine learning plays a significant role in improvement of performance, accuracy, and security of fog computing applications. Therefore, the challenges can be studied, researched, investigated, and addressed in these fog systems.

References

Al-Dulaimi H. B. A. H. & Ku-Mahamud K. R. (2019). Intelligent classification algorithms in enhancing the performance of Support Vector Machine. *J. Theor. Appl. Inf. Technol.*, vol. 97, no. 2, pp. 644–657.

Alharbi S., Rodriguez P., Maharaja R., Iyer P., Subhash Chandra Bose N., & Ye Z. (2017). Secure the internet of things with challenge response authentication in fog computing. *36th International Performance Computing and Communications Conference (IPCCC)*, IEEE, pp. 1–2.

Assunção M. D., Calheiros R. N., Bianchi S., Netto M. A., & Buyya R. (2015). Big data computing and clouds: Trends and future directions. *J. Parallel. Distrib. Comput.*, vol. 79, pp. 3–15.

Bagula A., Mandava M., & Bagula H. (2018). A framework for healthcare support in the rural and low income areas of the developing world. *J. Netw. Comput. Appl.*, vol. 120, pp. 17–29.

Chen M. & Leung V. (2018). From cloud-based communications to cognition-based communications: A computing perspective. *Comput. Commun.*, vol. 128, pp. 74–79.

Cutler D. R. (2007). Random forests for classification in ecology. *Ecology*, vol. 88, no. 11, pp. 2783–2792.

Goeschel K. (2016). Reducing false positives in intrusion detection systems using data-mining techniques utilizing support vector machines, decision trees, and naive Bayes for off-line analysis. *Southeast Con, 2016*, IEEE, pp. 1–6. doi: 10.1109/SECON.2016.7506774.

Granville V. (2017). *Types of Machine Learning Algorithm in One Picture*. Source: www.datasciencecentral.com/profiles/blogs/types-of-machine-learning-algorithms-in-one-picture. Access date: June 2, 2021.

Hall M., Frank E., Holmes G., Pfahringer B., Reutemann P., & Witten I. H. (2009). The WEKA data mining software: An update. *ACM SIGKDD Explor. Newslett.*, vol. 11, no. 1, pp. 10–18.

Homayoun S., Dehghantanha A., Ahmadzadeh M., Hashemi S., Khayami R., Choo K.-K. R., & Newton D. E. (2019). DRTHIS: Deep Ransomware threat hunting and intelligence system at the fog layer, Future Gener. *Comput. Syst.*, vol. 90, pp. 94–104.

Hong H.-J., Chuang J.-C., & Hsu C.-H. (2017, December). 'Animation rendering on multimedia fog computing platforms. *Proc. IEEE International Conference on Cloud Computing Technology and Science (CloudCom)*, IEEE, pp. 336–343.

Javatpoint, K-Nearest Neighbor (KNN) Algorithm for Machine Learning. Source: www.javatpoint.com/k-nearest-neighbor-algorithm-for-machine-learning. Access date: June 2, 2021.

Khan S., Parkinson S., & Qin Y. (2017). Fog computing security: A review of current applications and security solutions. *J. Cloud. Comput. Adv. Syst. Appl.*, vol. 6, no. 1, p. 19.

Kotsiantis S. B., Zaharakis I., & Pintelas P. (2007). Supervised machine learning: A review of classification techniques. *Emerg. Artif. Intell. Appl. Comput. Eng.*, vol. 160, pp. 3–24.

La Q. D., Ngo M. V., Dinh T. Q., Quek T. Q. S., & Shin H. (2018). Enabling intelligence in fog computing to achieve energy and latency reduction. *Digit. Commun. Netw.*, vol. 5, no. 1, pp. 3–9.

Li L., Ota K., & Dong M. (2018). Deep learning for smart industry: Efficient manufacture inspection system with fog computing. *IEEE Trans. Ind. Informat.*, vol. 14, no. 10, pp. 4665–4673.

Lu L., Xu L., Xu B., Li G., & Cai H. (2018). Fog computing approach for music cognition system based on machine learning algorithm. *IEEE Trans. Comput. Soc. Syst.*, vol. 5, no. 4, pp. 1142–1151.

Malathi D., Logesh R., Subramaniyaswamy V., Vijayakumar V., & Sangaiah A. K. (2019). Hybrid reasoning-based privacy-aware disease predic-tion support system. *Comput. Elect. Eng.*, vol. 73, pp. 114–127.

Muhammed T., Mehmood R., Albeshri A., & Katib I. (2018). UbeHealth: A personalized ubiquitous cloud and edge-enabled networked healthcare system for smart cities. *IEEE Access*, vol. 6, pp. 32258–32285.

Naha R. K., Garg S., Georgakopoulos D., Jayaraman P. P., Gao L., Xiang Y., & Ranjan R. (2018). Fog computing: Survey of trends, architectures, requirements, and research directions. *IEEE Access*, vol. 6, pp. 47980–48009.

Pedregosa Varoquaux F G., Gramfort A., Michel V., Thirion B., Grisel O., Blondel M., Prettenhofer P., Weiss R., Dubourg V., & Vanderplas J. (2011). Scikit-learn: Machine learning in Python. *J. Mach. Learn. Res.*, vol. 12, pp. 2825–2830.

Peralta G., Iglesias-Urkia M., Barcelo M., Gomez R., Moran A., & Bilbao J. (2017). Fog computing based efficient IoT scheme for the Industry 4.0. *2017 IEEE International Workshop of Electronics, Control, Measurement, Signals and their Application to Mechatronics (ECMSM)*, May 2017, pp. 1–6. doi: 10.1109/ECMSM.2017.7945879.

Pérez J. L., Gutierrez-Torre A., Berral J. L., & Carrera D. (2018). A resilient and distributed near real-time traffic forecasting application for Fog computing environments. *Future Gener. Comput. Syst.*, vol. 87, pp. 198–212.

Stojmenovic I. & Wen S. (2014). The fog computing paradigm: Scenarios and security issues. *Computer Science and Information Systems (FedCSIS), 2014 Federated Conference On*, IEEE, pp 1–8.

Tran, Hieu. (2019). *Survey of Machine Learning and Data Mining Techniques Used in Multimedia Systems*. no. 113, 13–42. https://www.researchgate.net/profile/Hieu-Tran-17/publication/340271573_A_SURVEY_OF_MACHINE_LEARNING_AND_DATA_MINING_TECHNIQUES_USED_IN_MULTIMEDIA_SYSTEM/links/5e8182fa92851caef4aca4f7/A-SURVEY-OF-MACHINE-LEARNING-AND-DATA-MINING-TECHNIQUES-USED-IN-MULTIMEDIA-SYSTEM.pdf. 10.13140/RG.2.2.20395.49446/1. (Preprint)

Van Loon, R. (2018). *Machine Learning Explained: Understanding Supervised, Unsupervised, and Reinforcement Learning.* Source: https://bigdata-madesimple.com/machine-learning-explained-understanding-supervised-unsupervised-and-reinforcement-learning/. Access date: June 2, 2021.

Vardhan V. (2020). *Detailed Explanation and Math Behind the Building of Decision Trees* (learners at Medium level). Source: https://laptrinhx.com/detailed-explanation-and-math-behind-the-building-of-decision-trees-learners-at-medium-level-2133379269/. Access date: June 2, 2021.

Yang M., Zhu T., Liu B., Xiang Y., & Zhou W. (2018). Machine learning differential privacy with multifunctional aggregation in a fog comput-ing architecture. *IEEE Access*, vol. 6, pp. 17119–17129. https://doi.org/10.1109/ACCESS.2018.2817523.

Yi S., Qin Z., & Li Q. (2015). Security and privacy issues of fog computing: A survey. *International Conference on Wireless Algorithms, Systems, and Applications*, Springer, pp. 685–695.

Zhang J. & Zulkernine M. (2006). A hybrid network intrusion detection technique using random forests. *The First International Conference on Availability, Reliability and Security, 2006, ARES 2006*, IEEE, pp. 8–269.

4

Application of Machine Learning in Fog Computing

Kabir Jaiswal

School of Computer Science
University of Petroleum and Energy Studies
Dehradun, India

Niharika Singh

School of Computer Science
University of Petroleum and Energy Studies
Dehradun, India

CONTENTS

4.1 Introduction to Machine Learning

Machine learning as a term was first used in a paper written by A. L. Samuel in 1959. According to the author, machine learning was a way for machines to behave the way human beings or animals would (Samuel, 1959). After decades, machine learning has been shaped from theory to reality. Today machine learning tries to address problems that are out of human understanding.

Significant progress in machine learning has brought accessibility to its applications. Due to the exponential amounts of data available to the public and the tools that make machine learning practically possible, like open-source libraries, frameworks, and programming languages built to cater to machine learning needs, the theoretical paradigm of machine learning has started to become viable and efficient. Applications of machine learning range from real-time decision-making in sectors like healthcare, investment banking, and fraud detection to learning over time and modelling changes in industries like e-commerce, social media, and policymaking. Machine learning has emerged as an excellent tool for artificial intelligence to develop efficient approaches to natural language processing, cognitive intelligence, predictive regression models, and much more (Jordan and Mitchell, 2015). Continuous research and development

DOI: 10.1201/9781003188230-4

TABLE 4.1

Applications of Machine Learning

Application	Description
Speech Recognition	Speech recognition systems help understand human and animal speech, and they respond with corresponding replies. Speech recognition relies heavily on machine learning algorithms that are engineered for natural language processing (NLP). NLP includes language understanding and language generation. Both of these processes are achieved using statistical manipulation of the speech input and converting the output generated by NLP algorithms to speech again.
Computer Vision	Computer vision deals with the understanding of image and video data. The applications of computer vision range from handwriting detection to facial recognition to issuing tickets to speeding vehicles by analyzing their speed and plate numbers.
Genetic Modelling	Genetic modelling tries to imitate the behaviour of nature by contemplating change factors like crossover and mutation. Genetic algorithms have applications in sectors like flight scheduling, algorithmic optimization, and early disease diagnosis.
Path Finding and Robot Automation	Path finding and robotic automation rely upon multiple machine learning models coming together at once. These are called multi-modal systems, and this is required as there are a number of factors and simulators that affect the functioning of an automated vehicle.

efforts have brought machine learning closer to commercial use. The development of new and efficient algorithms has democratized the field of machine learning for the better.

Although machine learning is still working its way from infancy and has many untapped research opportunities, it has proven to be resourceful in almost all sectors and businesses.

Machine learning was shaped by statistics and computer science coming together. It has divulged into several dimensions with almost infinite numbers of applications. Due to the continuous development process in learning, algorithms, and databases, ML has become proficient in effectively probing myriad problems at different levels of difficulty. Recounting all its applications is relatively impossible for the scope of this section. Nevertheless, Table 4.1 and this section seek to describe some of the most prominent and impactful applications of ML.

These applications present a corroborated indicator of machine learning's sound capabilities and ongoing development opportunities. The greatest challenge is discovering how these learn what they learn and to harness that understanding to create optimized machine learning models that can outperform state-of-the-art technology.

While understanding the actual workings of a machine learning model may be an endeavor worth researching, areas like cognitive intelligence, perception (Behera and Das, 2017), and complexity optimization can also provide for making machine learning accessible, reliable, and commercially viable.

4.1.1 A Review of Fog Computing

Cloud computing has changed the way we interact with data. Over the past few decades, with the development of efficient and reliant cloud computing infrastructure, industries have optimized their computational and physical costs related to storing and accessing data. Cloud has provided opportunities for small and medium-sized businesses to reach around the globe. While the cloud has not only aided data transfer, it has also made interactions with data more accessible.

These virtues have solved many problems but have created new ones too. With the introduction of the Internet of Things came millions and millions of devices that needed continuous sync with the cloud. This has proven to be a challenge as the networking devices become bottlenecked with the overwhelming number of data relays between the devices and the cloud. The lack of infrastructure around the cloud hindered latency and awareness, which were key to making the cloud architecture sustainable. This created a need for an intermediary to perform specific tasks related to the cloud without intercepting the cloud. Hence Cisco introduced fog computing. Fog computing is a cloud closer to the device layer and can store and manipulate data without the cloud's involvement. The fog layer helps prevent increased latency and creates a locational awareness.

Fog computing is built on the infrastructure, application, and platform. These three pillars help the fog architecture to execute efficiently. The infrastructure helps maintain the network and the devices in the fog layer. The application aids user and device requirements using application modelling. The platform is used to keep attributes like service requirements, security, and resource allocation in check (Naha et al., 2018).

Fog computing has become one of the necessary additions to the cloud and device layer. Fog has aided the following applications:

- Marine sciences (Yang et al., 2019) monitor and analyze the ocean's environment.
- Farming (Malik et al., 2020) uses analyzing to understand the requirements of the farms using sensors and taking appropriate actions using actuators.
- Healthcare (Fratu et al., 2015) has benefited enormously by using fog to monitor patients, creating a familiar environment.
- Fog computing has become an essential component in many cattle farms and helps early prognosis of diseases (Taneja et al., 2020) in young and adult cattle.

These are just a few ways fog computing has made cloud applications more accessible and industry ready. Although these applications work in real-time, they are a long way from being cost-efficient and viable. Table 4.2 describes the research and development toward fog computing that has been yielding positive results. The present state of fog has already demonstrated its prowess and will continue to become even more efficient with continuous efforts in the field.

4.1.2 Machine Learning in Fog Computing

When we examine the process behind using fog computing, we can gauge two main branches of procedures: networking and processing of data. Since fog computing resides

TABLE 4.2

Research and Development in Fog Computing

Field of research	Ongoing research and description
Security and Privacy	Fog computing exposes the current infrastructure to a lot of security threats like third-part intrusions, malfunctioning (Gedeon et al., 2018). Stojmenovic et al. (2016) have outlined the use of different authorization and authentication techniques to overcome these issues.
Fog Computing Infrastructure	Fog computing is an inconsequential addition to the cloud and hence has to be compatible with already existing infrastructure. Meurisch et al. (2015) talk about using WiFi routers as fog devices to bridge the gap between cloud and end nodes.
Resource Management	Fog computing relies on shared computing resources between the nodes in the fog layer. This creates a need for an efficient resource management mechanism. This mechanism needs to have capabilities to handle multiple heterogeneous devices and provide multiple tenancies at the same time. Tong et al. (2016) talk about a hierarchical architecture to distribute workloads efficiently amongst the edge nodes and the ways this process can be optimized.

on the lower levels of networking, it retains many undesirable traits like insufficient memory, resource allocation, heterogeneity, and operational management.

The core problem lies in that the amount of data and the computational power of a central server are often vastly disproportionate to local resources. As a result, it is not easy to scale cloud applications cost-effectively.

The architecture we use for fog computing is an extension of today's TCP/IP. Fog computing works by directly connecting computing resources, which makes it a decentralized computing environment. It features very low latency and high bandwidth between the different nodes in a fog computing architecture. Traditional cloud technologies are based on end-to-end network packet transport protocols that cannot scale efficiently in this type of architecture.

Machine learning has shown adequate ability to overcome these problems efficiently. Fadlullah et al. (2017) talk about a plethora of applications of machine learning in networking like:

- Bayesian inference technique and GPR for networking wireless sensor networks (WSNs)
- Using classification and clustering models to learn about network traffic
- Managing scarce networking resources by predicting network flow, i.e., data packets with a shared context
- Allocating resources based on learned characteristics from mobility prediction of the devices in the network
- Applications of self-organizing networks (SONs) using deep learning-based cognitive radio networks (CRNs)

These machine learning applications have shown how fog computing has benefited from machine learning to bridge the gap between shortcomings that arise at the fog layer in terms of networking and operating efficiently between the cloud and the edge devices.

Another promising advancement is machine learning for networking (MLN) (Wang et al., 2018). MLN is a more vivid approach and implicates various techniques of machine learning like prediction, classification, and clustering to tackle the problems in networking.

Figure 4.1 gives us an overview of the workflow of MLN. The process starts with the formulation of the problem and defines the machine learning approach to be followed while solving the problem. This is followed by relevant data collection and analysis to understand the data related to the problem. After the preprocessing and analysis of the data at hand, the process moves toward model construction and validation. If the model performs satisfactorily, it is deployed in an environment for the application.

The MLN workflow applies to a plethora of problems like the prediction of incoming traffic in a network (Zhitang Chen et al., 2016) using the Hidden Markov Model (HMM), which uses real-time traffic logs to understand the statistics behind the flow of traffic in the network and generates a prediction of traffic volume in the future.

MLN has also been used for resource scheduling (Mao et al., 2017) using deep belief networks (DBN). These networks work with traffic patterns in a router and try to characterize the patterns to embody the dynamism in a heterogeneous network like the fog layer to predict the following network node periodically.

These approaches have shown how the networking part of fog computing can benefit from machine learning. Another crucial aspect of fog computing, as discussed earlier in this section, is data processing. Storage and manipulation of data are paramount to decrease the computational costs of cloud computing via fog computing.

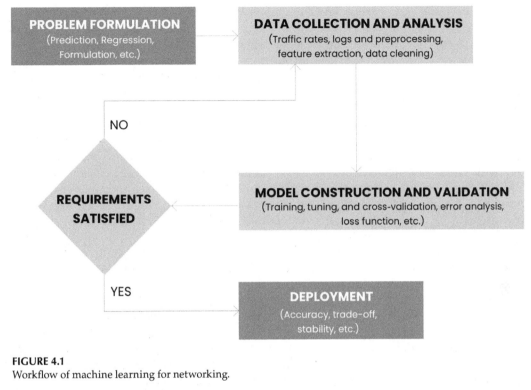

FIGURE 4.1
Workflow of machine learning for networking.

Source: Modified from Wang et al., 2018

Machine learning models like deep neural networks and logistic regression models could classify data in fog nodes according to different attributes. An intelligent storage system recognizes the type of data contained by a file without having to open it beforehand.

4.2 Applications

Most devices and services around us require sensors and actuators to collect data, interpret it, and perform functions. These devices, which are also referred to as the Internet of Things (IoT) devices, work on strict latency requirements while being dense and heterogeneous at the same time. This has made cloud computing handicapped and has been the reason for the emergence of fog computing. As discussed in the previous sections, what is fog computing, and how can machine learning aid the functional and operational requirements of fog computing?

Machine learning has exhibited astounding results as a crucial part of the core functioning of fog computing as well as with other applications that require fog computing for operations. Hogan and Esposito (2017) talk about using machine learning to perform real-time path selection in traffic lights. Traffic engineering is a highly latency-sensitive task as it requires optimized decisions to be made in real-time. The authors use financial modelling techniques that are generally used to predict the future of volatile financial investments, tools, and instruments. The chapter looks at the application of risk minimization derived by portfolio theory. The authors suggest that a Bayesian network yield results that are suitable for estimating latency's performance metric.

Schneible and Lu (2017) describe an efficient approach for anomaly detection. The authors implement an autoencoder model at each node in the fog layer to detect anomalous behavior in the network. *Autoencoders* are an ensemble-based deep learning model that tries to learn representational patterns in data. Autoencoders fall in the category of unsupervised learning algorithms, i.e., they do not follow a set of rules instead try to form their approaches to find patterns in a dataset. The paper describes using autoencoders in each fog node so that parallel and distributed computation can be performed, eliminating the requirement of extensive resources and continuous data exchange between the cloud and the edge devices. A centralized node aggregates observations and data and transports it to the cloud when a connection is made available. The whole architecture solves two problems at once: observing and detecting anomalies and reducing bandwidth and latency required for the overall operations.

Data collection and aggregation is a crucial aspect of fog computing and machine learning to make better decisions over time. However, since the fog layer is closer to the user, the information is predominantly sensitive. Yang et al. (2018) propose a novel method for multifunctional data aggregation in fog computing using machine learning models that train and learn through queries and predict the forthcoming queries. This process takes the burden off the cloud servers and does not require fog nodes to compute complex functions like encryption and decryption. The proposed schema by the author dictates that each sensor node split its data into n parts and sent it randomly to m fog nodes. These fog nodes receive split data from many different sensors and provide input to the training model, which learns to predict the aggregate of the split parts of data. Since each fog node's training and prediction infrastructure is isolated, there is no collusion in the learning parameters. After the training model has learned the data and can predict the query data, it takes advantage of these predictions to avoid differential attacks on the fog architecture.

There are a plethora of applications of machine learning in fog. Some of these applications provide better ways to understand the functional requirements; some provide better data understanding, while on the other machine learning also provides analytically intrinsic application in fog, keeping into account the scarce resource availability.

The applications discussed in this section have demonstrated how machine learning is a crucial addendum to fog computing. These applications have not only helped solve hardware scarcity issues but also software issues like security and privacy. However, machine learning has impacted majorly three sectors of fog computing: resource management; accuracy; and viability, security, and privacy.

4.2.1 Resource Management with Machine Learning

The nodes in the fog layer and the edge layer produce enormous amounts of data each day. This data requires processing at the edge level with the resources available at the edge. The fog layer has been built with abilities like multi-tenancy to cope with the scarcity of resources at the edge, but these abilities alone cannot suffice the resource requirements of fog computing. Sun and Lin (2017) describe a resource pooling technique by aggregation of distributed resources into one virtual pool of resources, which is also called 'crowdfunding.' Machine learning algorithms are used to reward devices that actively participate in this pool as well as to decide optimal approaches for distributing resources amongst the devices.

Li et al. (2018) talk about applying machine learning in a fog environment to detect defects in a manufacturing line. The authors design an experiment in which they use convolutional neural networks to understand the type and degree of defect in a product. Since each manufacturing facility has multiple production lines with hundreds of products being manufactured simultaneously, this increases the computational needs of automated systems like defect detection with convolutional neural networks. Therefore, the authors shifted the detection model from a centralized cloud server to distributed fog nodes. These fog nodes help perform the required functions while only reporting observations to the central server when they have enough data to add to the legacy dataset to improve the complete model.

There are several other machine learning algorithms and approaches that have made fog computing more relevant in industrial, commercial, and healthcare industries, like transforming healthcare with the transition from physical, locational requirements to patient-centric environments that help accumulate patients' vitals without the need for physical presence at healthcare institutions (Farahani et al., 2018).

Although resource management and allocation remain a prominent topic of research, the developments in the sector have made fog computing efficient and reliable to use in production settings.

4.2.2 Accuracy and Viability

Machine learning algorithms learn through data in a pursuit to form an understanding of the data's recurring patterns. These algorithms have limitations in terms of how accurate they can be and where their abilities converge. Therefore, the accuracy of these algorithms is studied to determine the confidence in the output they generate. Accuracy is dynamic for the type of model and the application. There are no preset thresholds for accuracy; it is at the user's discretion to decide whether a machine learning model with a certain amount of accuracy fits for real-time usage.

Qian et al. (2018) present a novel artificial intelligence-based efficient experience management model (AIEM), which combines machine learning models from AI and customer experience management (CEM) for a better understanding of emotional data and lays the foundation for better customer experience. The paper sought to accurately manage and classify a consumer's emotions in real time to increase the accuracy of results and recommendations it generates. VGG-net and Alexnet machine learning algorithms are used for facial recognition and speech analysis. These models are deployed on Affective Interaction through Wearable Computing and Cloud Technology (AIWAC) systems, which are edge nodes in a fog computing environment. The model accuracy and delays are measured, and it is noted in the experiment that these algorithms provide increased accuracy in real-time settings for emotion detection.

Continuous research and development in machine learning alone have provided for algorithms that can perform classification, predictions, and clustering with great accuracy and limited data. However, the introduction of fog computing and the quality of data produced in huge volumes can provide machine learning algorithms with new optimizations and applications.

4.2.3 Security and Privacy in Fog Computing with Machine Learning

IoT networks are distributed systems with seemingly scarce resources. This affects the development of secure IoT systems, as functional requirements are prioritized over a system that provides security robustness (Khan et al., 2017).

Machine learning algorithms have previously had astounding success in detecting outliers and anomalies in varied types of environments like fraud detection in banking transactions, natural disaster prediction using weather data, etc. Many researchers have implemented the same approaches to make fog networks secure with intrusion detection in the network, anomalous request flagging (Zissis, 2017), and various other security threats.

Abbas et al. (2019) propose a fog security service (FSS) as a novel method that works by offloading the security and privacy tasks to a fog node. The proposed architecture works in an end-to-end fashion by providing applications such as identification, authentication, and confidentiality. This architecture was tested on an Optimized Network Engineering Tool with a single topology and varied traffic loads. The paper uses two cryptography schemes: identity-based encryption as well as signature-based identity.

Security and privacy hence are crucial elements of fog computing as they deal with sensitive and confidential data. Fog systems are vulnerable to security threats at network, hardware, and data levels. All these aspects must be secured to provide for a robust fog network that can be applied in real-world scenarios. The increasing number of synergies being developed in security tools and algorithms and machine learning will benefit sectors like healthcare, social networking platforms, cloud storage, fog computing, and IoT networks.

This section has discussed why the scalability of fog computing relies upon abundant resource availability, which can perform functions and computation accurately and securely deliver solutions, and how it can be aided by machine learning. The following section will discuss the open questions and research areas in fog computing and machine learning.

4.3 Future of Machine Learning in Fog Computing

The ever-growing number of devices like sensors, actuators, routers, and mobile devices in the fog layer has made it practical. Fog computing has taken the burden from the cloud servers and distributed the workload to the devices in the fog layer. The previous sections have highlighted how machine learning has provided ways to make fog computing viable and production ready.

Although, even with the present research and ongoing efforts, some open-ended questions and areas need attention to make fog computing even more stable.

First and foremost, amongst these areas is intra-device communication and data processing. The devices in the fog computing layer are prone to failures due to many reasons like accidental power off, hardware failure, etc. The reliability of the device's performance or a group of devices can only be achieved by distributing the compute and storage units across multiple devices. This requires a robust communication mechanism between these various devices.

The second area is regarding memory management and data synchronization. Again, in a distributed computing scenario, it is almost impossible to have an accurate synchronization as each device has its memory hierarchy and context set up, making it difficult for them to provide correct data consistency.

The third area is in the implementation of the machine learning model on top of fog computing devices. This gives rise to challenges like scaling up applications, hardware design, and architectural setup.

These issues and vulnerabilities describe the areas that require further research and development to make fog computing in IoT networks reliable. Various other problems and questions unfold in fog computing and machine learning, which this chapter has sought to address and discuss. However, machine learning has impacted fog computing for the better and will continue to play an essential role in its wide adoption in various industries and sectors.

4.4 Summary and Conclusion

This chapter has aimed to outline the functions and features of fog computing and machine learning and how they can work in confluence to yield a production-ready environment. The chapter discusses various machine learning applications in fog computing, from software aspects like data processing and distribution to hardware aspects like energy consumption and resource allocation processes. The chapter also discusses how machine learning has served to enhance security and privacy in the fog network, as the data procured and produced by the fog and edge devices are sensitive to the user.

The chapter also discusses the open issues and topics of research in the later sections that will provide even more promising applications of fog computing in even more varied sectors.

Machine learning and fog computing are both new arenas of research that have rapidly found many applications in almost all sectors of commerce and life. These subjects together have shown astounding results and are ripe for even more research and development in the coming years.

References

Abbas, N., Asim, M., Tariq, N., Baker, T., & Abbas, S. (2019). A mechanism for securing IoT-enabled applications at the fog layer. *Journal of Sensor and Actuator Networks*, 8(1), 16. doi:10.3390/jsan8010016

Behera, R., & Das, K. (2017). A survey on machine learning: Concept, algorithms, and applications. *International Journal of Innovative Research in Computer and Communication Engineering*, 2.

Fadlullah, Z. M., Tang, F., Mao, B., Kato, N., Akashi, O., Inoue, T., & Mizutani, K. (2017). State-of-the-art deep learning: Evolving machine intelligence toward tomorrow's intelligent network traffic control systems. *IEEE Communications Surveys and Tutorials*, 19(4), 2432–2455. doi:10.1109/COMST.2017.2707140

Farahani, B., Firouzi, F., Chang, V., Badaroglu, M., Constant, N., & Mankodiya, K. (January 2018). Towards fog-driven IoT eHealth: Promises and challenges of IoT in medicine and healthcare. *Future Generation Computer Systems*, 78, 659–676. doi:10.1016/j.future.2017.04.036

Fratu, O., Pena, C., Craciunescu, R., & Halunga, S. (2015). Fog computing system for monitoring Mild Dementia and COPD patients—Romanian case study. *2015 12th International Conference on Telecommunication in Modern Satellite, Cable and Broadcasting Services (TELSIKS)*. IEEE. https://doi.org/10.1109/telsks.2015.7357752

Gedeon, J., Heuschkel, J., Wang, L., and Mühlhäuser, M. (2018). FOG computing: Current research and future challenges. https://www.semanticscholar.org/paper/Fog-Computing%3A-Current-Research-and-Future-Gedeon-Heuschkel/3eab46d43f6a09db797d5966c470732d17bd81a7

Hogan, M., & Esposito, F. (October/November 2017). Stochastic delay forecasts for edge traffic engineering via Bayesian networks. *Proceedings of the IEEE 16th International Symposium Network Computer Applications* (pp. 1–4). Cambridge, MA.

Jordan, M. I., & Mitchell, T. M. (2015). Machine learning: Trends, perspectives, and prospects. *Science (New York, NY)*, 349(6245), 255–260. doi:10.1126/science.aaa8415

Khan, S., Parkinson, S., & Qin, Y. (2017). Fog computing security: A review of current applications and security solutions. *Journal of Cloud Computing*, 6(1). doi:10.1186/s13677-017-0090-3

Li, L., Ota, K., & Dong, M. (October 2018). Deep learning for smart industry: Efficient manufacture inspection system with fog computing. *IEEE Transactions on Industrial Informatics*, 14(10), 4665–4674. doi:10.1109/TII.2018.2842821

Malik, A., Rahman, A. U., Qayyum, T., & Ravana, S. D. (2020). Leveraging fog computing for sustainable smart farming using distributed simulation. *IEEE Internet of Things Journal*, 1–1. doi:10.1109/JIOT.2020.2967405

Mao, B., Fadlullah, Z. M., Tang, F., Kato, N., Akashi, O., Inoue, T., & Mizutani, K. (2017). Routing or computing? The paradigm shift towards intelligent computer network packet transmission based on deep learning. *IEEE Transactions on Computers*, 66(11), 1946–1960. doi:10.1109/TC.2017.2709742

Meurisch, C., Seeliger, A., Schmidt, B., Schweizer, I., Kaup, F., & Mühlhäuser, M. (2015). Upgrading wireless home routers for enabling large-scale deployment of cloudlets. *Lecture Notes of the Institute for Computer Sciences, Social Informatics and Telecommunications Engineering*, 162, 12–29. doi:10.1007/978-3-319-29003-4_2

Naha, R. K., Garg, S., Georgakopoulos, D., Jayaraman, P. P., Gao, L., Xiang, Y., & Ranjan, R. (2018). Fog computing: Survey of trends, architectures, requirements, and research directions. *IEEE Access*, 6, 47980–48009. doi:10.1109/ACCESS.2018.2866491

Qian, Y., Lu, J., Miao, Y., Ji, W., Jin, R., & Song, E. (2018). AIEM: AI-enabled affective experience management. *Future Generation Computer Systems*, 89, 438–445. doi:10.1016/j.future.2018.06.044

Samuel, A. L. (July 1959). Some studies in machine learning use the game of checkers. *IBM Journal of Research and Development*, 3(3), 210–229. doi:10.1147/rd.34.0210

Schneible, J., & Lu, A. (2017). Anomaly detection on the edge. *MILCOM 2017 – 2017 IEEE Military Communications Conference (MILCOM)*. IEEE. https://doi.org/10.1109/milcom.2017.8170817

Stojmenovic, I., Wen, S., Huang, X., & Luan, H. (2016). An overview of fog computing and its security issues. *Concurrency and Computation: Practice and Experience*, 28(10), 2991–3005.

Sun, Y., & Lin, F. (2017). Non-cooperative differential game for incentive to contribute resource-based crowdfunding in fog computing. *Boletin Tecnico/Technical Bulletin*, 55, 69–77.

Taneja, M., Byabazaire, J., Jalodia, N., Davy, A., Olariu, C., & Malone, P. (2020). Machine learning based fog computing assisted data-driven approach for early lameness detection in dairy cattle. *Computers and Electronics in Agriculture*, 171. doi:10.1016/j.compag.2020.105286

Tong, L., Li, Y., & Gao, W. (2016). A hierarchical edge cloud architecture for mobile computing. *IEEE INFOCOM 2016 – The 35th Annual IEEE International Conference on Computer Communications*. IEEE. https://doi.org/10.1109/infocom.2016.7524340

Wang, M., Cui, Y., Wang, X., Xiao, S., & Jiang, J. (March–April 2018). Machine learning for networking: Workflow, advances and opportunities. *IEEE Network*, 32(2), 92–99. doi:10.1109/MNET.2017.1700200

Yang, J., Wen, J., Wang, Y., Jiang, B., Wang, H., & Song, H. (2019). Fog-based marine environmental information monitoring toward ocean of things. *IEEE Internet of Things Journal*, 1–1. doi:10.1109/JIOT.2019.2946269

Yang, M., Zhu, T., Liu, B., Xiang, Y., & Zhou, W. (2018). Machine learning differential privacy with multifunctional aggregation in a fog computing architecture. *IEEE Access*, 6, 17119–17129. doi:10.1109/ACCESS.2018.2817523

Zhitang Chen, Jiayao Wen, & Yanhui Geng. (2016). Predicting future traffic using Hidden Markov Models. *2016 IEEE 24th International Conference on Network Protocols (ICNP)*. IEEE. https://doi.org/10.1109/icnp.2016.7785328

Zissis, D. (2017). Intelligent security on the edge of the cloud. *2017 International Conference on Engineering, Technology and Innovation (ICE/ITMC)*. IEEE. https://doi.org/10.1109/ice.2017.8279999

5

Simulation and Modeling Tools for Fog Computing

Antonio A. T. R. Coutinho

State University of Feira de Santana
Bahia, Brazil

Elisangela O. Carneiro

State University of Feira de Santana
Bahia, Brazil

Fabíola Greve

Institute of Computing
Federal University of Bahia
Salvador, Brazil

CONTENTS

DOI: 10.1201/9781003188230-5

5.1 Introduction

Extensive research efforts have been made to address platform constraints of a cloud based Internet of Things (IoT). As an extension of cloud computing, the fog computing model (Iorga et al. 2018) offers a hierarchic conceptual architecture that integrates cloud resources with core network devices. Its infrastructure may include a wide number of fog nodes running fog services and applications between end-user devices and the cloud data centers. Therefore, to validate such large-scale systems, it is essential to test their parts in an appropriate facility to evaluate characteristics such as performance, scalability, and safety (Coutinho et al. 2018b).

A real-world testbed is ideal for verifying how proposed fog system components and algorithms operate with realistic system parameters and conditions. Evaluating solutions with a small number of devices and nodes does not ensure that they will operate correctly in the fog large-scale context, both in terms of performance and quality. A broad infrastructure is needed in this regard, with networking, computation, and storage resources deployed in a hierarchy of tiers from the data source to the data center. Fog testbeds can be difficult or even unfeasible to use for the following reasons:

- *Cost and accessibility*: Real-world testbeds are expensive, and their access is limited to members of consortiums or lead industries (Industrial Internet Consortium n.d.). Therefore, a real-world fog infrastructure may be beyond the budget of low-cut research projects. It is fair that more active experimentation in the fog field should pay big dividends. However, the most significant value will come when the knowledge gained from testbeds is accessible for all academic and professional communities.

- *Configuration complexity and time demands*: Existing open IoT testbeds may be adapted to evaluate fog solutions. Adjih et al. (2015) and Sanchez et al. (2014) describe public large-scale infrastructures that allow authorized users to run IoT applications over many resources. However, these infrastructures require extra work to test fog solutions as they were not initially designed to accommodate a fog system (Coutinho et al. 2018b). Also, fog developers must deal with the system complexity introduced by many involved items and the interplay of different technologies and applications. In this case, the time demanded to set up a fog testbed to harness the advantage of real-world experimentation may be a weighted requirement.

- *Does not provide a controllable environment*: Testing and validation of solutions for fog computing using testbeds are challenging for researchers. According to Aral and De Maio (2020), computational scientists often use computing resources that are provided by commercial cloud providers, and the use of commercial public or private infrastructures may affect the reproducibility of experiments. Also, due to privacy issues, Aral and De Maio (2020) pointed out that some capabilities and measures might not be available on commercial public infrastructures, since they are managed by other organizations.

Therefore, before testing solutions on real large-scale fog platforms, other faster and cost-benefit options should be explored to exclude inefficient algorithms and methods. The research community has widely used modelling and simulation of cloud distributed systems to evaluate cutting-edge protocols, services, and architectures. In the same way, the adoption of fog modelling frameworks has the potential to shorten deployment time, reduce the costs involved with real-world infrastructure, and improve the quality of the services provided.

This chapter provides an overview of frameworks and modelling tools that allow the design and testing of fog solutions. In the elaboration of this chapter, several surveys (Margariti, Dimakopoulos, and Tsoumanis 2020; Svorobej et al. 2019; Markus and Kertesz 2020; Perez Abreu et al. 2020; Usha 2020; Ashouri et al. 2019; Gill and Singh 2021) that examine different aspects of modelling and simulation in fog scenarios were summarized. Beyond the studies considered in this chapter, the relationship of fog computing with recent and similar paradigms such as edge computing (Ashouri et al. 2019) has produced specific modelling proposals (Ashouri et al. 2019; Taheri and Shuiguang Deng 2020) that also extend cloud computing to the edge of the network but focus on supporting IoT devices and services close to the end users. Although dealing with similar problems of fog computing, these modelling and simulating tools are out of the scope of this chapter.

The rest of the chapter is organized as follows. Section 5.2 introduces fog modelling concepts, motivations, and challenges. Sections 5.3 and 5.4 describe the goals of the model and the main features of the most widely referenced fog modelling tools, classified respectively into fog simulators and fog emulators. Section 5.5 offers a short practical tutorial on installing and configuring fog virtualized testing environments running on a host machine and a cluster of computers in a local network. Finally, Section 5.6 concludes this chapter by discussing the current stage of development, challenges, and research directions in fog simulation.

5.2 Modeling Fog Systems

As defined in Margariti, Dimakopoulos, and Tsoumanis (2020), a model is an entire or partially idealized depiction of a realistic or proposed system. The study of the models helps to acquire a better knowledge of systems, interpret different phenomena and interactions between its components, develop predictions about the entire system behavior or some of its parts, and then act based on those predictions.

According to Svorobej et al. (2019), distributed system research has used a variety of analytical modelling techniques such as Markov chains, Petri nets, reliability graphs, fault trees, and reliability block diagrams in order to describe and estimate cloud systems behavior. In Margariti, Dimakopoulos, and Tsoumanis (2020) a brief description of these techniques and case studies are presented. However, Svorobej et al. (2019) pointed out that there are situations when mathematical modelling methods are hard to use due to the heterogeneity, scale, and complexity of the studied systems. In such situations, simulation frameworks may offer a viable alternative. For example, Sarkar and S. Misra (2016) employed a theoretical fog model in a wide-scale setting using numerical simulations.

According to Banks (2005), simulation is a methodology based on reproducing the functioning of systems. In this method, there is the possibility to change the system inputs to investigate and validate the different properties of the model. Birta and Arbez (2007) define a simulator as a device that reproduces characteristics of specific systems considered essential for different finalities such as training of administrators and operators and developing new systems features, identifying problems, and involved costs. Therefore, a simulator is a powerful tool to experiment solutions before deploying them on a real infrastructure.

One of the system domains that can benefit from simulation methods is fog computing. The fog model was proposed as a current solution in several areas that impact society, such as health, energy, and industrial applications. From the first proposals in Bonomi et al. (2012) to the present, emphasis has been placed on creating a suitable fog framework that can be employed as a model for developers. Nevertheless, despite growing investments in this area, fog platforms and applications have not yet reached a required maturity level, and current approaches try to prototype emerging solutions mainly using modelling tools.

As one of the earliest companies in the fog computing field, Cisco provides commercial fog products and an open testbed environment based on the IOx platform. The IOx Fog Director ("Cisco Fog Director—Cisco" n.d.) and Cisco IOx Sandbox permit developers with a low-cost laptop to reserve a virtual environment and remotely deploy and test IOx fog applications based on virtual machines (VM). The IOx Sandbox is an appropriate strategy for driving the teaching-learning of the Cisco platform. However, being limited to a small number of nodes is insufficient for widely distributed experiments.

The widespread acceptance of the fog paradigm and the challenges of deploying and testing real-world fog infrastructures and management strategies have motivated the development of extensible fog model simulation frameworks. The development of fog simulators that allow analyzing different requirements of these systems is not trivial. Margariti et al. (Margariti, Dimakopoulos, and Tsoumanis 2020) identify the main deployment requirements associated with fog simulation tools:

- *Infrastructure modelling*: The fog architecture is hierarchically distributed with at least three tiers to represent the cloud, fog, and IoT/end-user devices. In terms of functionality, the fog infrastructure can be represented as a linked graph, where the most popular resource types such as storage, compute, and communication must be supported and distributed. Also, different functionalities, capacities, and characteristics of resources need to be modelled. In large-scale scenarios, the scalability of simulation or the capacity of adding devices while maintaining simulation accuracy is a requirement that must be maintained.

- *Technology modelling*: In fog environments, virtualization technology provides scalability systems while several distributed computing methods are used to process requests in an autonomous way. The research community has proposed new resource management mechanisms to distribute application tasks across available and most efficient well-located fog nodes. As evaluation tools, simulators need to support different factors that allow the examination of key resource management approaches (Ghobaei-Arani, Souri, and Rahmanian 2019) such as load balancing, task offloading, application placement, resource scheduling, resource provisioning, and resource allocation.

- *Applications modelling*: Fog computing demands models and simulators that can execute services and applications. A vast array of applications in different domains and their requirements for low latency, time sensitivity, efficiency, and accessibility for mobile users are foreseen in the fog paradigm. Simulation tools should provide control and data management mechanisms to support vertical applications, the concurrent execution of applications and services, and the sharing of cloud and fog resources. Also, the inclusion of application performance aspects in simulators may help provide responsive solutions to end users.

- *Cost Modelling*: The concept of cost is present in environments such as fog computing, where services are provided to user applications. Therefore, different metrics involved with fog computing costs such as operational, communication, processing, storage, migration, software, energy, security, and sensors should be considered in simulation and modelling tools. These metrics can be used to propose, for example, cost-aware schemes for resource allocation. Simulators that support cost models can help deploy eligible and competitive fog computing applications.

Different characteristics and requirements of modelling and simulation tools that support fog models are described in other surveys. Svorobej et al. (2019) address the main deployment challenges associated with the simulation of fog and edge sceneries and the requirements of fog simulation tools. Perez Abreu et al. (2020) present an overview of six fog simulation tools, outlining their key features and functionality. Markus and Kertesz (2020) provide an analysis, taxonomy, and categorization of fog simulators using viewpoints such as software metrics and properties related to the fog models present in these environments. Usha and Kompalli (Usha 2020) present a comparative analysis of resource management and simulation tools in conjunction with a comparison of various edge computing concepts. Ashouri et al. (2019) evaluate available simulators in order to identify qualities and assess which ones they support. Gill and Singh (2021) employed a systematic search strategy to identify relevant tools in the literature of fog computing and help researchers to explore related proposals.

However, even faced with these challenges and requirements, researchers have used system modelling to investigate and answer emergent questions in deploying resources and applications at intermediate layers between the cloud and end-user's devices. In addition, the professional community uses fog simulation and modelling tools to identify problems; evaluate performance; propose new techniques, applications, or services; and minimize risks for users and fog providers. The recent proposal of new fog simulation and modelling tools and the release of new versions with additional functionalities in earlier fog environments indicate that the development of these frameworks is still in progress and helpful in this area.

The following sections present the most referenced fog simulation frameworks and modelling tools from the literature search. In addition, the properties and requirements of simulation platforms and modelling tools are summarized, seeking to help researchers and professionals find a suitable environment to develop or evaluate their technical proposals.

5.3 Fog Computing Simulators

Simulation has been used extensively by researchers and practitioners to model traditional network infrastructures. Currently, there are several network simulation systems such as Wireless Sensor Networks (WSNs), NS-2, ATEMU, OMNeT++, Avrora, and J-Sim. However, these tools are not originally designed for use in fog experiments. According to Svorobej et al. (2019), there are many cloud computing simulators, but only some of them can be configured to model edge/fog computing scenarios.

Table 5.1 resumes the fog simulation environments listed in the second column. The year of the latest release of each simulator software is listed in the first column. The underlying platform is specified in the third column, and the technology used to develop the

TABLE 5.1

Simulator Tools for Fog Computing

Year	Fog Simulator	Underlying Platform	Programming Language	Mobility Model	Cost Model	Energy Model	Failure Model
2016	Edge-Fog cloud (Mohan and Kangasharju 2016; Mohan and Kangasharju 2017)		Python	Y	Y	N	N
2016	iFogSim (Gupta et al. 2016)	CloudSim	Java	N	Y	Y	N
2017	MyiFogSim (Lopes et al. 2017)	iFogSim	Java	Y	Y	Y	N
2017	FogTorch (Brogi and Forti 2017)		Java	N	N	N	N
2017	FogTorchPI (Brogi, Forti, and Ibrahim 2017)	FogTorch, Monte Carlo Simulator	Java	N	Y	N	Y
2017	RECAP (Byrne et al. 2017; Ostberg et al. 2017)	N/A	Java	Y	Y	Y	Y
2018	FogExplorer (Hasenburg, Werner, and Bermbach 2018a; Hasenburg, Werner, and Bermbach 2018b)	N/A	JavaScript	N	Y		N
2018	FogNetSim++(Qayyum et al. 2018)	OMNeT++	C++	Y	Y	Y	N
2019	FogBus (Tuli et al. 2019)	Aneka	Java, PHP, RESTfulAPI	N	N	N	N
2019	FogDirMime (Forti, Ibrahim, and Brogi 2019)	Cisco IOx	Python	N	N	N	Y
2019	FogWorkFlowSim (Liu et al. 2019)	iFogSim, WorkflowSim	Java	N	Y	Y	N
2019	YAFS (Lera, Guerrero, and Juiz 2019)	SimPy	Python, JSON	Y	N	N	Y
2018	FogDirSim (Forti, Pagiaro, and Brogi 2020)	FogDirMime	Python, RESTfulAPI	N	N	Y	Y
2020	MobFogSim (Puliafito et al. 2020)	iFogSim, MyiFogSim	Java	Y	Y	Y	N
2021	FoBSim (Baniata and Kertesz 2021)		Python	N	N	N	N

simulator is indicated in the fourth column. The following columns indicate whether the simulator implements mobility, cost, energy, and failure models. Some simulators provide models quite limited. The simulators will be briefly described in this section.

5.3.1 Edge-Fog Cloud

The Edge-Fog cloud[1] (Mohan and Kangasharju 2016, 2017) simulator is a node-oriented, fully decentralized hybrid of edge and fog computing cloud model. The decentralized architecture enables decoupling processing time from network delays by handling processing close to data generators (Mohan and Kangasharju 2016).

The proposed Edge-Fog cloud architecture comprises three layers, which contain different resource types: (i) edge layer; (ii) fog layer; and (iii) data store. The layers are described briefly here but can be found in detail in Mohan and Kangasharu (2016).

- *Edge layer:* It has a set of loosely coupled devices operated by humans with different computing capabilities, such as computers, tablets, small data centers, etc. These resources are one-two hops away from IoT devices and clients. The resources at the edge layer are connected to each other. The communication between the edge layer and the fog layer is considered reliable.

- *Fog layer:* The devices present in the fog layer have high computation capabilities and run cloud applications. These devices are interconnected with edge devices from high-speed and reliable links. Fog efficiently manages the computationally tasks that are delegated by edge devices.

- *Data store:* It consists only of servers that store all the data in the cloud that are accessed by the fog and edge layers.

In addition, the Edge-Fog cloud simulator implements the Least Processing Cost First (LPCF) algorithm to allocate tasks to nodes (Mohan and Kangasharju 2016). The goal is to allocate tasks to nodes that produce optimal processing time and near optimal network costs. Thus, it is possible to minimize the processing time and network costs.

According to Mohan and Kangasharju (2017), the Edge-Fog cloud has the following benefits: (i) *reduced network load;* (ii) *native support for mobility;* (iii) *providing context;* and (iv) *no single point of failure.*

The Edge-Fog cloud simulator is designed and implemented in Python. The simulator creates a network with edge and fog resources and a job dependency graph from user-defined parameters (Mohan and Kangasharju 2016).

5.3.2 iFogSim

Gupta et al. (2016) added new functionalities to the CloudSim simulator (Calheiros et al. 2011) and developed an event-based simulator toolkit for fog computing, the iFogSim[2] (Gupta et al. 2016). The iFogSim is one of the most popular tools used to model and simulate IoT and fog environments. iFogSim measures the impact of resource management techniques in terms of latency, network congestion, energy consumption, and operational cost (Gupta et al. 2016).

The hierarchical architecture of iFogSim maintains physical, logical, and management components (Margariti, Dimakopoulos, and Tsoumanis 2020). The architecture involves a hierarchical arrangement of sensors, fog nodes, and the cloud at the core of the network. Fog devices, actuators, and sensors are used as physical components. While the logical components are the processing modules and their interaction as a directed graph, the management components are three main services: (i) monitoring components; (ii) resource management; and (iii) power monitoring. Aral and De Maio (2020) describe the elements of the hierarchical architecture of the iFogSim in a bottom-up approach, as follows.

- *IoT sensors and actuators* are responsible for sensing the environment and emitting observed values to upper layers, and controlling a mechanism or system, respectively. Typically, sensors detect changes in the environment, and actuators respond to those changes.

- *Fog devices* are usually located between the cloud and edge network or IoT devices. The fog device maintains modules to connect the sensors to the Internet (gateways) and provide cloud resources provisioned on demand.

- *Data generated* are a sequence of immutable values emitted by sensors or fog devices.

- *Infrastructure monitoring* collects data from sensors, actuators, fog devices, and network elements and monitors the performance and status of the applications and services deployed on the infrastructure. Besides, monitoring components provide this information to other services.

- *Resource management* is essential to ensure quality of service (QoS) constraints and minimize wasted resources. It is the central component of the architecture, where placement and scheduling decisions are maintained, and controls the state of available resources.

- *Applications models* designed for use in the fog are directed graphs based on the distributed data flow (DDF) model. iFogSim (Gupta et al. 2016) offers two models to be used in IoT applications:

  i. *Sense-Process-Actuate model:* Sensor emits data as a data stream that is processed in the fog. Based on the resulting data, commands are sent to the actuators.

  ii. *Stream processing model:* Fog devices continuously process data streams received from sensors. Processed data is stored in data centers for analytics and large-scale.

- *IoT applications* in iFogSim are modelled as a collection of modules that perform processing on incoming data.

iFogSim (Gupta et al. 2016) is written in Java, and physical topologies are built from a JSON file format or Java APIs. The GUI allows the user to create physical elements that communicate through message passing, specify their properties, and build their topology. iFogSim supports the simulation of entities and services and provides a management component aids in the placement, scheduling, and monitoring of applications (Gupta et al. 2016).

5.3.3 MyiFogSim

MyiFogSim[3] (Lopes et al. 2017) is an extension of iFogSim (Gupta et al. 2016) to support mobility through the migration of virtual machines (VMs) between fog computing. The simulator has used VMs to host applications and data of the users. This action is possible due to the migration capabilities of MVs, which can be used to move applications and data between fog servers based on device mobility. The VM migration is essential in fog computing to support user mobility.

Lopes et al. (2017) describe the features needed to the MyiFogSim add to iFogSim to simulate user VM migration:

- *User device mobility* includes positioning on map coordinates (x, y) in a Cartesian plane. All simulated entities have a placement assigned from their coordinates. MyiFogSim users can define the map boundaries.

- *Radio base stations* add the responsibilities and features of a wireless network access point, including connection/disconnection of devices and handoff management system.

- *Migration of virtual machines* is a parallel task that can start and end anytime, independently of the handoff process. MyiFogSim (Lopes et al. 2017) implements migration of AppModules, which represents the application components.

- *Migration strategies* determine the fog server for which the VM is going and how the migration is performed.

- *Migration policies* consider user speed, direction, and geographic location to define when a user VM should be migrated.

MyiFogSim explored different strategies to determine the destination fog server and to implement VM migration. A developer can design different migration policies and strategies and determine which elements must be monitored to implement them.

5.3.4 FogTorch and FogTorchPI

Borgi et al. (Brogi and Forti 2017) propose a general and extensible model to support QoS-aware deployments of IoT applications to fog infrastructures. This model is supported by FogTorch,[4] a simulator written in Java that allows developers to customize the fog infrastructure, define QoS policies for latency and bandwidth, and specify application requirements (Margariti, Dimakopoulos, and Tsoumanis 2020). FogTorch does not include a cost and mobility model.

FogTorchPI[5] (Brogi, Forti, and Ibrahim 2017) is an extension of FogTorch; inherits hardware, software, and QoS parameters; and provides facilities for configuring QoS for communication links. Thus, the FogTorchPi allows the express processing capabilities (e.g., CPU, RAM, storage) and average QoS attributes as latency and bandwidth of a fog infrastructure.

The FogTorchPI (Brogi, Forti, and Ibrahim 2017) approach is based on the formal model and algorithms presented in FogTorch (Brogi and Forti 2017). The authors relate the concept of QoS profile as a set of pairs (l, b), where l and b denote the average latency and bandwidth required for a communication link, respectively. Fog infrastructure is considered as a 4-tuple (T, F, C, L) where each one represents a set of things (T), fog nodes (F), cloud datacenters (C), and fog-to-fog, fog-to-cloud, and cloud-to-fog communication hyperlinks (L), respectively. The communication link (L) is associated with its respective QoS profile.

FogTorchPI uses probability distributions based on historical data to model QoS of communication links that describe changes in the featured latency or bandwidth over time as a function of network conditions (Brogi, Forti, and Ibrahim 2017).

According to the authors, FogTorchPi handles input probability distributions and estimates a QoS guarantee of different deployments using the Monte Carlo method (Dunn and Shultis 2011). FogTorchPI simulates the various runtime behaviors of communication links and aggregates the results from all runs by computing two metrics, QoS assurance and fog resource consumption (Brogi, Forti, and Ibrahim 2017). These metrics enable the comparison of alternative deployments and assess the impact of potential changes to the fog infrastructure/applications. Thus, the IT experts decide where to deploy the components of an application to get the best QoS assurance.

5.3.5 RECAP

RECAP[6] simulator (Byrne et al. 2017; Ostberg et al. 2017) is an open-source simulation framework that enables the testing of infrastructure using a variety of different workloads, user distribution, network topology, and (physical and virtual) resource placement models. The RECAP aims to simulate large-scale scenarios in cloud, fog, and edge computing to assist with decision-making and control in the administration of data center resources and applications. The decision-making and control are possible through the simulation of applications and applications subsystems, infrastructure resources and resource management systems, experimentation, and validation of simulation results (Ostberg et al. 2017).

The RECAP simulator operates with other tools designed to realize ideas relating to resource management, data analytics, and intelligent automation for cloud/edge/fog computing. These tools include the RECAP data collector and analyzer, the RECAP application modeler, the RECAP workload modeler, and the RECAP optimizer (Ostberg et al. 2017).

The RECAP simulator assists the RECAP optimizer in evaluating various deployment and infrastructure management alternatives in terms of cost, energy, resource allocation, and utilization.

According to Ostberg et al. (2017), the RECAP simulator consists of the following components:

- *Experiment Manager:* The objective is to collect all models and configuration settings for the simulation experiment. An event generator determines available options and launches the specified simulation instance with the specified parameters.
- *Simulation Manager:* Controls the simulation cycle by connecting RECAP infrastructure models (RIM) and simulation engine model elements using the ModelMapper.
- *Event Coordinator:* Is responsible for managing optimization and failure events and serializing simulation results to database storage.
- *Event Generator:* Creates a distribution of failures or new virtual entity (VE) arrivals for the simulation duration. Additionally, it can be extended to incorporate additional types of events into the simulation routine.

The output of the RECAP simulation framework varies depending on the use case. However, it is typically a collection of user-defined metrics such as bandwidth, resource consumption (CPU, memory, storage), network delay, energy consumption, active number of virtual machines, and cache hits and misses (Ostberg et al. 2017). The simulated behavior encompasses context-aware service and mobility for various user, thing, and service categories.

5.3.6 FogExplorer

FogExplorer[7] (Hasenburg, Werner, and Bermbach 2018a, 2018b) is an interactive simulation tool for evaluating the QoS and cost evaluation of fog-based IoT applications early in the design phase. The simulator is built using an iterative modelling and simulation process. The developer begins by developing a high-level infrastructure model and an application model that enable a high-level abstract description of their respective assets (Hasenburg, Werner, and Bermbach 2018b).

- *Infrastructure model:* Specifies the machines and their connections. The properties of this model include a performance indicator, memory size and cost, connection latency between machines, and bandwidth size and cost for each connection.
- *Application model:* Specifies the application modules and all inter-module data streams. This model has three general types of modules: sources, services, and sinks. Data is generated by sources that are processed and forward results by services and received by sinks. Module properties include the memory requirements to run correctly, the estimated processing time on the reference machine, and data output rates per module.

In the FogExplorer, users can specify infrastructure and application models, create deployment maps, and analyze the effects on QoS and cost metrics (Hasenburg, Werner, and Bermbach 2018b). FogExplorer is an open-source project and is built as a front-end JavaScript application. The tool runs on a modern web browser, where graph visualization is possible.

5.3.7 FogNetSim++

FogNetSim++[8] (Qayyum et al. 2018) is an event-driven simulator with the primary goal of providing a static or dynamic environment for sensors, fog nodes, distributed data centers, and a broker node. This framework supports various mobility models and enables the simulation of realistic network characteristics such as packet loss, bandwidth, and error rate.

The FogNetSim++ provides the energy model and pricing model. The energy model is the combination of device energy and energy consumed at a fog node. The pricing model applies to network, storage, and compute components used for network, storage, and other tasks.

According to Qayyum et al. (2018), FogNetSim++ is built at the top of OMNET++ and is composed of diverse modules. The main modules are described as follows:

- *Broker node:* This is responsible for handling connections, computing requests, transfers, and keeping track of all fog nodes. In addition, the broker connects with the user nodes and fog nodes and manages all the fog nodes. The fog nodes inform the available resources to the broker. The broker uses a scheduling algorithm to assign tasks as per incoming requests to the best fog resource available. The broker can communicate with other devices over UDP, TCP, SCTP, or MQTT protocols. This module is considered the core of FogNetSim++ (Qayyum et al. 2018).

- *User nodes:* These can be static or mobile nodes. Static nodes are physically connected to the broker via an Ethernet cable, while mobile nodes are connected via a wireless network. FogNetSim ++ supports various wireless device mobility models, classified as trace-based, deterministic, stochastic, or combined (Qayyum et al. 2018).

The simulator provides detailed configuration options to users. It includes modules for configuring the network environment. Due to the open-source nature of FogNetSim++, researchers can easily replace the existing resource-sharing algorithm with another and add new modules and test cases.

5.3.8 FogBus

FogBus[9] (Tuli et al. 2019) is a framework that enables end-to-end IoT-fog(edge)-cloud integration to deal with limitations of platform independence, security, resource management, and multi-application execution in real-world frameworks. FogBus provides platform-independent interfaces and computing instances for the execution and interaction of IoT applications. FogBus assists users in running multiple applications concurrently and service providers in managing their resources (Tuli et al. 2019). Additionally, FogBus employs blockchain technology, authentication, and encryption techniques to ensure data integrity while transferring confidential data and applies authentication for data privacy. FogBus was developed to analyze sleep apnea.

In FogBus, the various hardware instruments are connected through software components that allow structured communication and application execution on any platform (Tuli et al. 2019). According to Tuli (2019), an integrated IoT-fog-cloud environment using FogBus consists of hardware, software, and network structure, which are briefly described as follows:

- The hardware elements are IoT devices, fog gateway nodes (FGN), fog computational nodes (FCN), and cloud data centers that form the base for FogBus.

- FogBus provides several interconnected software components capable of coping with the operating system (OS) and peer-to-peer (P2P) communication-level heterogeneity of various hardware instruments to facilitate IoT-fog-cloud integration. These components are classified into three types of system services: broker service, computing service, and network structure. The system services are described in Tuli et al. (2019).
- Network structure facilitates the interaction among hardware instruments to share numerous data and information among software components. The FogBus communication is persistent, stable, secure, scalable, and fault tolerant. Different aspects of the network structure of FogBus, such as topology, scalability, reliability, security, and performance are detailed in Tuli et al. (2019).

In FogBus, the built-in blockchain feature is generic, developed in Java, and located in different FCNs. Blockchain on fog nodes can be disabled to reduce network usage, as few security attributes need to be transferred across infrastructures (Tuli et al. 2019).

The FogBus system services are written in PHP and Java and are used with the application layer protocol (HTTP). Thus, it is possible to overcome the heterogeneity of OS and communication links of different fog nodes. In addition, FogBus integrates cloud-fog environments by a platform-as-a-service (PaaS) model holding customized services, service providers, and managing resources to users according to the system context (Tuli et al. 2019).

5.3.9 FogDirMime

The FogDirMime[10] (Forti, Ibrahim, and Brogi 2019) simulator is an open-source prototype in Python that aims to model the behavior of the Cisco FogDirector,[11] a tool for managing Internet of Things (IoT) applications on fog systems. FogDirMime enables the evaluation of different management policies in the presence of probabilistic variations in end-to-end communication links and hardware resources of fog nodes (Forti, Ibrahim, and Brogi 2019).

The FogDirMime class implements all basic operations of FogDirector, infrastructure management, application management, and monitoring. The modelling and FogDirMime can be advantageously used to comprehend FogDirector functioning through concise and unambiguous operational rules and to test different infrastructure. The infrastructure can vary due to executing operations in FogDirector or interactions with the system outside of FogDirector (Forti, Ibrahim, and Brogi 2019). This evolution of the infrastructure was modelled as an extension to the transition of the system.

The purpose of FogDirMime is to compare various management policies for applications and infrastructure, taking into account energy consumption, uptime, and resource utilization. Although FogDirMime refers to resource availability and quality of service, it makes no mention of costs.

5.3.10 FogWorkFlowSim

FogWorkflowSim[12] (Liu et al. 2019) is a flexible and efficient toolkit for evaluating task allocation and resource management strategies in a fog environment using user-defined workflow applications. According to authors, the FogWorkflowSim is capable of automatically: (i) configuring a fog computing environment for workflow applications; (ii) executing workflow applications submitted by the user; and (iii) evaluating and comparing the performance of various task scheduling and computation offloading strategies using three fundamental metrics as cost, energy, and time.

FogWorkflowSim is a Java-based application that combines the functionality of iFogSim (Gupta et al. 2016) and WorkflowSim (Chen and Deelman 2012), modifying the resource allocation techniques to obtain the integration between the two simulators.

The architecture of FogWorkflowSim (Liu et al. 2019) is organized into three layers that perform distinct functions and assist the higher levels in their operations. The layers are described here in a down-top approach:

- *Fog computing environment:* It consists of three layers that represent the types of devices present in a fog environment, namely: end device, fog node, and a cloud server. The Fog Device class represents all types of resources in the fog environment, simulating different devices by altering hardware specifications (computing and storage capacity) and bandwidth (uplink/downlink). In addition, the Fog Device class provides an interface to manage and allocate hardware resources, including methods to simulate the computation, storage, and execution of allocated workflow tasks (Liu et al. 2019).

- *Workflow system:* It includes a set of modules responsible for starting the simulation, representing the workflow tasks in the system, clustering multiple tasks into a job using clustering algorithm, performing the scheduling algorithm for initiating the virtual machine, submission, updating, and return of the workflow tasks.

- *Resource management:* It is divided into four components responsible for various functions: (i) the virtualization of various types of storage resources and computation; (ii) strategies for offloading and task scheduling; and (iii) control that is composed of various metrics to assess performance application (Liu et al. 2019).

The FogWorkflowSim supports personalized workflow structures with multiple task numbers that must be converted to the XML format. In addition, the simulator presents a user interface divided into pages that are described in Liu et al. (2019).

5.3.11 YAFS

The other fog simulator (Yet Another Fog Stimulator [YAFS]) is a discrete event simulator proposed by Lera et al. (Lera, Guerrero, and Juiz 2019) for simulated scenarios involving fog and edge computing and mobile IoT. This simulator aims to analyze application design and deployment and incorporate scheduling, placement, and routing strategies. According to Lera, Guerrero, and Juiz (2019), the YAFS includes the following functionalities:

- *Network:* YAFS allows the visualization of communication links between devices through a graph or network view model. Besides, it allows the creation or removal of any link or network entity during the simulation using custom tags and timing distributions, allowing for efficient and flexible scenario definition.

- *Workload sources:* Each workload source corresponds to an IoT sensor, an actuator, or a user requesting a service. The request services are generated based on a well-defined distribution, and each source is connected to a network entity. The YAFS models the user movements within an environment by dynamically creating, changing, or removing workload sources (Lera, Guerrero, and Juiz 2019).

- *Customized placement, scheduling, and routing algorithms:* The user defines which algorithm to use. By default, YAFS defines the placement of each entity and the selection of the shortest path between two entities.

- *Custom processes:* The simulator allows the implementation of events such as work-load source movement, network failure generation, and data collection via third-party applications by customized functions that can be invoked at runtime. YAFS supports dynamic scenarios in service orchestration, placement, user movement, path routing, and workload (Lera, Guerrero, and Juiz 2019).

- *Post-simulation data analysis:* The results are analyzed and presented to the user post-simulation to reduce the overhead. Thus, it eliminates the need to repeat the simulation to analyze additional indicators and share raw results. YAFS includes functions for obtaining network utilization metrics such as network delay, waiting time, response time, among others. The link transmissions and events of computation and workload generation are automatically logged in CSV files.

- *JSON-based scenario definition:* Scenarios can be defined by importing JSON files or allowing other tools to generate scenarios in this format. Furthermore, the simulator allows the use of basic functionality by non-specialist developers.

The components of the YAFS architecture consist of application, selection, placement, population, topology, and core (Lera, Guerrero, and Juiz 2019). YAFS is developed in Python[13] and distributed under the MIT license and includes tutorial, documentation, and examples.

5.3.12 FogDirSim

FogDirSim[14] (Forti, Pagiaro, and Brogi 2020) is a discrete-event simulation environment compliant with Cisco FogDirector RESTful API ("Cisco Fog Director—Cisco" n.d.) for application and infrastructure management. FogDirSim enables the comparison of various application management policies using a set of well-defined performance indicators (e.g., uptime, energy consumption, resource usage, and type of alerts) and by taking into account probabilistic variations in the application workload and failures of the underlying infrastructure.

FogDirSim is built on a microservices architecture consisting of a collection of independently deployable services that communicate via RESTful APIs. The simulator consists of four significant microservices (Forti, Pagiaro, and Brogi 2020), which are described as follows:

- *API Gateway:* This is implemented with the Python Flask micro-framework, and it exposes an API (FD) compliant with a feature-complete subset of the actual Cisco FogDirector API (FD). This micro-service also exposes a custom API (SIM) to retrieve data about the current simulation.

- *Database:* The database microservice manages two non-relational databases implemented with MongoDB. The first (InfrastructureDB) stores all the information about the monitored infrastructure devices and the probabilistic distributions of their available resources (CPU, RAM). The second database (SimulationDB) maintains state information about the simulated infrastructure resources and application deployments.

- *Simulation engine:* This is a discrete-event simulator implemented in Python. It runs a simulation loop that: (i) samples a particular state of the infrastructure and application workload based on the probability distributions defined in the database microservice; (ii) updates statistics on device and application status and checks for alerts triggered during the sampled state; and (iii) pops and executes the next client request to be simulated from the event queue.

- *GUI:* A web-based graphical user interface (GUI) displays key performance indicators (KPIs) for the currently running simulation. Additionally, it is responsible for data aggregation and computation of some of the results output by the simulator.

The FogDirSim can be used to assist in determining when and where to migrate a particular application, how to handle failures and node workload variations best, how many application replicas are required to achieve the desired uptime, and how to reduce energy consumption caused by an inefficient management policy.

5.3.13 MobFogSim

MobFogSim[15] (Puliafito et al. 2020) is an open-source that extends iFogSim (Gupta et al. 2016) (Section 5.3.2) and to MyiFogSim (Lopes et al. 2017) (Section 5.3.3) to enable modelling of device mobility and service migration in fog computing. Migrating a fog service may be one mitigation strategy, ensuring that the service is always close enough to a user (Puliafito et al. 2020). The simulator is implemented in Java.

MobFogSim extends the mobility concepts introduced preliminarily to MyiFogSim (Lopes et al. 2017) by modelling more generalized aspects of device mobility and virtual machine/container migration in the fog, such as user position and speed, connection handoff, migration policies and strategies, to name a few. In addition, they are integrating MobFogSim with the mobility tool Simulation of Urban Mobility (SUMO) (Krajzewicz et al. 2012) to allow more generalized mobility simulation in fog computing. MobFogSim accepts custom user mobility patterns as input data. MobFogSim implements the following data flow in a simulation:

- The SUMO interprets the source mobility database in file .XML format.
- The result of SUMO is then saved in.csv format; each line in this file contains data about devices, such as position x and y on the map, speed in meters per second, the direction in radians, and the simulation time in which these data were collected (Puliafito et al. 2020).
- This new database is used as a basis to define the user mobility in MobFogSim. The simulator interprets this database and modifies it to fit its mobility model.
- A new database is created after the simulation that contains user behavior results for local resource management. These results include (i) the average and maximum latency presented by the application along the path of the user, (ii) the migrations performed; (iii) the packages requested and attended; and (iv) the number of handovers.

MobFogSim is capable of static and dynamic migration. Static migration begins at a known point in time and may depend on the distance to the edge of the area covered by a network access point. The dynamic migration starts based on the parameters of (i) the speed movement of the user, (ii) the network connection between the source and destination fog device, and (iii) the data volume to transmit. A dynamic migration event can significantly reduce the delay experienced by a mobile user. However, static migration decisions are of limited benefit when a user moves quickly or when network conditions between fog devices are poor.

5.3.14 FoBSim

FoBSim[16] is a fog-blockchain simulator proposed by Baniata and Kertesz (Baniata and Kertesz 2021) with the main objective of facilitating the experimentation and validation of integrated fog-blockchain approaches. According to Baniata and Kertesz (2021) the main properties of FobSim are as follows:

- FoBSim includes a variety of consensus algorithms (CA) that are available to be used in any scenario, being proof of work (PoW), proof of stake (PoS), and proof of authority (PoA).
- FoBSim enables easy deployment of blockchain miners in either the fog or end-user layer.
- FoBSim enables the blockchain network to provide various services reliably, including data management, identity management, computational services (via smart contracts [SC]), and payment/currency transfer services (Baniata and Kertesz 2021).
- FoBSim supports both parallel and non-parallel mining processing. A distributed chain remains consistent across various network topologies while gossiping is carried out efficiently.
- FoBSim is the first simulation environment dedicated to simulating any scenario involving fog computing and blockchain technologies.

FoBSim is implemented according to the conceptual workflow to cover all architectural elements to fog computing and blockchain. To start the simulation with FoBSim, the user needs to choose the function of the blockchain that can be (i) data management; (ii) computational services; (iii) payment/incentivization; and (iv) identity management. After the choice of the function, the user can choose the placement of the blockchain, localizing it into the end-users layer or fog layer. Then the user can choose the consensus algorithm among the PoW, PoS, and PoA protocols. After that, the fog nodes, end-users, miners, and genesis block are initiated. Then the simulation is started, and once it provides analysis, the simulation is finished.

The definition of *network topology* is facilitated in FoBSim. It allows the user to indicate the number of nodes in each layer and the number of neighbors of each blockchain node. Additionally, regardless of whether they were deployed in the fog layer or end-user layer, all blockchain nodes are automatically connected into a single giant component. Thus, the effect of modifying the topology of simulated networks can easily be captured (Baniata and Kertesz 2021). FoBSim supposes that the data flows from end-users to fogs and from fogs to the blockchain network. However, it is possible to have additional data flow schemes simulated, for example, from end-users to the blockchain network. FoBSim allows the modifications necessary for the simulated application to be quickly made.

The FoBSim environment is written in Python v3.8 and is a freely available open-source simulation tool. FoBSim can be cloned and run directly, as all variables, lists, dictionaries, and sets have been initialized (Baniata and Kertesz 2021). However, these parameters can be modified in the Sim_parameters.json file before running the code. Specific properties, such as Merkle Trees, Digital Signatures, and Mining Pools, are not implemented in the current version of FoBSim.

5.4 Fog Computing Emulators

The emulation model is defined in McGregor (2002) as a non-pure simulation model where a part of the real system performs some functional part of the model. According to I. McGregor (McGregor 2002), the motivation for using the emulation model lies in the invariable fact that there will exist measurable differences between the performance of the real system and the equivalent simulation model. As models are approximations of real systems, these differences often lead to a lack of credibility that an emulation model attempts to minimize by bringing the model closer to reality (McGregor 2002).

However, the reason for the use of the emulation model does not have a single motivation. According to Coutinho et al. (2018b), although useful, a pure simulation framework does not address the problems relating to its practical implementation. The proposed solutions need to operate in real-world conditions with realistic system parameters and technologies. Since the definition of the emulation model remains valid when turned around, the use of emulation frameworks allows testing solutions under realistic conditions by replacing part of real systems with a proposed model.

The emulation approach has piqued the interest of researchers and developers of fog systems. Coutinho et al. (2018b) point out that, although desirable, the use of a real-world fog testbed facility is expensive, time-consuming, and in some cases difficult to access, configure, and operate. The use of fog emulation frameworks offers a low cost-effective alternative to deploy fog components, algorithms, and applications with real-party systems and technologies. In the following sections of this chapter, the fog emulation frameworks found in the literature will be briefly described.

5.4.1 EmuFog

EmuFog[17] (Mayer et al. 2017) is an extensible emulation framework built on top of MaxiNet (Wette, Draxler, and Schwabe 2014) and optimized for fog computing scenarios. It enables the design of fog computing infrastructures from the ground up and emulates real applications and workloads. EmuFog enables researchers to design network topologies based on use cases, embed fog computing nodes within the topology, and run Docker[18]-based applications on those nodes connected via an emulated network (Mayer et al. 2017).

The design objectives implemented by EmuFog are (i) scalability, allowing the emulation of large-scale fog computing scenarios; (ii) emulation of real applications and workloads, enabling developers to package and run real-world applications in an emulated environment; and (iii) extensibility, to allow that all components of EmuFog architecture are extensible and replaceable by custom-built components that are tailored to the emulated scenario or policies being evaluated. According to Mayer (Mayer et al. 2017), the workflow for simulating fog computing in EmuFog is divided into four distinct stages:

- *Topology generation*: The network topology is generated from a topology generator such as BRITE (Medina et al. 2001) or loaded from a file, allowing for the inclusion of real-world topology datasets.
- *Topology transformation*: The generated or imported network topology is converted into an EmuFog network topology model, representing the network as an undirected graph. Network devices (routers) are connected through links with a

specified latency and throughput. Network devices are grouped into autonomous systems.

- *Topology enhancement*: Fog nodes are used to enhance the network topology. The sub-steps involved in this process are (1) the edge of the network topology is determined; and (2) fog nodes are placed according to a placement policy in the network topology (Aral and De Maio 2020). The user specifies the fog nodes and their computational capabilities in a fog configuration file. Additionally, the user specifies the expected number of clients at the network edge connecting to the application deployed in the fog infrastructure (Mayer et al. 2017).

- *Deployment and execution*: In this phase, a network topology and fog nodes are deployed to the emulated network, and the application components are provided as Docker containers in fog nodes.

An EmuFog experiment is implemented according to user specifications. On the other hand, EmuFog already includes a collection of suitable implementations for a wide variety of fog computing emulation scenarios (Mayer et al. 2017). EmuFog includes a topology generation component that is based on the BRITE network topology generator (Medina et al. 2001). This component generates Internet-scale topologies. Additionally, an adapter is provided to convert BRITE and real-world network topologies from the CAIDA[19] Internet Topology Data Kit (ITDK) to the network topology model of EmuFog.

5.4.2 MockFog

MockFog[20] (Hasenburg et al. 2019) is a system for emulation of fog computing infrastructure in arbitrary cloud environments. Edge machines are also deployed in the cloud and configured to closely resemble the real (or planned) fog infrastructure in an emulated fog environment.

The developers must first model the properties of the desired (emulated) fog infrastructure, including the number and type of machines and the properties of their interconnections to use MockFog (Hasenburg et al. 2019). MockFog includes a visual editor that aids in the modelling phase. Once an infrastructure model has been created, it can be persistently stored and reused. MockFog can automatically instantiate the described infrastructure in the cloud as a bootstrapping infrastructure phase.

A fog infrastructure consists of edge machines, cloud machines, and possibly additional machines located between the edge and cloud. This infrastructure can be described as a graph with machines as vertices and networks connecting them as edges at the most abstract level. Additionally, machines and network connections in this graph can have properties such as compute power of a machine or the available bandwidth of a connection. The developer begins specifying such an abstract graph in the modelling phase before assigning properties to vertices and edges. Hasenburg et al. (2019) describe the properties that MockFog supports as follows:

- *Machine properties*: Machines are the components of the infrastructure that run application code. Fog machines can take various forms, from small edge devices to machines within a server rack to virtual machines provisioned via a public cloud service. The properties of the machines must be described adequately, such as compute power, memory, and storage capacity to emulate the fog environment accurately.

- *Network properties*: Networks connect machines within the infrastructure graph; only connected machines can communicate. In real-world deployments, these connections frequently exhibit a range of network characteristics, such as slow and unreliable connections at the edge and fast and reliable connections near the cloud (Hasenburg et al. 2019). All connections significantly impact the applications that run on them. For example, these characteristics of the connections need to be modelled as delay, dispersion, package loss, corruption, reorder, or duplicate.

In most cases, machines are not directly connected but connected to switches and routers, which are connected to each other. The MockFog includes such virtual routers in the infrastructure model to reduce the complexity of the infrastructure graph by dimensions (Hasenburg et al. 2019).

The bootstrapping infrastructure phase instantiates the existing infrastructure model in the cloud. Each fog machine in the infrastructure model is mapped to a single cloud VM for this purpose; selecting a VM type is simple when the cloud service accepts the machine properties directly (Hasenburg et al. 2019). MockFog has two primary components for instantiating infrastructure models: the node manager and the node agents. Each MockFog configuration contains a single node manager instance. It parses the infrastructure model, establishes a connection to the appropriate cloud provider, configures virtual machines and networks, and installs a node agent on each virtual machine. By contrast, node agents manipulate their respective virtual machines to display the desired network characteristics to applications.

MockFog provides capabilities for injecting various failures during runtime, allowing developers to analyze the fault tolerance of their applications. For instance, it is possible to reduce available memory abruptly (e.g., due to noisy neighbors), disable certain connections, increase messaging delays or package loss probabilities, or render a machine completely unreachable, in which case all communication to and from the respective VM is blocked (Hasenburg et al. 2019). Because these failures are triggered by the same mechanism as the fog emulation, MockFog can save snapshots of current property settings. Developers can then easily preconfigure complex failure scenarios and switch between scenario snapshots in a matter of seconds.

MockFog creates a virtual machine for each node; this is inefficient when the infrastructure model is composed of hundreds of machines. Another limitation is that the MockFog works well for larger edge machines, at least as large as a Raspberry Pi, but fails with smaller devices, as they cannot be accurately emulated. The same limitation applies to IoT sensors and actuators (Hasenburg et al. 2019).

5.4.3 Fogify

Fogify[21] (Symeonides et al. 2020) is an interactive fog computing emulation framework that enables repeatable, measurable, and controllable IoT service modelling, deployment, and experimentation under realistic environment assumptions, faults, and uncertainties.

Fogify allows users to emulate key aspects of fog environments and focus exclusively on evaluating and testing their services, deploying, and managing scalable IoT microservices on top of the emulated environment. Fogify takes care of heterogeneity of resources and network links, controllable faults and alterations, monitor capabilities, rapid application deployment, and relieves users of the burden of dealing with these issues. At a high level, Symeonides et al. (Symeonides et al. 2020) described the Fogify architecture as follows:

- *SDK level*: The deployment of Fogify starts with a description of an IoT microservices application, workload, and fog topology at the SDK level. Fogify extends the docker-compose specification to encapsulate a broad range of fog infrastructure properties, including computing resources, network capabilities, quality of service constraints, and placement policies.

- *Fogify controller*: It acts as a coordinator between the SDK level and the execution environment when an application is ready to deploy. More precisely, the controller validates the submitted description to identify potential issues such as insufficient underlying resources and instantiated the (micro-) services and distributed (any) network restrictions to Fogify agents at the execution layer. For this, the controller communicates via the orchestrator connector with the resource management layer.

- *Cluster orchestrator*: It ensures that containerized services are executed efficiently across the fog environment. The cluster orchestrator manages each local Docker engine process of each fog node and manages container execution.

- *Fogify agents*: They are lightweight processes deployed on each cluster node. According to Symeonides (Symeonides et al. 2020), each agent is composed of three modules that perform a specific function: (i) a server, which accepts requests from the Fogify controller and executes them on the host node; (ii) a listener, which monitors for updates via the container socket; and (iii) a monitor, capturing performance and user-defined metrics in a non-intrusive manner directly from Docker containers. All monitored metrics are stored at the local storage of the agent.

Fogify SDK includes some built-in analytics functions that can be used to analyze monitoring data and plotting functionality that simplifies metric examination. With interactive topology changes and the ability to inspect the effects of those changes, the Fogify SDK enhances the programmability of the platform. It enables developers to incorporate more complex behavior into their components, such as external modules or connections to their tools. The Fogify controller bounds the scalability of Fogify with performance impacted by the number of Fogify agents (Symeonides et al. 2020).

5.4.4 Fogbed Framework

The Fogbed framework (Coutinho et al. 2018a) was created with the support of the SOFT-IoT project (Andrade et al. 2018) as a virtual infrastructure that seeks to facilitate the deployment and testing of scalable fog computing solutions. It is founded on open-source technologies backed by the research community such as Docker containers, Mininet (de Oliveira et al. 2014) network emulators, and Vim-emu (Peuster, Karl, and van Rossem 2016) resource API. The proposed Fogbed architecture seeks to meet the following main requirements pointed out in Coutinho et al. (2018a and 2018b): low cost, flexible configuration, support for third-party systems, and distributed emulation.

An emulation scenario in Fogbed is established by deploying different types of virtual elements such as virtual fog nodes, virtual switches, virtual connections, and virtual fog instances. Furthermore, regarding execution scalability, the virtual environment can be configured to run on a single host fashion or different host machines in a local network.

The Fogbed API allows the user to dynamically add, connect, and remove elements from the virtual network using a desktop-centric approach. An emulation in Fogbed begins by executing a script that creates the topology of the network. When defining an experimental scenario, it is possible to create and deploy virtual fog nodes based on existing Docker containers images, and these images can be arranged in different network topologies.

Then, using a command-line interface (CLI), it is possible to alter runtime virtual fog node parameters such as CPU time and available memory limits of the containers.

As shown in Figure 5.1, Fogbed uses different open-source tools to compose its emulation framework architecture (Coutinho et al. 2018b):

- *Mininet*[22] is a framework that modifies the Linux kernel to emulate a network and its elements. It provides a virtual abstraction of communication channels, network nodes, and switches with native OpenFlow support for flexible custom routing.
- *Containernet*[23] is a core extension that replaces the native virtual nodes of the Mininet framework with Docker containers. This extension isolates resources from the virtual nodes once native virtual nodes of Mininet share the same file system of the host machine by default.
- *Fogbed*[24] introduces cloud, fog, and edge node abstractions. They are represented through a virtual instance that aggregates one or more virtual nodes and virtual switches as a unique manageable virtual element.
- *Topology, instance, and resource APIs* allow configuration of virtual environment, manage virtual instances, and define resource models in emulation.
- *Maxinet*[25] is a project that extends Mininet in a distributed way. It allows the parallel execution of a simulated environment in different host machines.

In the Fogbed framework architecture, emulation scalability and flexible setup are targeted requirements (Coutinho et al. 2018b). Using Maxinet, it is possible to improve scalability by splitting and balancing the emulated environment into independent instances of Fogbed, where each instance runs on a different host machine on a local network. Furthermore, by defining pre-built container images in the topology API, it is possible to obtain a flexible and heterogeneous fog network configuration. Each image can be built

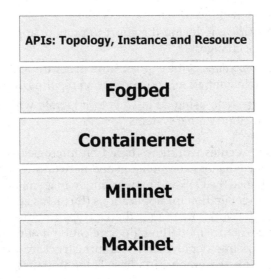

FIGURE 5.1
Fogbed emulation framework architecture.

to run particular services and protocols, representing virtual nodes with different roles and capabilities.

In the Fogbed model, virtual instances represent cloudlets (mini clouds) capable of running one or more applications and services. A specific resource model for each virtual instance must be applied to set out how its resources are managed. For example, an over-provisioning model is used in a virtual cloud instance to emulate cloud data centers. In virtual edge instances, resource allocation can be defined in a restrictive way to simulate low-cost devices.

In addition to the system CLI, Fogbed allows starting and controlling virtual instances using third-party management systems. A well-defined instance may be API is used to communicate between a virtual instance and the management system (Coutinho et al. 2018a). More details about the Fogbed emulation framework are provided in Section 5.5, where a practical example of its use is described through a brief tutorial.

5.4.5 Osmotic Computing

Osmotic Computing[26] (OC) (Buzachis et al. 2021) is an emulator with a similar architecture to Fogbed to deal with scalable, interoperable, configurable solutions for delivering IoT applications in complex, heterogeneous, and dynamic computing environments. According to Buzachis et al. (2021), an OC emulator provides advances in the following aspects:

- *Hybrid cloud-fog/edge-IoT architecture*, allowing the generation of topologies to be more realistic

- *Dynamicity*, distributing the computation dynamically across nodes following QoS requirements and available infrastructure resources

- *Resource provisioning and orchestration*, allowing dynamic and flexible resource provisioning and monitoring mechanisms in complex scenarios in IoT with different QoS, service level agreements (SLA), processing, and mobility

- *Execution of realistic applications* on top of the infrastructure topology, minimizing the effort in preparing applications, avoiding costly changes in stack and tools

- *Real application execution*, reducing the effort to prepare applications by avoiding costly stack and tool changes

- *Well-defined usage procedure*, with explicit infrastructure and application modelling, infrastructure instantiation, and application pipeline deployment

- *Service-oriented integration*, using APIs/CLIs to integrate with appropriated automated osmotic and cloud-native systems

The OC emulation tool executes workflows based on microelements (MELs) under specific conditions where the edge has computation and networking capabilities limited. The MELs run on IoT to enhance the QoS and networking management and the interoperability and efficiency of next-generation IoT applications (Buzachis et al. 2021).

In the high-level design workflow of OC, the DevOps Engineer (DOE) is involved in several phases: (i) infrastructure modelling; (ii) application modelling; (iii) infrastructure instantiation; and (iv) pipeline deployment. The infrastructure topology and the application are modelled as directed graphs. In phase 3, the initializer middleware loads the template primitive containing the infrastructure description and instantiates it by deploying instances and links into an emulated environment. This system is managed by the orchestrator node (ON) for efficiently controlling and managing this complex osmotic eco-system. The DOE communicates with the pipeline via the orchestrator APIs to manage the status of the MELs, perform updates, tear down the pipeline, or deploy a new one.

In the same manner as Fogbed emulator, the core Osmotic toolkit is based on Containernet (Peuster, Karl, and van Rossem 2016), extending the Mininet emulation framework by adding Docker containers as compute instances within the emulated topology during runtime. Also, the Osmotic toolkit core offers similar APIs, although including additional models as Topology API, Instance API, and Resource API (Buzachis et al. 2021).

The *initializer middleware* is written in Python and executes on the DOE host system or within the build pipeline. Its primary function is to initialize the emulation by loading the infrastructure topology definition template. The OC toolkit is beneficial for comprehending the impact of processing power, workloads, and QoS requirements while preserving the service level agreements (SLAs) of the user (Buzachis et al. 2021).

5.5 An Example of Use: A Basic Virtual Fog Testbed Environment

This section will provide a brief tutorial on building a virtual fog testbed to demonstrate how to use a fog modelling tool practically. This tutorial is based on the Fogbed framework, which joins and extends different tools to create fog testbeds in virtualized environments. The sequence of commands and script of example is available and can be obtained from the public and open Fogbed documentation in the Readthedocs.[27]

5.5.1 Installation

In the current release, there are two options for installing Fogbed: (i) it can be installed natively (bare metal) on top of the operating system; or (ii) can run as a privileged Docker container. Both options require at least Linux Ubuntu version 16.04 LTS on a host machine. In option (i), an automatic installation is provided via an Ansible tool playbook.

The following sequence of commands can be applied to a host Linux terminal, where the administrator user password can be requested to allow the sudo command to run:

```
$ sudo apt-get install ansible git aptitude
$ git clone https://github.com/fogbed/fogbed.git
$ cd fogbed/ansible
$ sudo ansible-playbook -i "localhost," -c local install_metis.yml
$ sudo ansible-playbook -i "localhost," -c local install_docker.yml
$ sudo ansible-playbook -i "localhost," -c local --skip-tags "notindocker"
install_fogbed.yml
```

Unless you are trying to get the best emulation performance, use a VM instead of installing in your own machine, since the Fogbed installation process changes the system settings and may mess with your native OS installation or damage it in any way if unsuccessful.

In option (ii), the Fogbed environment runs in a privileged Docker container. Like any Linux-based application, Fogbed can also be containerized as a Docker image. These Fogbed images can then be replicated, distributed, and instantiated on different host machines. A precompiled Docker image of Fogbed is available over the Internet through the public Docker Hub image library.

5.5.2 Fog Environment Configuration

An emulation in Fogbed is configured by defining virtual instances, virtual nodes, virtual switches, and virtual connections. These settings are used to create a virtual fog environment running on a host machine. Flexible environment configuration is achieved using Docker container images. Each virtual node is instantiated from a pre-configured container image that comprises part of a distributed application, as well as its services and protocols. Different types of container images can be used to instantiate virtual nodes. Note that if the Fogbed environment is running as a privileged container, the virtual nodes are running as either containers within containers or nested container deployment.

Before starting an emulation, creating a script that defines the fog topology and its virtual elements is necessary. A predefined topology script is provided to demonstrate the basic configuration of the environment. Thus, after installing Fogbed in a virtual machine or Docker container, and inside the VM or container with Fogbed installed, it is possible to start an emulation through the following command applied in a guest machine terminal:

```
$ python examples/virtual_instance_example.py
```

In the topology script, the environment definition is performed using Python. First, all virtual elements are described and, after their initialization, a predefined experiment can be run over the environment. If the Fogbed installation procedures were performed correctly, the execution of the script should instantiate the fog topology defined in it and run some basic test commands (ifconfig and ping) on virtual nodes of this topology. In the example, looking at the topology script file, we find in its first lines the following declarations:

```
1. topo = FogTopo()
2. c1 = topo.addVirtualInstance("cloud")
3. f1 = topo.addVirtualInstance("fog")
4. e1 = topo.addVirtualInstance("edge")
```

In the first declarations, we have the instantiation of a fog topology followed by the definition of three virtual instances. A virtual instance is an abstraction of Fogbed that allows managing a set of virtual nodes and related virtual switches as a single entity. For example, a virtual instance can be formed by one or more virtual nodes connected by a single virtual switch where, during emulation, new virtual nodes can be allocated in a virtual instance.

The following command can then be applied to a terminal on the host Linux system to build a Fogbed image locally:

```
$ docker build -t fogbed .
```

Or, It is also possible to use the most recently built image:

```
$ docker pull fogbed/fogbed
```

Finally, the following command is used to instantiate a Fogbed container:

```
$ docker run --name fogbed -it --rm --privileged --pid='host' -v \
/var/run/docker.sock:/var/run/docker.sock fogbed /bin/b
```

Next, in the following lines of the topology script, three different resource models are defined. Each template is assigned to one of the virtual instances:

```
erm = EdgeResourceModel(max _ cu=20, max _ mu=2048)
frm = FogResourceModel()
crm = CloudResourceModel()
e1.assignResourceModel(erm)
f1.assignResourceModel(frm)
c1.assignResourceModel(crm)
```

Each virtual instance in Fogbed is associated with a resource model that defines how many resources this instance has to distribute among its virtual nodes (containers) and what is the management strategy for these resources. It defines how many resources this instance must distribute among its virtual nodes (containers) and the management strategy for these resources. Each resource model would define a *max_cu* and *max_mu* value, representing the maximum processing and memory units assigned to the virtual instance. Thus, it is possible to determine how many processing units (*cu*) and memory units (*mu*) the containers can consume during emulation by calculating their values as fractions proportional to the total resources available in the virtual instance where the containers are running. These values are converted to real CPU time and available memory limit. For example, if container *a* is assigned four processing units, and container *b* two processing units, and if they are both in the same virtual instance, container *a* will have twice as much CPU time as container *b*.

There are three types of resource models predefined in Fogbed: EdgeResourceModel, FogResourceModel, and CloudResourceModel, where the default values of *max_cu* and *max_mu* are 32 and 2048, respectively. The management strategy used in EdgeResourceModel has a fixed limit. Therefore, if a container requests resources and all the virtual instance capacity has already been allocated, an exception warns the virtual instance that it cannot allocate new containers. In FogResourceModel and CloudResourceModel, an overprovisioning strategy like the one employed in cloud computing is used. In this case, if a container requests resources, and all the capacity of the virtual instance has already been allocated, the new container is started anyway. However, in FogResourceModel, the value of *max_cu* and *max_mu* remain the same after the new container is started, and the CPU time limit and memory of each container is recalculated.

The following excerpt from the topology script is like examples of other Mininet-based emulators and defines the other virtual elements of fog:

```
d1 = c1.addDocker('d1', ip='10.0.0.251', dimage="ubuntu:trusty")
d2 = f1.addDocker('d2', ip='10.0.0.252', dimage="ubuntu:trusty")
d3 = e1.addDocker('d3', ip='10.0.0.253', dimage="ubuntu:trusty")
d4 = topo.addDocker('d4', ip='10.0.0.254', dimage="ubuntu:trusty")
d5 = e1.addDocker('d5', ip='10.0.0.255', dimage="ubuntu:trusty",
     resources=PREDEFINED _ RESOURCES['medium'])
d6 = e1.addDocker('d6', ip='10.0.0.256', dimage="ubuntu:trusty",
     resources=PREDEFINED _ RESOURCES['large'])
```

As shown, each new virtual node is started passing as a parameter its settings (identifier, IP address, and the used Docker container image), where each one, except node d4, is started inside a virtual instance. The resource parameter in d5 and d6 describes the virtual instance resources the container should receive. If not specified, the *small* resource is set to default. The predefined list of resources is described in the following excerpt from the topology script:

```
PREDEFINED _ RESOURCES = {
    "tiny": {"cu": 0.5, "mu": 32},
    "small": {"cu": 1, "mu": 128},
    "medium": {"cu": 4, "mu": 256},
    "large": {"cu": 8, "mu": 512},
    "xlarge": {"cu": 16, "mu": 1024},
    "xxlarge": {"cu": 32, "mu": 2048}
}
```

If none of the predefined values is suitable for a given virtual node, a new entry can be defined for the specific container. After creating all the virtual nodes, two virtual switches are instantiated, followed by the definitions of their virtual connections using the parameters of class (*cls*), delay (*delay*), and bandwidth (*bw*) between the virtual nodes, as virtual instances, and virtual switches:

```
s1 = topo.addSwitch('s1')
s2 = topo.addSwitch('s2')
topo.addLink(d4, s1)
topo.addLink(s1, s2)
topo.addLink(s2, e1)
topo.addLink(c1, f1, cls=TCLink, delay='200ms', bw=1)
topo.addLink(f1, e1, cls=TCLink, delay='350ms', bw=2)
```

5.5.3 Executing and Interacting with the Fog Environment

A fog application and its services run on one or more virtual nodes within a virtual instance. In the architecture of Fogbed, there are different ways to interact with the environment during an experiment. The first way is by defining procedures in the topology script itself. These procedures will be performed after starting the fog environment in the topology script:

```
exp = FogbedExperiment(topo, switch=OVSSwitch)
exp.start()
```

Where following procedures determine the steps that the experiment must perform:

```
try:
    print exp.get _ node("cloud.d1").cmd("ifconfig")
    print exp.get _ node(d2).cmd("ifconfig")
    print "wait 5 seconds for controller routing algorithms to converge"
    time.sleep(5)
    print exp.get _ node(d1).cmd("ping -c 5 10.0.0.252")
    print exp.get _ node("fog.d2").cmd("ping -c 5 10.0.0.251")
finally:
    exp.stop()
```

In the example, the *ifconfig* command is executed on virtual node d1 running on the virtual cloud instance. Then, the same command is executed inside virtual node d2, this time using a reference variable instead of passing the string identifier of virtual node as a parameter. After five seconds of waiting, the experiment ran the *ping* command from d1 to d2 and vice versa.

In addition to procedures in the topology script itself, container images instantiated as virtual nodes can include preconfigured scripts so that, after their initialization, they run services, applications, and procedures on the emulation environment. For ease of management, the CLI in Fogbed enables users to interact with virtual nodes, examine log files, change container configurations, or run arbitrary commands while the Fogbed platform executes an emulation environment.

Another way to interact with an experiment is to implement one or more processes responsible for launching and managing virtual instances in the Fogbed emulation environment. The management software needs to interact with the emulated environment to control the virtual nodes in virtual instances. In this case, communication between a virtual instance and the management system is performed through a standardized and extensible instance API. The instance API provides infrastructure as a service (IaaS) semantics to manage virtual nodes adaptively. It is designed as an abstract interface to allow for the integration and testing of third-party systems. A developer can implement their own management interface over a virtual instance API. Once implemented, the interaction of the management system with the virtual instance happens through a communication port defined in the topology script. The following example adds an instance-specific API to each virtual instance type:

```
api1 = EdgeApi(port=8081)
api1.connectInstance(e1)
api1.start()
api2 = FogApi(port=8082)
api2.connectInstance(f1)
api2.start()
api3 = CloudApi(port=8083)
api3.connectInstance(c1)
api3.start()
```

Implementing different instance APIs allows each virtual instance to use a different management system or process. With this flexible design, it is possible to execute different management strategies for each virtual instance in the emulated environment.

5.5.4 Distributed Emulation

The previous topics explored emulation on a single host machine. Fogbed can be adapted, using an interface like the one provided by Maxinet (Wette, Draxler, and Schwabe 2014), to run a distributed topology over different machines in a local network (Coutinho et al. 2018b). To run MaxiNet, it is necessary to reserve a set of physical machines called workers. Each worker machine must run an instance of Fogbed that emulates a specific part of the virtual network. Maxinet is responsible for distributing virtual nodes and virtual switches across different workers, interconnected through GRE tunnels. Also, it maintains a list of which virtual element resides on which worker machine on a specific worker called the front-end. Thus, a centered API on the front-end machine makes it possible to control and access all emulated elements.

However, before running the distributed configuration, it is necessary to check: (i) whether all the host machines that will run the distributed environment have Fogbed installed; and (ii) whether host machines can communicate over the local network.

Then it is necessary to start the POX controller in one of the machines present in the network. The POX controller is a software defined network (SDN) application that manages flow control. It is installed in the *pox* subfolder in the Fogbed directory. In the case of running Fogbed as a privileged Docker container, the commands to run the POX controller are:

```
$ cd /pox
$ ./pox.py forwarding.l2 _ learning
```

After running the SDN controller on a machine on the network, it is necessary to configure Maxinet. One machine on the local network will be the front-end of the distributed emulation, and the other machines will be workers. On the network front-end copy, the contents of the */usr/local/share/maxinet/config.example* file to the */etc/MaxiNet.cfg* directory. In the copied file, replace the IP address of the controller attribute with the IP address of the machine running the POX controller:

```
controller = 172.17.0.2:6633
```

In the IP attribute of *[FrontendServer]*, the address of the machine that will run the front-end server must be filled:

```
[FrontendServer]
ip = 172.17.0.2
```

Below the *[FrontendServer]* setting, the name and IP address of each worker machine on the network must be entered. In the following example, two machines are configured:

```
[worker1-hostname]
ip = 172.17.0.2
share = 1
[worker2-hostname]
ip = 172.17.0.3
share = 1
```

It is possible to check the name and IP of a machine running in the terminal:

```
$ hostname
$ ip -4 addr show
```

Then, to finish the Maxinet configuration, it is necessary to run the following command on the machine defined as the front-end:

```
$ sudo FogbedFrontendServer
```

And on each worker machine on the network, it is necessary to run the command:

```
$ sudo FogbedWorker
```

After starting the Maxinet emulation cluster, its status can be checked with the command:

```
$ FogbedStatus
MaxiNet Frontend server running at 172.17.0.2
```

```
Number of connected workers: 2
--------------------------------
worker1-hostname              free
worker2-hostname              free
```

Next, it is necessary to change the topology script to run in a distributed manner. It is possible by changing the experiment class in the topology script to *FogbedDistributedExperiment*:

```
exp = FogbedDistributedExperiment(topo, switch=OVSSwitch)
```

And finally, running the topology script on the front-end machine:

```
$ python examples/virtual _ instance _ example.py
```

After running the distributed environment, it is possible to check from a CLI running on the front-end machine which nodes and switches are emulated on which physical machine. The interactive CLI of the front-end also helps debug experiments, allowing the execution of arbitrary commands centrally on any of the emulated virtual nodes.

5.5.5 Data Collection from Experiments

As in real-world IoT fog environments, the data collected from experiments in Fogbed depends on the experiment being performed and can be implemented in different ways. However, a general scheme for observing the behavior of the environment can be implemented by monitoring the data flows at the interfaces of virtual nodes and virtual switches. In Coutinho et al. (2018a), NetFlow (Claise, Ed. 2004) was employed as the flow-monitoring technology, and NFDUMP[28] as the collection and analysis software. According to Coutinho et al. (2018a), flow records were sent to a specified *nfcapd* flow capture daemon using the *fprobe* command on virtual nodes and the *ovs-vsctl* command on virtual switches. The *nfdump* flow analysis tool was used to study the traffic collected on each virtual interface. In this scheme, the containers were configured to run the capture and monitoring daemons during their startup.

In the case of a distributed emulation, MaxiNet functionalities automatically record and evaluate the use of physical resources throughout the experiment. MaxiNet monitors different parameters such as network utilization, memory consumption and CPU utilization, and of all active workers. Upon completing an experiment, the generated data can be analyzed to ensure that no physical resources have been overloaded during the experiment.

5.5.6 Adapting Fogbed for Testing of Solutions

This chapter covers the basics of installing and configuring the Fogbed framework for local and distributed fog emulation. However, in this tutorial, no IoT architecture was instantiated but only a virtual environment or infrastructure where these architectures can be designed, executed, and evaluated. Different IoT solutions can employ different Docker container images, each comprising part of a particular distributed fog architecture, services, and protocols. Although this framework is motivated by the SOFT-IoT platform, its project was elaborated in an open, generic, and extensible way, being able to be adapted for testing other fog and IoT architectures. More information about Fogbed and its source code can be found on the project page on GitHub.[29]

5.6 Challenges, Research Directions, and Conclusion

This chapter discusses current fog modelling tools for fog computing and presents the most recent studies found in the literature. However, the evolution of fog computing brings new insights and open questions. According to Svorobej et al. (2019), fog and edge simulator frameworks face significant challenges in infrastructure and network management, resource management, mobility, scalability, application architecture design and deployment. Currently, requirements for simulating resource management strategies are a critical feature of simulation analysis at fog and edge domains. In addition, Svorobej et al. (2019) pointed out that there are challenges associated with validating large-scale simulation in terms of accuracy. Therefore, choosing a suitable simulation tool remains based on the type of application.

According to Law (2019), creating a simulation system to address a wide variety of aims is difficult since an appropriate model for one aim may not be appropriate for another. As a result, it is necessary to create a simulation model for a specific set of requirements (Law 2019). Margariti, Dimakopoulos, and Tsoumanis (2020) point out that, at the current stage, fog modelling tools target certain problems and provide specific and limited solutions. Although various requirements are met in different tools, it is a fact that no framework incorporates complete capabilities to simulate fog systems.

However, different authors considered that most current simulators are adapted from previous cloud simulation frameworks. Margariti, Dimakopoulos, and Tsoumanis(2020) also point out that fog computing is an active research area with different real-world implementations emerging commercially. Thus, improvements to the new tools and enhanced simulators that meet current modelling needs are expected in the coming years.

In the current fog computing literature, few works were found comparing fog simulators. As a research direction and future works, different authors consider systematic comparisons of available fog modelling tools and simulators. According Margariti, Dimakopoulos, and Tsoumanis (2020), these studies may involve an assessment of the potential of each simulator and its applicability to specific issues. Also, the study can assess the efficiency of each simulation framework by simulating an equivalent system based on general metrics such as simulation time, memory consumption, and scalability. And finally, by comparing simulation results with measurements from a real system implementation, the research can assess the accuracy of the simulation frameworks.

Notes

1 Edge-Fog cloud: https://github.com/nitindermohan/EdgeFogSimulator
2 iFogSim: https://github.com/Cloudslab/iFogSim
3 MyiFogSim: www.lrc.ic.unicamp.br/fogcomputing/
4 FogTorch: https://github.com/di-unipi-socc/FogTorch
5 FogTorchPI: https://github.com/di-unipi-socc/FogTorchPI
6 RECAP: https://recap-project.eu/simulators/
7 FogExplorer: https://openfogstack.github.io/FogExplorer/
8 FogNetSim++: https://github.com/rtqayyum/fognetsimpp
9 FogBus: https://github.com/Cloudslab/FogBus

10 FogDirMime: https://github.com/search?q=fogdirmime
11 Fog Director: www.cisco.com/c/en/us/products/cloud-systems-management/fog-director/index.html
12 FogWorkFlowSim: https://github.com/ISEC-AHU/FogWorkflowSim
13 www.python.org/dev/peps/pep-0008/
14 FogDirSim: https://github.com/search?q=fogdirsim
15 MobFogSim: https://github.com/diogomg/MobFogSim
16 FoBSim: https://github.com/sed-szeged/FobSim
17 EmuFog: https://github.com/emufog/emufog
18 Docker: www.docker.com
19 www.caida.org/catalog/datasets/internet-topology-data-kit/
20 MockFog: https://github.com/OpenFogStack/MockFog-Meta
21 Fogify: https://github.com/UCY-LINC-LAB/fogify
22 http://mininet.org/
23 https://containernet.github.io/
24 https://github.com/fogbed/fogbed
25 https://maxinet.github.io/
26 OsmoticToolkit: http://github.com/alinabuzachis/OsmoticToolkit
27 https://fogbed.readthedocs.io/en/latest/index.html
28 http://nfdump.sourceforge.net/
29 https://github.com/fogbed/fogbed

References

Adjih, C., E. Baccelli, E. Fleury, G. Harter, N. Mitton, T. Noel, . . . and T. Watteyne. 2015, December. FIT IoT-LAB: A Large Scale Open Experimental IoT Testbed. In *2015 IEEE 2nd World Forum on Internet of Things (WF-IoT)*, 459–464. IEEE.

Andrade, Leandro, Cleber Lira, Brenno Mello, Andressa Andrade, Antonio Coutinho, Fabiola Greve, and Cássio Prazeres. 2018. "SOFT-IoT Platform in Fog of Things." In *Proceedings of the 24th Brazilian Symposium on Multimedia and the Web*, 23–27. WebMedia '18. New York, NY: Association for Computing Machinery. https://doi.org/10.1145/3243082.3264604.

Aral, Atakan, and Vincenzo De Maio. 2020. "Simulators and Emulators for Edge Computing." 10.1049/PBPC033E_ch14.

Ashouri, Majid, Fabian Lorig, Paul Davidsson, and Romina Spalazzese. 2019. "Edge Computing Simulators for IoT System Design: An Analysis of Qualities and Metrics." *Future Internet* 11 (11): 235. https://doi.org/10.3390/fi11110235.

Baniata, Hamza, and Attila Kertesz. 2021. "FoBSim: An Extensible Open-Source Simulation Tool for Integrated Fog-Blockchain Systems." *PeerJ Computer Science* 7 (April): e431. https://doi.org/10.7717/peerj-cs.431.

Banks, J. 2005. *Discrete Event System Simulation*. Delhi, India: Pearson Education.

Birta, L. G., and G. Arbez. 2007. *Modelling and Simulation: Exploring Dynamic System Behaviour*. Ottawa: School of Information Technology and Engineering.

Bonomi, Flavio, Rodolfo Milito, Jiang Zhu, and Sateesh Addepalli. 2012. "Fog Computing and Its Role in the Internet of Things." In *Proceedings of the First Edition of the MCC Workshop on Mobile Cloud Computing*, 13–16. MCC '12. New York, NY: Association for Computing Machinery. https://doi.org/10.1145/2342509.2342513.

Brogi, Antonio, and Stefano Forti. 2017. "QoS-Aware Deployment of IoT Applications Through the Fog." *IEEE Internet of Things Journal* 4 (5): 1185–1192. https://doi.org/10.1109/JIOT.2017.2701408.

Brogi, Antonio, Stefano Forti, and Ahmad Ibrahim. 2017. "How to Best Deploy Your Fog Applications, Probably." In *2017 IEEE 1st International Conference on Fog and Edge Computing (ICFEC)*, 105–114. Madrid, Spain: IEEE. https://doi.org/10.1109/ICFEC.2017.8.

Buzachis, Alina, Daiana Boruta, Massimo Villari, and Josef Spillner. 2021. "Modeling and Emulation of an Osmotic Computing Ecosystem Using OsmoticToolkit." In *2021 Australasian Computer Science Week Multiconference*, 1–9. Dunedin, New Zealand: ACM. https://doi.org/10.1145/3437378.3444366.

Byrne, J., S. Svorobej, A. Gourinovitch, D. M. Elango, P. Liston, P. J. Byrne, and T. Lynn. 2017, December. "RECAP Simulator: Simulation of Cloud/Edge/Fog Computing Scenarios." In *2017 Winter Simulation Conference (WSC)*, 4568–4569. IEEE.

Calheiros, Rodrigo N., Rajiv Ranjan, Anton Beloglazov, César A. F. De Rose, and Rajkumar Buyya. 2011. "CloudSim: A Toolkit for Modeling and Simulation of Cloud Computing Environments and Evaluation of Resource Provisioning Algorithms." *Software: Practice and Experience* 41 (1): 23–50. https://doi.org/10.1002/spe.995.

Chen, W., and E. Deelman. 2012, October. "WorkflowSim: A Toolkit for Simulating Scientific Workflows in Distributed Environments." In *2012 IEEE 8th International Conference on E-Science*, 1–8. IEEE.

"Cisco Fog Director—Cisco." n.d. Accessed June 19, 2021. www.cisco.com/c/en/us/products/cloud-systems-management/fog-director/index.html.

Claise, B., Ed. 2004. "Cisco Systems Netflow Services Export Version 9." https://datatracker.ietf.org/doc/html/rfc3954.html.

Coutinho, A., F. Greve, C. Prazeres, and J. Cardoso. 2018a, May. "Fogbed: A Rapid-Prototyping Emulation Environment for Fog Computing." In *2018 IEEE International Conference on Communications (ICC)*, 1–7. IEEE.

Coutinho, A., H. Rodrigues, C. Prazeres, and F. Greve. 2018b, June. "Scalable Fogbed for Fog Computing Emulation." In *2018 IEEE Symposium on Computers and Communications (ISCC)*, 00334–00340. IEEE.

de Oliveira, R. L. S., C. M. Schweitzer, A. A. Shinoda, and L. R. Prete. 2014, June. "Using Mininet for Emulation and Prototyping Software-Defined Networks." In *2014 IEEE Colombian Conference on Communications and Computing (COLCOM)*, 1–6. IEEE.

Dunn, William L., and J. Kenneth Shultis. 2011. *Exploring Monte Carlo Methods*. Elsevier.

Forti, S., A. Ibrahim, and A. Brogi. 2019. "Mimicking FogDirector Application Management." *SICS Software-Intensive Cyber-Physical Systems* 34 (2): 151–161.

Forti, Stefano, Alessandro Pagiaro, and Antonio Brogi. 2020. "Simulating FogDirector Application Management." *Simulation Modelling Practice and Theory* 101 (May): 102021. https://doi.org/10.1016/j.simpat.2019.102021.

Ghobaei-Arani, M., A. Souri, and A. A. Rahmanian. 2019. "Resource Management Approaches in Fog Computing: A Comprehensive Review." *Journal of Grid Computing* 18: 1–42. https://doi.org/10.3390/s21051832.

Gill, Monika, and Dinesh Singh. 2021. "A Comprehensive Study of Simulation Frameworks and Research Directions in Fog Computing." *Computer Science Review* 40 (May): 100391. https://doi.org/10.1016/j.cosrev.2021.100391.

Gupta, Harshit, Amir Vahid Dastjerdi, Soumya K. Ghosh, and Rajkumar Buyya. 2016. "IFogSim: A Toolkit for Modeling and Simulation of Resource Management Techniques in Internet of Things, Edge and Fog Computing Environments." *ArXiv:1606.02007 [Cs]*, June. http://arxiv.org/abs/1606.02007.

Hasenburg, Jonathan, Martin Grambow, Elias Grunewald, Sascha Huk, and David Bermbach. 2019. "MockFog: Emulating Fog Computing Infrastructure in the Cloud." In *2019 IEEE International Conference on Fog Computing (ICFC)*, 144–152. Prague, Czech Republic: IEEE. https://doi.org/10.1109/ICFC.2019.00026.

Hasenburg, Jonathan, Sebastian Werner, and David Bermbach. 2018a. "FogExplorer." In *Proceedings of the 19th International Middleware Conference (Posters)*, 1–2. Middleware '18. Rennes, France: Association for Computing Machinery. https://doi.org/10.1145/3284014.3284015.

Hasenburg, Jonathan, Sebastian Werner, and David Bermbach. 2018b. "Supporting the Evaluation of Fog-Based IoT Applications During the Design Phase." In *Proceedings of the 5th Workshop on Middleware and Applications for the Internet of Things*, 1–6. Rennes France: ACM. https://doi.org/10.1145/3286719.3286720.

Industrial Internet Consortium. n.d. "Testbeds | Industrial Internet Consortium." Accessed June 4, 2021. www.iiconsortium.org/test-beds.htm.

Iorga, Michaela, Larry Feldman, Robert Barton, Michael J. Martin, Nedim S. Goren, and Charif Mahmoudi. 2018. "Fog Computing Conceptual Model." *Special Publication (NIST SP), National Institute of Standards and Technology.* Gaithersburg, MD, March. https://doi.org/10.6028/NIST.SP.500-325.

Krajzewicz, Daniel, Jakob Erdmann, Michael Behrisch, and Laura Bieker-Walz. 2012. "Recent Development and Applications of SUMO – Simulation of Urban MObility." *International Journal on Advances in Systems and Measurements* 3&4.

Law, A. M. 2019, December. "How to Build Valid and Credible Simulation Models." In *2019 Winter Simulation Conference (WSC)*, 1402–1414. IEEE.

Lera, Isaac, Carlos Guerrero, and Carlos Juiz. 2019. "YAFS: A Simulator for IoT Scenarios in Fog Computing." *IEEE Access* 7: 91745–91758. https://doi.org/10.1109/ACCESS.2019.2927895.

Liu, Xiao, Lingmin Fan, Jia Xu, Xuejun Li, Lina Gong, John Grundy, and Yun Yang. 2019. "FogWorkflowSim: An Automated Simulation Toolkit for Workflow Performance Evaluation in Fog Computing." In *2019 34th IEEE/ACM International Conference on Automated Software Engineering (ASE)*, 1114–1117. San Diego, CA: IEEE. https://doi.org/10.1109/ASE.2019.00115.

Lopes, Márcio Moraes, Wilson A. Higashino, Miriam A. M. Capretz, and Luiz Fernando Bittencourt. 2017. "MyiFogSim: A Simulator for Virtual Machine Migration in Fog Computing." In *Companion Proceedings of the 10th International Conference on Utility and Cloud Computing*, 47–52. Austin, TX: ACM. https://doi.org/10.1145/3147234.3148101.

Margariti, Spiridoula V., Vassilios V. Dimakopoulos, and Georgios Tsoumanis. 2020. "Modeling and Simulation Tools for Fog Computing—A Comprehensive Survey from a Cost Perspective." *Future Internet* 12 (5): 89. https://doi.org/10.3390/fi12050089.

Markus, Andras, and Attila Kertesz. 2020. "A Survey and Taxonomy of Simulation Environments Modelling Fog Computing." *Simulation Modelling Practice and Theory* 101 (May): 102042. https://doi.org/10.1016/j.simpat.2019.102042.

Mayer, R., L. Graser, H. Gupta, E. Saurez, and U. Ramachandran. 2017, October. "EmuFog: Extensible and Scalable Emulation of Large-Scale Fog Computing Infrastructures." In *2017 IEEE Fog World Congress (FWC)*, 1–6. IEEE.

McGregor, I. 2002. "The Relationship between Simulation and Emulation." *Proceedings of the Winter Simulation Conference*, 2: 1683–1688. https://doi.org/10.1109/WSC.2002.1166451.

Medina, A., A. Lakhina, I. Matta, and J. Byers. 2001, August. "BRITE: An Approach to Universal Topology Generation." In *MASCOTS 2001, Proceedings Ninth International Symposium on Modeling, Analysis and Simulation of Computer and Telecommunication Systems*, 346–353. IEEE.

Mohan, Nitinder, and Jussi Kangasharju. 2016. "Edge-Fog Cloud: A Distributed Cloud for Internet of Things Computations." In *Cloudification of the Internet of Things (CIoT)*, 1–6. IEEE.

Mohan, Nitinder, and Jussi Kangasharju. 2017. "Edge-Fog Cloud: A Distributed Cloud for Internet of Things Computations." *ArXiv:1702.06335 [Cs]*, March. http://arxiv.org/abs/1702.06335.

Ostberg, Per-Olov, James Byrne, Paolo Casari, Philip Eardley, Antonio Fernandez Anta, Johan Forsman, John Kennedy, et al. 2017. "Reliable Capacity Provisioning for Distributed Cloud/Edge/Fog Computing Applications." In *2017 European Conference on Networks and Communications (EuCNC)*, 1–6. Oulu: IEEE. https://doi.org/10.1109/EuCNC.2017.7980667.

Perez Abreu, David, Karima Velasquez, Marilia Curado, and Edmundo Monteiro. 2020. "A Comparative Analysis of Simulators for the Cloud to Fog Continuum." *Simulation Modelling Practice and Theory* 101 (May): 102029. https://doi.org/10.1016/j.simpat.2019.102029.

Peuster, M., H. Karl, and S. van Rossem. 2016, November. "MeDICINE: Rapid Prototyping of Production-Ready Network Services in Multi-PoP Environments." In *2016 IEEE Conference on Network Function Virtualization and Software Defined Networks (NFV-SDN)*, 148–153. IEEE.

Puliafito, Carlo, Diogo M. Gonçalves, Márcio M. Lopes, Leonardo L. Martins, Edmundo Madeira, Enzo Mingozzi, Omer Rana, and Luiz F. Bittencourt. 2020. "MobFogSim: Simulation of Mobility and Migration for Fog Computing." *Simulation Modelling Practice and Theory* 101 (May): 102062. https://doi.org/10.1016/j.simpat.2019.102062.

Qayyum, Tariq, Asad Waqar Malik, Muazzam A. Khan Khattak, Osman Khalid, and Samee U. Khan. 2018. "FogNetSim++: A Toolkit for Modeling and Simulation of Distributed Fog Environment." *IEEE Access* 6: 63570–63583. https://doi.org/10.1109/ACCESS.2018.2877696.

Sanchez, Luis, Luis Muñoz, Jose Antonio Galache, Pablo Sotres, Juan R. Santana, Veronica Gutierrez, Rajiv Ramdhany, et al. 2014. "SmartSantander: IoT Experimentation Over a Smart City Testbed." *Computer Networks*, Special issue on Future Internet Testbeds—Part I, 61 (March): 217–238. https://doi.org/10.1016/j.bjp.2013.12.020.

Sarkar, Subhadeep, and Sudip Misra. 2016. "Theoretical Modelling of Fog Computing: A Green Computing Paradigm to Support IoT Applications." *IET Networks* 5 (2): 23–29. https://doi.org/10.1049/iet-net.2015.0034.

Svorobej, Sergej, Patricia Takako Endo, Malika Bendechache, Christos Filelis-Papadopoulos, Konstantinos Giannoutakis, George Gravvanis, Dimitrios Tzovaras, James Byrne, and Theo Lynn. 2019. "Simulating Fog and Edge Computing Scenarios: An Overview and Research Challenges." *Future Internet* 11 (3): 55. https://doi.org/10.3390/fi11030055.

Symeonides, Moysis, Zacharias Georgiou, Demetris Trihinas, George Pallis, and Marios D. Dikaiakos. 2020. "Fogify: A Fog Computing Emulation Framework." In *2020 IEEE/ACM Symposium on Edge Computing (SEC)*, 42–54. San Jose, CA: IEEE. https://doi.org/10.1109/SEC50012.2020.00011.

Taheri, Javid, and Shuiguang Deng, eds. 2020. "Simulators and Emulators for Edge Computing." In *Edge Computing: Models, Technologies and Applications*, 291–311. Institution of Engineering and Technology. https://doi.org/10.1049/PBPC033E_ch14.

Tuli, Shreshth, Redowan Mahmud, Shikhar Tuli, and Rajkumar Buyya. 2019. "FogBus: A Blockchain-Based Lightweight Framework for Edge and Fog Computing." *Journal of Systems and Software* 154 (August): 22–36. https://doi.org/10.1016/j.jss.2019.04.050.

Usha, Vadde. 2020. "Resource Management and Simulation Tools in Fog Computing—A Comparative Study." *International Journal of Advanced Trends in Computer Science and Engineering* 9 (1): 875–882. https://doi.org/10.30534/ijatcse/2020/125912020.

Wette, Philip, Martin Draxler, and Arne Schwabe. 2014. "MaxiNet: Distributed Emulation of Software-Defined Networks." In *2014 IFIP Networking Conference*, 1–9. Trondheim, Norway: IEEE. https://doi.org/10.1109/IFIPNetworking.2014.6857078.

6

Security and Privacy Issues in Fog Computing

Smriti Gaba

Reliance Jio Infocomm Limited
Mumbai, India

Susheela Dahiya

School of Computer Science
University of Petroleum and Energy Studies
Dehradun, India

Keshav Kaushik

School of Computer Science
University of Petroleum and Energy Studies
Dehradun, India

CONTENTS

DOI: 10.1201/9781003188230-6

6.1 Introduction

In the past few years, technology has grown exponentially with growing needs such as the emergence of cloud computing to fulfil the need of storing and processing huge amounts of data brought a major change in different sectors like healthcare, finance, education, e-commerce and many more. Because the concept of cloud computing comes with traffic congestion and latency issues, limitation of bandwidth and other factors affecting the performance of technologies like 5G and Internet of Things (IoT), it is necessary to find a solution that can solve these issues.

The term *IoT* requires no introduction, and the number of IoT-driven smart devices are proliferating. Now each of these devices generates vast amounts of data including variety and velocity factors (Sagiroglu and Sinanc, 2013). The processing and storing of huge amounts of data requires an effective technology that cloud computing could not fulfil due to low latency, bandwidth limitation and many other factors. Therefore, edge computing came into existence, where data from these IoT devices is processed at the device itself or nearby (maybe at a local computer or server). The edge computing solution brought better performance but did not solve the problem as while processing data or while transmitting it to the cloud the latency may highly affect time-sensitive decisions, response to critical system failures get delayed and above all these concerns, cloud computing and edge computing come with their own security and privacy concerns.

Because of the need for effective performance, reduced latency gave birth to a technology based on decentralized infrastructure that could handle the abounding data and its processing. The technology is termed as *fog computing*, found and introduced by Cisco. A foggy environment (where fog computing is deployed) acts like a catalyst for analysis and processing of data leading to the emergence of a more efficient model. The most promising factor of fog computing is providing secure and immediate response to extremely critical data including time-sensitive decisions and response to critical alerts reducing latency delays.

Basically, data is created at the edge of a device, stored and computed on the cloud, and then fog acts as a missing link between these, further providing functionality to analyze what data needs to be pushed to the cloud and which could be processed locally at edge. Working with fog nodes and a foggy network raises security and privacy concerns, which are discussed in detail in this chapter.

6.2 Fog Computing: Applications and Security

Fog computing provides a wide variety of applications for IoT devices. Although many cloud services are implemented widely in commercial solutions, they do not provide efficient solutions to IoT devices such as applications sensitive to location, latency like Smart Grids and Smart Meter (Wei et al., 2014), Connected Vehicular Network, smart wearables and many more.

A large volume of data is being generated in high velocity by these applications; while this data is on its way to a cloud solution for analysis, the immediate response that is required at this point of time to enable an IoT device to act on time may not happen, further leading to critical instances including latency in medical applications that if not given immediate response could result in life-critical scenarios. Therefore, fog computing provides support to these applications for immediate response, storage, computation and other services as per the requirement of the device.

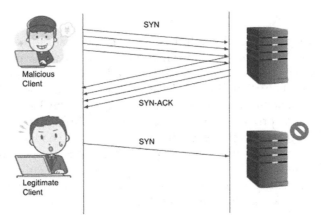

FIGURE 6.1
SYN flood attack illustration.

While considering a basic overview of fog computing being a link between cloud and edge device, it is observed that the security issues that apply to cloud computing could be inherited by the fog computing platform. These security threats may include:

(i) **Denial-of-Service (DoS) attacks:** Excessive requests are sent to the network making resources unavailable to legitimate users. For example, a SYN Flood attack where the attacker sends excessive SYN messages continuously and does not send ACK messages so that SYN requests floods the server as illustrated in Figure 6.1 and due to absence of ACK message, none of the requests gets terminated, resulting in a DoS attack.

(ii) **Access Control Issues:** Access control issues allow an unauthorized user to gain access, acquire data and permissions to modify configurations.

(iii) **Insecure APIs:** Insecure APIs that are provided to a third-party to give services to customers could lead to access of security keys, sensitive information, decryption of customer's encrypted data and modification of parameters affecting endpoints.

(iv) **Account Hijacking:** An attacker may steal account credentials via cross-site scripting (XSS) malicious payload attacks, phishing attacks, execution of buffer overflow by sending extra bytes of data in the username or password field, resulting in voiding the password and gaining complete access to the account.

(v) **Shared Technology Vulnerabilities:** Due to the absence of isolation between virtual machines, sharing of infrastructure, platform and software gives birth to many vulnerabilities increasing the potential attack surface for unauthorized access, privilege escalation, VM based attacks, weak segregation, etc.

6.3 Foggy Internet of Things

A foggy environment provides efficiency to IoT applications in terms of latency, bandwidth, resource allocation, etc. These IoT applications are widely deployed with the concept of fog computing that provide low latency, location awareness and real-time decisions.

The role of fog computing in IoT and related security concerns could be elaborated with following applications:

6.3.1 Smart Meter

A Smart Meter as termed extends the functionality of calculating the generated and utilised electricity along with remotely controlled supply cut-off as per requirement.

Smart Meter generates large amounts of data, which is collected and processed using data aggregation at these units; furthermore, while processing data aggregation (Nazmudeen et al., 2016) at these units, a lot of time is consumed due to low bandwidth. However, the existence of the fog computing model provides the solution to optimize throughput of these devices. The data collected and aggregated is processed through deployed fog nodes that acquire readings of the meters in a defined time frame (Merino et al., 2021). One of the involved fog nodes is dedicated to the data reduction process so that performance can be enhanced.

Therefore, a fog-based approach creates advanced metering infrastructure that reduces overheads in the network and thus improves throughput.

Security Concern:

- The solution could allow an external illegitimate node to replicate data from hardware units used for aggregation and modify the data, leading to compromise of confidentiality, integrity and availability of data (Feng et al., 2010).

- As a fog-based approach is decentralized, it could increase attack surface for access control vulnerabilities via which an attacker can maintain access and configure parameters to own the data that is being processed and transmitted between fog nodes. This could further result in data loss or compromised integrity of data (Rial and Danezis, 2011).

6.3.2 Healthcare System

IoT devices and sensors are widely used in medical equipment and healthcare sectors. Deploying many sensors for pulse rate, oxygen levels, cardiac functions, etc. form a Smart Healthcare Infrastructure. Considering the processing and analysis of large amounts of data from these sensors, latency issues can lead to delay of response, causing life-critical issues. Therefore, the fog computing model is to be deployed (Gia et al., 2015) for better performance. The classification of data being processed and generated from sensors could be performed at fog nodes (Prieto González et al., 2016). Distributed databases extend functionality to store heterogeneous data, and integration of fog computing in medical infrastructures will reduce latency and prevent critical situations by providing immediate response and on-time decisions.

One of the applications includes the electrocardiogram (ECG), which is used for diagnosis of cardiac diseases. Several sensors transmit data that is stored across distributed databases by fog node while providing real-time graphical results of ECG diagnosis. The detection of critical stroke is carried out efficiently by fog nodes providing quick response.

Security Concern:

- Medical records consist of sensitive data of patients, and the application used could be exploited while the data is in transit; an attacker may intercept the traffic using a proxy tool and obtain data or even modify real-time data.

- The real-time data being transmitted over sensors may use insecure MQTT implementation, which could be exploited by attackers who can subscribe to MQTT topics and obtain data or in some cases may even publish data by issuing MQTT broker commands.

- Attackers may also try to perform DoS attacks, as the sensors work wirelessly providing unauthorized access to the communication and flooding with malicious packets or requests.

6.3.3 Software Defined Network

The emergence of software defined networking (SDN) enabled organizations to have customized network services that can be controlled centrally using software applications. The SDN technology separates the control plane of network devices from the data plane that forwards data in the network, enabling automated provisioning and policy-based management. With the implementation of SDN, the network could be controlled intelligently, which makes it easier to manage the entire network with consistency.

SDN has extended applications like the software-defined wide area network (SD-WAN) that controls and manages connections between the network and user over WAN. The deployment of SD-WAN enhances performance and provides customized services on the basis of its intelligence.

6.3.3.1 SDN and Vehicular Network

The intelligence of SDN with its controlled management if integrated with the fog computing model results in a high performance extended application like a "Vehicular Network using Fog based Software Defined Network" (FSDN) [16] which consists of a SDN controller that controls the entire network along with resource management for the fog node, SDN wireless nodes (vehicles), SDN Road-Side-Unit (fog device), a cellular base station and SDN controller for RSU, which controls the network of fog devices that perform data forwarding services. The fog-enabled base stations and the fog devices (SDN Road-Side-Unit) send vehicle information to the SDN controller and provide faster communication.

Security Concern:

- As per the scenario it could be observed that the number of connections due to the rising number of vehicles will result in a large network with multiple routes between same nodes that indicate mismanagement of a centralized system. This could become a potential attack surface for DoS attack.
- Communication is wireless leading to distortion issues, impersonation and MITM attacks.

6.3.3.2 SDN and Virtualized Network

Fog-based models of SDN also provide management of the network at the Virtualized level by providing Network Level Virtualization (NLV), which includes SDN controller (Virtual software). This virtual SDN controller mostly resides in a cloud that manages and receives data from local virtual controllers present in fog. After receiving the data, the SDN controller intelligently processes data and decides based on policies whether data is to be processed at local controller or SDN controller and responds on time without any latency issues as it consumes low energy and low network overhead while providing load balancing.

Security Concern:

- Networking in this case is based on a virtualized approach that incorporates security issues of shared technology such as exploitation of insecure hypervisors that may affect the entire platform and lead to hypervisor-based attacks and privilege escalation attacks.

- Virtualization security issues also extend the potential attack surface for gaining privileged access and exploit available fog resources.

6.3.4 Web Applications

The fog computing model is widely used to optimize the performance of web applications. In a basic web application model, HTTP requests are made each time a resource is required and called; for example a script or content which is required at multiple places in the applications is requested multiple times for which HTTP request response goes through a round trip to the server and comes back to the client. This increases latency issues, delay in response time and ultimately affects the performance of web applications.

Implementation of a fog model in these web applications would enable the fetching and execution of such resources only once at the fog node, after which each time the request is sent for a specific resource. The fog node working as a cache management block would fulfil the request and thus reduce time delays as well as reducing redundancy of requests to the server, further reducing overhead of server, and optimizing the web application while enhancing the performance.

Security Concerns:

- The implementation will bring web-security issues covering OWASP Top-10, which includes critical injection attacks such as SQL injection, command injection and execution, header injection, which may reveal critical database information.
- Cross-site scripting attacks, insecure web APIs, session and cookie replay attacks, account hijacking, insecure direct object reference exploitation for illegitimate access of data, gain of unauthorized access and privilege escalation attacks are some of the possible scenarios.
- Cache poisoning attacks can also be executed to exploit the cache system of the fog node.

6.3.5 5G and Telecom Sector

The extensive use of mobile devices consumes mobile data at high rates causing congestion and low data speed rates due to which the need of a high-performance mobile network arises, further leading to the emergence of 5G. Fog computing provides high performance, reduces latency, extends functionality of load balancing that further reduces congestion issues, and a large number of users can consume data at higher speed rate simultaneously without compromising speed and quality of the signals.

Techniques like SDN (Luan et al., 2015) mesh network topologies and cloud computing, together forming a distributed network management of fog nodes that makes the implementation of 5G technology more efficient.

Security concern:

- A 5G network consists of several fog nodes connected to each other in different topologies; compromise of a single fog node will allow an attacker to perform a man-in-the-middle attack (MITM) (Desmedt, 2011).

- Attackers may intercept, sniff over the communication and access sensitive information of users connected in the network.
- Attackers may hijack one or two fog nodes, gain access and tamper data or send malicious requests to perform DoS attacks.

6.4 Security and Privacy in Fog Computing

The fog computing model enables a wide range of services and benefits including reduced latency, decreased bandwidth, real-time time-sensitive decisions and many more. However, the deployment of fog devices and the involvement of cloud and edge models incorporate many security and privacy threats. Existing cloud solutions address many security and privacy issues; fog introduces fog nodes and other new concepts to increase security and address privacy concerns to enhance security.

6.4.1 Security Issues

6.4.1.1 Authentication

Authentication is one of the important and critical security issues in the case of fog computing (Stojmenovic et al., 2015), as the implementation has applications in healthcare, vehicular and network-critical infrastructure where weak authentication will allow attackers to take control of the device, further exploiting or tampering real-time data, stealing sensitive information and leading to compromise of confidentiality, integrity and availability.

Many IoT devices have low memory and power to handle cryptographic calculations, so they require fog nodes for such computations and execution of authentication protocol. For instance, if we consider the scenario of the Smart Meter application, authentication takes place at different stages including authentication to gateways, authentication to Smart Meter devices, its web interface, etc. In such cases, attackers may bypass authentication, gain access to devices and tamper or modify parameters, further raising false readings. This may happen due to following reasons:

- Use of weak or default passwords for authentication that could easily be brute forced or cracked by specialized tools.
- Use of weak cryptographic techniques, which may allow attackers to sniff communication and obtain keys for authentication.

For preventing such attacks, the following measures are recommended:

- Use of multi-factor authentication.
- Implementing strong cryptographic techniques such as public key infrastructure (PKI) as these involve multicast authentication and Deffie-Hellman key exchange for encryption of data sent over fog devices.
- Use of AES encryption algorithm, as according to (Vishwanath et al., 2016) it is suitable for fog platforms.

6.4.1.2 Intrusion Detection

In a foggy network, there are several fog nodes and devices connected to each other. One of the fog devices may act as an intruder and try to attack other connected devices, or further may attempt to flood it with malicious requests resulting in DoS attacks, taking down other devices or the entire network.

Intrusion detection techniques must be implemented to monitor any suspicious activities and to identify insider attacks and DoS attacks in fog (Modi et al., 2013). For instance, detection of suspicious behaviours by using a signature-based or anomaly-based approach can verify the pattern or signature in the existing databases. If the pattern or signature does not match, alerts could be raised for suspicious behaviour. Any modifications of input values can be detected with intrusion detection techniques and thus appropriate action can be taken.

6.4.1.3 Network Security

With the implementation of fog networking, wireless security issues increase potential attack surface. Wireless devices connected in a foggy environment transmit private data; if this communication is not secure, it may lead to sniffing attacks and leakage of private data. Wireless access points are also visible to the devices that are not connected. Moreover, implementation of weak encryption techniques makes the communication insecure due to which the attacker can enter the network via impersonation attack or sybil attack and execute DoS attacks or even try to intercept network traffic by MITM and obtain sensitive information (Pathan et al., 2006). For prevention of these attacks, communications in fog networks must be encrypted and authenticated.

6.4.1.4 Data Security

Data is continuously being transmitted, stored, and processed in a fog environment. If the data is not encrypted, it increases possibilities of data loss and data tampering. Therefore, data at rest or in motion or even in the state of processing if encrypted with strong encryption algorithms will not allow any unauthorized access.

The communication channel via which the data is being sent must also be encrypted using Secure Socket Layer (SSL) and encryption of data being transmitted with strong cryptographic standards such as AES (Vishwanath et al., 2016).

6.4.1.5 Access Control

To secure authority of users, access control techniques must be implemented. In case no access level and policies are applied, it may allow unauthorised access to resources and data. Specifying authorization level and policies for fog nodes will enhance security.

Access control techniques such as role-based access control, rule-based access control, mandatory access control and discretionary access control can be used for implementation of authorization at different levels based on roles and policies.

6.4.2 Privacy Issues

Fog nodes collect a lot of sensitive information from the end-user, which raises privacy concerns. To preserve privacy in fog computing models, secure techniques are proposed for different solutions (Cao et al., 2014).

6.4.2.1 Data Privacy

IoT devices are resource-constrained due to which they may not use strong cryptographic techniques to encrypt or decrypt data being generated or processed. If data is transmitted unencrypted, it can be obtained by attackers, compromising the privacy of the data.

To preserve privacy of data, strong authentication algorithms must be used so that data is transmitted encrypted. The following techniques can be used:

- Homomorphic encryption allows computations on encrypted data without actually decrypting it (Lu et al., 2012), which along with providing security also reduces computations of the decryption mechanism so that resource-constrained devices can process services and operations efficiently.
- Differential privacy (Dwork, 2011) can be utilised to collect and transmit data while maintaining privacy.

6.4.2.2 Usage Privacy

The usage pattern of users of fog services incorporates privacy issues that need to be protected. For instance, a Smart Meter user may have different usage patterns based on which Smart Meter generates data or readings (McLaughlin et al., 2011). These readings may disclose privacy-sensitive information including the presence of users at home by analysing the readings of turning off lights and appliances connected to Smart Meters along with their consumption pattern.

Privacy issues are also present in data collected or generated by smart video surveillance revealing private information of households and the places where it is deployed. Similarly, privacy of healthcare systems must be preserved, as if breached it may result in sharing of critical information and private data. Implementation of privacy-preserving techniques is crucial for enhancing security.

6.4.2.3 Location Privacy

Many IoT and fog applications provide services based on location. This location-based information when generated and transmitted among different fog nodes opens a door for privacy issues (Novak and Li, 2014). Location of a fog client is critical information, which if compromised may lead to identity theft, life threats and more adversaries. Therefore, preserving privacy of location is important and can be accomplished by identity obfuscation (Shen et al., 2014) of fog clients such that nearby fog could not identify the client. In that case fog nodes will only be aware of the rogue location of the client.

6.5 Security Measures and Challenges

(i) Data that is being generated, transmitted and processed among fog devices needs to be secured. That is achieved by encryption of data by strong cryptographic techniques. Since implementation of cryptographic algorithms will require more resources for computations, however, devices being used are resource-constrained or may also affect the performance of the application. Data that is sensitive and crucial can only be encrypted to save computation operations and resource utilization.

(ii) In a foggy environment of application, a fog node may specifically be used for caching mechanisms, mostly in case of web optimization. However, the cache mechanisms are prone to attacks that may result in leakage of keys and sensitive information. For these scenarios "newcache" (Liu and Lee, 2013) could be implemented as a security solution. Implementation of proper security mechanisms will prevent insecure APIs, service-based vulnerabilities, sniffing attacks and data leakage while ensuring the privacy of users' data (Qin et al., 2014).

(iii) The fog platform involves several internal and external communications wirelessly, which allow sniffing attacks and rogue access points. These can be reduced by the implementation of authentication mechanisms and encryption mechanisms such as SSH and SSL for communication. Communication of wireless sensors in IoT can be encrypted using Wi-Fi security algorithms such as WPA (Wi-Fi protected access) and WPA2 (Mamta and Prakash, 2016).

(iv) IoT devices generate and process large volumes of data that is continuously being transmitted in fog systems. Handling this amount of data is difficult for fog systems (Hu et al., 2014), therefore monitoring techniques are deployed for handling data securely, detecting suspicious activities inside the network by use of policy-based rules for enhancing the security of the fog network.

(v) In a multi-user fog network, it is necessary that access control is enabled on data and network to prevent any unauthorized access. Along with this constraint, policies must also be deployed so that resource allocation is managed, failing to which one user could lock resources for unlimited time intentionally resulting in unavailability of resources or may even deploy a DoS attack scenario in the network. To prevent this, appropriate access control policies must be incorporated in a multiuser environment. Sharing of resources among multiple users may affect performance and security of data, resulting in potential insider attacks compromising confidentiality, integrity and availability of resources (Bezemer and Zaidman, 2010). Therefore, a role-based authentication mechanism must be implemented. According to Khan and Parkinson (Khan and Parkinson, 2017), deployment of security solutions in the fog network can be illustrated as in Figure 6.2.

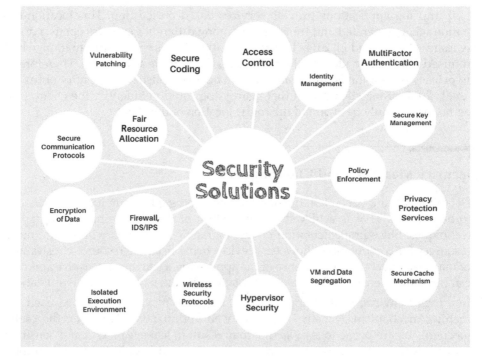

FIGURE 6.2
Deployment of security solutions.

Conclusion

The purpose of the presented study is to identify possible security and privacy concerns that are neglected by many IoT devices and their applications. The need of fog computing in real-world applications and related security concerns are also discussed. It can be observed that a wide range of implemented fog models in different applications mainly focus on functionalities and lack security, resulting in increasing attack surfaces of these applications. These fog systems need to implement security measures to protect user data and maintain confidentiality, integrity and availability across fog systems. Security and privacy concerns related to user data being transmitted across fog platforms are discussed along with the security measures that need to be implemented for enhancing security across the fog system.

Furthermore, IoT is a growing field, and new applications based on extended functionality of fog computing will soon come into existence and further lead to new security and privacy concerns. Therefore, development of a security model specific to fog computing and its application will enhance implementation of a secure fog model during the development and designing stages, with efficiency in performance along with security.

References

Bezemer C.P. & Zaidman A. (2010). Multi-tenant saas applications: Maintenance dream or nightmare? In: *Proceedings of the Joint ERCIMWorkshop on Software Evolution (EVOL) and International Workshop onPrinciples of Software Evolution (IWPSE)*. ACM, pp 88–92.

Cao N., Wang C., Li M., Ren K. & Lou W. (2014). Privacy-preserving multi-keyword ranked search over encrypted cloud data. *IEEE Transactions on Parallel and Distributed Systems*, vol. 25, no. 1, pp. 222–233. doi:10.1109/TPDS.2013.45.

Desmedt Y. (2011). Man-in-the-middle attack, encyclopedia of cryptography and security. *Jurnal Pendidikan Teknologi Informasi*, vol. 2, no. 2, pp 759–759, Springer.

Dwork C. (2011). Differential privacy. In: van Tilborg, H.C.A., Jajodia, S. (eds.) *Encyclopedia of Cryptography and Security*. LNCS, vol. 2011. Springer, Heidelberg.

Feng H., Li G. & Wang G. (2010). Efficient secure in-network data aggregation in wireless sensor networks. *2010 Second International Conference on Networks Security, Wireless Communications and Trusted Computing*, vol. 1, pp. 194–197. IEEE. doi:10.1109/NSWCTC.2010.52.

Gia T.N., Jiang M., Rahmani A., Westerlund T., Liljeberg P. & Tenhunen H. (2015). Fog computing in healthcare Internet of Things: A case study on ECG feature extraction. *2015 IEEE International Conference on Computer and Information Technology; Ubiquitous Computing and Communications; Dependable, Autonomic and Secure Computing; Pervasive Intelligence and Computing*, pp. 356–363. IEEE. doi:10.1109/CIT/IUCC/DASC/PICOM.2015.51.

Hu F., Hao Q. & Bao K. (2014). A survey on software-defined network and OpenFlow: From concept to implementation. *IEEE Communications Surveys & Tutorials*, vol. 16, no. 4, pp. 2181–2206, Fourth quarter 2014. doi:10.1109/COMST.2014.2326417.

Khan S. & Parkinson S. (2017). Fog computing security: A review of current applications and security solutions. *Journal of Cloud Computing: Advances, Systems and Applications*, vol. 6, Article 19.

Liu F. & Lee R.B. (2013). Security testing of a secure cache design. *Proceedings of the 2nd International Workshop on Hardware and Architectural Support for Security and Privacy*. ACM, p 3.

Lu R., Liang X., Li X., Lin X. & Shen X. (2012). EPPA: An efficient and privacy-preserving aggregation scheme for secure smart grid communications. *IEEE Transactions on Parallel and Distributed Systems*, vol. 23, no. 9, pp. 1621–1631. doi:10.1109/TPDS.2012.86.

Luan T.H., Gao L., Li Z., Xiang Y. & Sun L. (2015). Fog computing: Focusing on mobile users at the edge. *arXiv:1502.01815*.

Mamta & Prakash S. (2016). An overview of healthcare perspective based security issues in Wireless Sensor Networks. *3rd International Conference on Computing for Sustainable Global Development (INDIACom)*, pp. 870–875. IEEE.

McLaughlin S., McDaniel P. & Aiello W. (2011). Protecting consumer privacy from elec-tric load monitoring. *Proceedings of the ACM Conference on Computer and Communications Security*, pp. 87–98. https://doi.org/10.1145/2046707.2046720

Merino X., Otero C., Nieves-Acaron D. & Luchterhand B. (2021). Towards orchestration in the cloud-fog continuum. *Southeast Con 2021*, pp. 1–8. doi:10.1109/SoutheastCon45413.2021.9401822.

Modi C., Patel D., Borisaniya B., Patel H., Patel A. & Rajarajan M. (2013). A survey of intrusion detection techniques in cloud. *Journal of Network and Computer Applications*, vol. 36, no. 1, pp. 42–57.

Nazmudeen M. S. H., Wan A. T. & Buhari S. M. (2016). Improved throughput for Power Line Communication (PLC) for smart meters using fog computing based data aggregation approach. *2016 IEEE International Smart Cities Conference (ISC2)*, pp. 1–4. IEEE. doi:10.1109/ISC2.2016.7580841.

Novak E. & Li Q. (2014). Near-pri: Private, proximity based location sharing. *IEEE INFOCOM 2014—IEEE Conference on Computer Communications*, pp. 37–45. IEEE. doi:10.1109/INFOCOM.2014.6847922.

Pathan A.-S.K., Lee H.W. & Hong C.S. (2006). Security in wireless sensor networks: issues and challenges. *ICACT 2006. The 8th International Conference on Advanced Communication Technology*. IEEE, vol. 2, p 6.

Prieto González L., Prieto González L., Jaedicke C., Jaedicke C., Schubert J., Schubert J., Stantchev V. & Stantchev V. (2016). Fog computing architectures for healthcare: Wireless performance and semantic opportunities. *Journal of Information, Communication and Ethics in Society*, vol. 14, no. 4, pp. 334–349. doi:10.1108/JICES-05-2016-0014.

Qin Z., Yi S., Li Q. & Zamkov D. (2014). Preserving secondary users' privacy in cognitive radio networks. *IEEE INFOCOM 2014—IEEE Conference on Computer Communications*, pp. 772–780. IEEE. doi:10.1109/INFOCOM.2014.6848004.

Rial A. & Danezis G. (2011). Privacy-preserving smart metering. *Proceedings of the10th Annual ACM Workshop on Privacy in the Electronic Society*, pp 49–60. https://doi.org/10.1145/2046556.2046564.

Sagiroglu S. & Sinanc D. (2013). Big data: A review. *International Conference on Collaboration Technologies and Systems (CTS)*, IEEE, pp 42–47.

Shen N., Yuan K., Yang J. & Jia C. (2014). B-Mobishare: Privacy-preserving location sharing mechanism in mobile online social networks. *Ninth International Conference on Broadband and Wireless Computing, Communication and Applications*, pp. 312–316. IEEE. doi:10.1109/BWCCA.2014.80.

Stojmenovic I., Wen S., Huang X. & Luan H. (2015). An overview of fog computing and its security issues. *Concurrency and Computation: Practice and Experience*, vol. 28, no. 10.

Vishwanath A., Peruri R. & He J.S. (2016). Security in fog computing through encryption. *International Journal of Informational Technology and Computer Science, (IJITCS)*, vol. 8, no. 5, pp. 28–36.

Wei C., Fadlullah Z. M., Kato N. & Stojmenovic I. (2014). On optimally reducing power loss in microgrids with power storage devices. *IEEE Journal on Selected Areas in Communications*, vol. 32, no. 7, pp. 1361–1370. doi:10.1109/JSAC.2014.2332077.

7

Leveraging Fog Computing for the Internet of Medical Things

Avita Katal

School of Computer Science
University of Petroleum and Energy Studies
Dehradun, India

CONTENTS

DOI: 10.1201/9781003188230-7

7.1 Introduction to Fog Computing

The number of Internet of Things (IoT) sensors and computers has grown significantly in recent years. A modern computing model known as fog computing has been developed to fulfil the applicants' criteria that require less response time of increasingly geo-distributed IoT sensors and computers. Fog computing (FC), in general, is located closer to IoT sensors/devices and expands cloud computing, storage, and networking capabilities.

It is a distributed computing architecture that serves as an intermediary layer among the Internet of Things sensors and devices and cloud layer. It offers networking, compute, running, and storage capabilities to bring cloud-based services closer to IoT sensors and smartphones (Katal et al., 2021). Cisco first introduced the fog computing idea in 2012 to solve the problems of IoT implementations of standard cloud computing (Bonomi et al., 2012). The environment of fog computing has components such as proxy servers, switches, routers and so on, and can be positioned near IoT sensors and devices. These modules are equipped with a wide range of processing, storage, and networking features, allowing them to facilitate the execution of service applications. As a result of the networking elements, fog computing can distribute cloud-based applications over a wide geographical area. Fog computing also helps with location awareness, connectivity assistance, real-time communications, interoperability, and scalability (*Fog Computing and the Internet of Things: Extend the Cloud to Where the Things Are What You Will Learn*, 2015). In this way, fog computing, as opposed to exclusively using cloud computing, best satisfies the criteria for IoT applications (Sarkar et al., 2018).

7.1.1 General Architecture of Fog Computing

A major research subject in fog computing is its reference model. Fog computing architectures have been suggested in recent years in a variety of ways. Most of them are taken from the basic three-layered structure. Figure 7.1 shows the general architecture of fog computing. The following three-layer elements make up the architecture:

- *Terminal layer*—It is the layer that is nearest to the user and their physical surroundings. Sensors, cell phones, smart cars, and other IoT products are among the modules. These devices are placed in different parts of the system. The main responsibility of these devices is to capture the data and transfer the captured data to the upper layer.

- *Fog layer*—At the network's edge, the fog layer can be detected. A variety of fog nodes, including gateways, routers, switches, base stations, access points, and unique fog servers, make up the fog computing layer. Cafes, shopping malls, bus stations, sidewalks, beaches, and other public places serve as fog nodes for end devices and the cloud. Sensor nodes can simply connect with fog nodes to receive services. They are capable of calculating, relaying, and temporally archiving the detected data that they gather. They are responsible for connecting and working with the cloud to improve storage and distribution capacity.

- *Cloud layer*—The cloud infrastructure layer is made up of a collection of devices for storage and high-performance servers that support a wide range of application services, including smart houses, smart transportation, and smart factories. It has strong computational and storage facilities to enable intensive computation

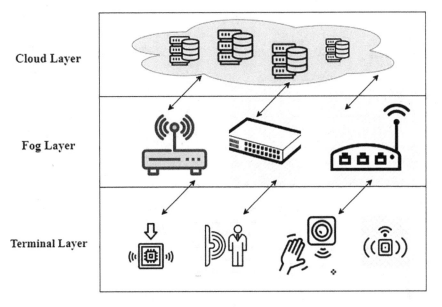

FIGURE 7.1
General architecture of fog computing.

and analysis, as well as the long-term storage of massive amounts of data. The cloud core modules are effectively handled and scheduled according to demand-load by certain management strategies to increase cloud resource usage (Sarkar & Misra, 2016).

7.1.2 Characteristics of Fog Computing

Fog computing uses network edge gadgets that are near to a user to perform computation, interaction, and storage. Its proximity to end users is one of its service capabilities. This is the most fundamental feature of fog computing, as well as its most noticeable advantage over other conventional computing models. Figure 7.2 shows the characteristics of fog computing. In addition, the following traits and benefits are listed:

- *Less response time*—Data is retrieved from sensors and devices by fog nodes at the network edge, which also stores and processes data from network edge devices in the LAN. It significantly reduces data flow via the Internet while providing endpoints with better and faster organizational solutions. As a consequence, it has low latency and satisfies the need for real-time communications, which is extremely useful for applications that require less response time (Bonomi, 2011).

- *Saves bandwidth*—Using fog computing, information may be analyzed and kept between end nodes and the traditional cloud, bringing computation and storage to the network edge. Some computing tasks are done locally, such as pre-processing of data, redundancy removal, data cleaning and filtering, and practical knowledge extraction.

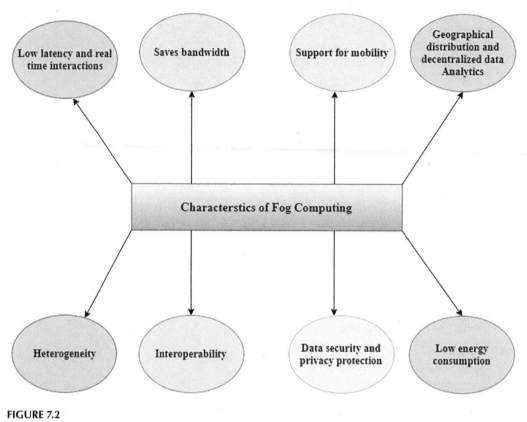

FIGURE 7.2
Characteristics of fog computing.

- *Mobility support*—In fog computing environments, some mobile devices enable movement at the terminal layer, while other end devices, such as traffic cameras, remain stationary. Similarly, a mobile or static computing utility network may be a fog node in a fog layer. It can be found in airports and coffee shops, as well as on trains and mobile cars.

- *Decentralized data analytics and distribution*—In contrast to more clustered cloud infrastructure, fog computing platforms and applications encourage geographically dispersed distribution. It is made up of a vast number of geographically dispersed nodes that can monitor and deduce the positions of end devices to enable movement. The decentralized feature of fog computing helps with quicker big-data processing, improved location-based applications, and more efficient real-time decision-making capability.

- *Heterogeneity*—Fog nodes come in a variety of form/factors and can be used as a physical or virtual node in a variety of contexts. The hardware platform has varying degrees of computation and storage capacity. Furthermore, fog computing's network architecture is heterogeneous, encompassing lightning-fast connections to the data center and wireless communication technology to the edge computers.

TABLE 7.1

Comparison of Fog Computing and Cloud Computing

Parameters	Fog Computing	Cloud Computing
Response Time	Low	High
Costs for Bandwidth	Low	High
Consumption of Energy	Low	High
Geographical Distribution	Decentralized	Centralized
Location Awareness	Supported	Partially supported
Location of Service	Local network edge	Within the Internet
Mobility	Supported	Limited
Latency	Less	High

7.1.3 Comparison of Fog Computing and Cloud Computing

Table 7.1 shows the comparison of the FC and CC on the basis of different parameters.

7.2 Integration of Fog Computing in the Medical Internet of Things

The healthcare sector is becoming increasingly interested in the growing number of medical instruments, sensors, and smartphones that are connected via Internet. The Internet of Things (IoT) is being utilized as a potential healthcare alternative because it would enable patients to seek care online, self-manage their circumstances, and obtain emergency aid through a mobile architecture (Miorandi et al., 2012). Data sharing, interoperability, and resource effectiveness, as well as security and privacy, are all obstacles that IoT must overcome (Atzori et al., 2010). The cloud infrastructure solution was used to solve the IoT issues described earlier. The cloud storage model allows convenient accessibility to a common resource pool for storing, processing, and handling the increasing amount of generated by IoT autonomous systems (Mell & Grance, 2011). From the user's perspective, cloud computing offers many benefits, including ubiquitous access to resources and software without the need to store massive storage archives or manage powerful computing devices (Botta et al., 2016). Anything is available as a service over the Internet with the cloud computing solution. Using his or her mobile phone, the patient may connect to distant medical data or preserve fresh content in data centers. Despite the fact that the unified cloud solution allows healthcare practitioners to provide remote access to patients' medical information and exchange vast volumes of information through their smartphones, the cloud's centralized structure prevents it from delivering low latency, position recognition, and geo-distribution, which are critical for IoT apps (Yi et al., 2015). Because any smartphone or computer will theoretically connect to the Internet, the number of mobile-enabled devices is expected to exceed the number of people on the planet by the end of 2018, with 1.4 mobile devices per person expected by the end of 2018 (Cisco Global Cloud Index: Forecast and Methodology, 2015–2020, 2016), and 24 billion devices expected by 2020 (Gubbi et al., 2013). Even though cloud computing (CC) has a high scalability and can accommodate the rapid rise in the devices related to IoT, the requirement for a large number of devices to be linked to the Internet for transferring signal to one another, transferring data on a regular basis, and gathering medical records places additional strain on network and cloud resources. The CC solution requires high operational, consistent Internet connectivity with enough traffic and minimal delay (*ECall: Time Saved = Lives Saved " Europe Direct Aldershot*, 2016). Moreover, the continuous connectivity of sensor nodes to the cloud results in energy usage. As a result, CC cannot meet the needs of IoT implementations for real-time data analysis that requires continuous and effective exchanges among IoT systems and low-latency healthcare providers.

Fog computing, as earlier stated, is a cloud computing extension that connects end devices to the cloud and offers on-demand storage, computation, and network services. Fog can gather, filter, and archive vast amounts of data, allowing it to bring storage and processing closer to end devices. Because medical sensors produce so much data, delivering analysis of data and making decisions based on local policy and network services to end users will enhance real-time analysis accuracy. Fog can manage data automatically without relying on the network due to its proximity to the client. The lower the latency, delay, and jitter, the closer the fog is to the end user. As a result, without migrating data to the cloud, it would enhance the quality of healthcare facilities and deliver prompt response activities and trustworthy healthcare services. End users will benefit from fog computing's thick spatial coverage, which can help with the massive distribution of medical data and IoT devices.

As a result, combining IoT and fog computing to provision healthcare facilities is a potential approach that can dramatically minimize data forwarding and filtering through network networks, resulting in lower latency and more efficient healthcare service provisioning.

7.3 Fog Computing in Healthcare

7.3.1 Deployment Scenarios

- *Mobile*—Users' cell phones function as a hub between sensor systems and the cloud in this case.
- *Home treatment*—The patient's Internet connection is often used to provide connectivity while the patient is at home. This has an impact on system ownership, as well as the required usability and maintainability and on how disruptions can be mitigated.
- *Hospital*—Tools in hospitals are mostly patented, and they are typically owned and operated by the hospital. The programs are significantly more sophisticated, necessitating the use of skilled practitioners as device users.
- *Non-hospital premises*—This scenario covers specialist points-of-care, but it has fewer resources and facilities than hospitals, although the clinic owns and retains the core hardware.
- *Transport*—The communication of an ambulance or helicopter is covered in this case. It's close to the non-hospital implementation situation, but with the extra complication that the infrastructure must be mobile, such as via a cellular network.

7.3.2 Implementation Scenarios' Use Cases

- *Mobile*—A smartphone serves as a mobile base station, collecting data from a variety of sensors, processing it, and sending back to the server. The goal of incorporating FC into a smartphone is to extend the life of the peripheral sensor's battery.

- *Home treatment*—The home implementation situation is demonstrated by the Parkinson speech recognition solution in (Monteiro et al., 2016). The LAN level of the network hierarchy is where a fog node can be located. FC is being used to collect, preserve, and compute raw data prior uploading it to the cloud for long-term storage, similar to how smartphones are used. FC's main goal is to decrease network load and latency.

- *Hospital*—In the hospital deployment situation, a common example of a configuration can be found in López et al. (2010). Patients' physiological data and location are tracked using smart shirts with built-in beacons. Fog computing is done across several nodes. Before submitting data to the wireless transmission board, the data acquisition and processing board (DAPB) gathers, analyzes, and integrates data from the sensors (WTB). The tracking system uses data from the DAPB and Beacon Points (BPs) to track patient medical parameters, locate the patient within the facility, and confirm whether a notification has been allowed.

- *Non-hospital premises*—The non-hospital implementation situation is exemplified by the real-time epileptic seizure monitoring system (Hosseini et al., 2016). The mobile device cloud, which is situated in the middle tier, handles extraction of features, collection of feature, pre-processing and classification of the patterns of Electroencephalogram (EEG).

- *Transport*—The approach for exchange of information discussed in Oladimeji et al. (2011) uses the transport implementation scenario. Fog computing's challenge is disseminating data across numerous fog nodes.

7.4 Healthcare Services in the Fog Layer

Figure 7.3 shows the services provided by fog layer.

7.4.1 Management of Data

Data processing is important in fog computing because sensory data is collected locally to retrieve significant information for user input and alerts. Because the fog layer gets a huge volume of sensory data from the sensor network in a shorter span of time, it must handle the incoming data to respond quickly to different users and system conditions according to the system architecture. In healthcare scenarios, this challenge becomes much more relevant because latency and confusion in decision-making will result in permanent harm to patients.

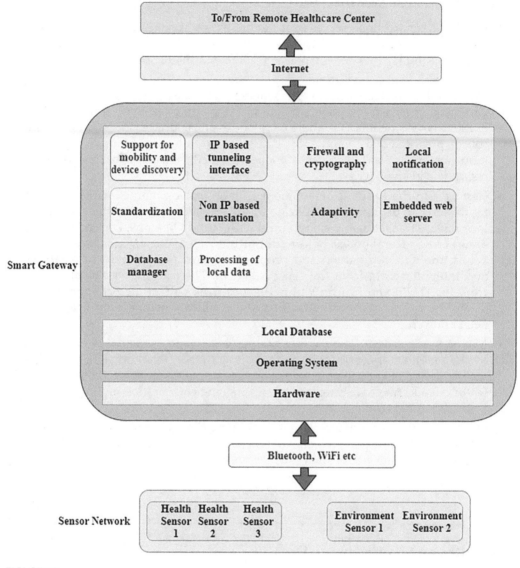

FIGURE 7.3
Services given by the fog layer.

Source: Based on Negash et al., 2018

7.4.1.1 Local Storage

In addition to using information obtained from various sources in the near future, the gateway must store it locally. The gateway's operational program contains a file server and a subdirectory for data gathering and restoration. Based on the kind, amount, and importance of the data, the gateway's internal memory may be utilized to store files in encoded files. Other gateway features rely on temporary storage as well, such as data interpretation, filtering, amplification, and authentication. As a result, if the calculation and transmitting times are different, the local storage acts as a local cache memory to keep data flowing.

When the gateway's Internet connection to the cloud provider is down, local storage will help keep records safe. The stored data is transferred to the cloud after the gateway reconnects to the Internet.

7.4.1.2 Data Compression

Data may be compressed using lossless or lossy compression techniques to reduce the volume of data transferred over a transmission network. In most cases, lossless encoding is desirable in healthcare IoT applications because missing data will lead to incorrect treatment of disease. Consequently, they are unsuitable for sensor nodes that are resource-limited in terms of battery power, computing, or memory. Many kinds of sensors, for example, cannot run lossless ECG compression methods (Lu et al., 2000).

7.4.1.3 Data Fusion

Data Fusion is a unit in which data processing occurs that combines the data retrieved from sensors from different sources to provide more reliable and useful data. This computing device significantly lowers the quantity of data gathered from the sensors by removing old information and replacing it with new information. As a result, the reduction of data and local data processing is improved. There are three types of data fusion: complementary, collaborative, and cooperative (Durrant-Whyte, 2016). In the fog layer, complementary data fusion incorporates two separate data sets to gain a more detailed information.

7.4.1.4 Data Analysis

A data processing device at the base would allow the sensory data to be processed locally by the hospital system. By reducing response time and data transfer to cloud storage, this device boosts system efficiency. For instance, in the event of a patient's health worsening, the emergency event is identified and responded to, quickly and easily because the data is stored directly rather than being sent to the cloud and waiting for response. Apart from this, the data processing unit increases data consistency and data efficiency.

7.4.2 Management of Event

The healthcare system should process sensory data locally using a data processing device at the base. By eliminating the response time and transmission of data to cloud servers, this device enhances system performance. Furthermore, the data processing unit improves the consistency and efficiency of data. Because the patient may engage in a variety of activities in a variety of environments, connectivity losses and decreased data processing capacity in long-term remote health monitoring are inevitable.

7.4.3 Resource Efficiency

Resource reliability is one of the most important criteria of healthcare IoT implementations because resource management failure may have significant repercussions, ranging from sensor node loss to inaccurate treatment of diseases. The consumption of energy by sensor nodes, as well as the response time in data gathered exhibited at end-user terminals, should be considered carefully. These will be discussed in detail as follows:

7.4.3.1 Energy Efficiency of Nodes

In the networks that are used for health monitoring, have sensor nodes that are normally limited in the form of resources, such as having a small battery size, but they must be able to run for an extended period, such as a day or even several days. Sensor nodes must function effectively based on usage of energy to satisfy these specifications. A variety of methodologies, including program and device solutions, can be used to complete the task. The hardware of a sensor node, for example, should be optimized for specific purposes rather than general activities. By avoiding unused or high-power-consuming elements, this approach helps to reduce energy usage. Designing energy-efficient nodes, on the other hand, is more complex than customizing applications running on the nodes. The program must be capable of performing primary tasks for sensor nodes while still being incredibly easy to reduce computing time.

7.4.3.2 Latency

Latency is important in health tracking systems because it can lead to incorrect disease analysis and judgement delays. In many environments, transmission latency and processor latency are also traded off. However, processing data does not necessarily mean that the overall delay can be minimized. Data processing can also increase overall latency in some instances. A special approach must be used for each sensor node and device to minimize overall latency and satisfy the time criteria of real-time health monitoring. In other situations, basic filtering techniques for removing noise and invalid data can assist in reducing both the volume of data transmitted and the overall latency.

7.4.4 Management of Device

Device control covers a wide range of IoT infrastructure topics. The emphasis of this section is on system management from the standpoint of device exploration and preserving compatibility when on the move.

7.4.4.1 Mobility and Discovery

Sensor and actuator resource limitations in the network of actuators and sensors were briefly mentioned previously. Battery life is important in battery-powered devices, and it necessitates careful maintenance. When machines become idle, they should be put to sleep in a regulated fashion. The fog layer is responsible for any contact that happens when the system is in sleep mode. Another system that wants to connect to a sleeping sensor node will use the device discovery service to locate it and gracefully navigate the sleeping period.

7.4.4.2 Interoperability

IoT is made up of several networking protocols, channels, and data formats. Traditionally, interoperability has been hampered by the bulk of end devices' resource restrictions. The fog computing layer is critical for delivering services that take advantage of the layer's proximity to end devices and thus promote interoperability. Preliminary work at the fog layer should also be done to provide seamless integration in the cloud, allowing data from sensors to be contextualized.

7.4.5 Personalization

For various fog computing applications, system behavior may be optimized in advance or at run time. However, in clinical scenarios, this may be ineffective, and users may have a variety of medical problems. As a result, a sophisticated system approach is necessary to not only customize behavior of the system depending on the demands of the user but also to automate behavior of the system and to modify the system adaptively over time. It enhances applications related to health and optimizes system efficiency in this regard (e.g., energy efficiency). Rule-based methods and deep learning algorithms may be used to describe personalized device actions for a variety of health applications. Various priorities and modes for device parameters are defined for this purpose, and reasonable values are determined based on the patient's circumstances. Furthermore, the goals become tailored depending on the patient's medical records. In a simplistic example, if a patient's heart disease was observed during testing, the device would learn to prioritize heart-related parameters higher.

7.5 Proposed Framework

In the proposed architecture, various sensors are available for data collection. The different types of sensors are: body temperature sensor, oxygen saturation sensor, heart rate sensor, etc. The main task of sensors is to collect the data from the body of the patient. Once the data collection is done, the collected data is sent to the smart gateways for pre-processing. The smart gateways filter, compress, and perform analytics on the collected data to get the useful data. Once the pre-processing is done, emergency alert or notifications are sent to the local doctor if the data is not similar to the normal values. The complete data set is transferred to a data center for prolonged term. Figure 7.4. shows the proposed framework.

- *Medical sensors and actuators*—These serve as a subject identifier, receiving information, and responding in reaction to the fog layer. They are primarily linked via low-power wireless communication protocols.
- *Smart e-health gateways*—The fog layer is made up of a distributed network of gateways that act as the underlying network for the actuator and sensors. Fog layer serves as a gateway to the cloud and hosts a multitude of applications.
- *Cloud platform*—This is a system in which data is stored and stakeholders can access it through a web or mobile interface.

7.6 Case Studies

Table 7.2 shows the case studies that uses fog computing in the domain of healthcare.

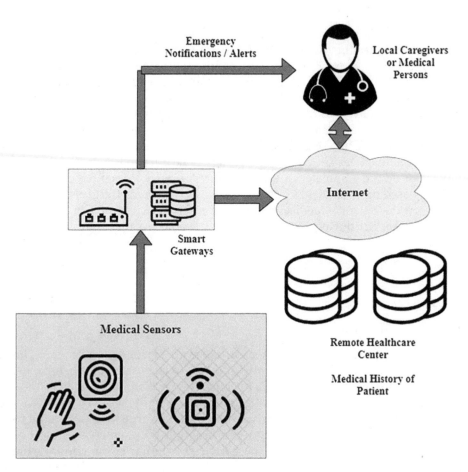

FIGURE 7.4
Proposed framework.

TABLE 7.2

Different Projects that Use Fog Computing in the Domain of Healthcare

Project	Company	Aim	URLs
TCSrobust FC	TCS	It enables real-time online patient control and vital care intervention, resulting in cost-effective preventive care.	www.tcs.com/remote-patient-monitoring
OpenFog Consortium	Cisco, Dell, etc.	These establish guidelines and best practices for the construction of fog computing systems.	https://opcfoundation.org/markets-collaboration/openfog/
Fog Director	Cisco	Healthcare technologies rely on networking that is easy, smart, and automatic.	https://bit.ly/3bFVJ0t
Edge Intelligence	FogHorn Technology	Its goal is to investigate the value of big data at the edge.	www.foghorn.io/
The HIKARI Artificial Intelligence Solution	Fujitsu Ltd.	Its goal is to check the right risk of a specific patient.	https://bit.ly/3foW88w

7.7 Research Challenges in Medical IoT

7.7.1 Management of Resources

When three separate paradigms are combined in one scheme, resource management becomes a top priority. Even when using fog computing without the cloud, management of resources can be a challenging task because of the fog's lower availability of computational and storage capacity as compared to the cloud. When it comes to managing resources for IoT artefacts and fog layer interaction, the data that is exchanged and stored between them must have a meaning, so that redundant data is not reused, wasting limited resources. When multiple customers or sections of a system share the same facilities, resource planning becomes even more critical to guarantee that the devices utilized are not delayed.

7.7.2 Offloading

Offloading, or the transition of responsibilities from one entity to another, is a significant problem. To maintain the low latency characteristic of fog computing, offloading is required. The decision-making involved in offloading is what makes this a fog computing problem. To meet the fog's standard of operation (QoS), this decision-making can be achieved with as little delay as possible. The prediction of offloaded tasks may be helpful in offloading decision-making because it will help determine whether offloading the task would have any benefits. If done incorrectly, offloading may be harmful to healthcare systems. If job offloading creates further delay, it can influence real-time management of patient conditions.

7.7.3 Data Management

The challenges encountered by IoT in other fields are close to those faced by eHealth. The eHealth info, on the other hand, comes from medical sensors worn by people. The human body is a dynamic structure whose state is continually evolving. Information diversity in IoT is a lot fresher issue than it was 10 years ago. Dozens of file formats are accessible in health, based on the end module. ECG data, for instance, might be supplied in XML form, while skin disorders may be identified using camera based IoT. Manufacturers and their target customers determine which data formats are supported by edge computers. In comparison to the edge data format, the cloud data model differs, necessitating standardization. The abilities of fog computing equipment for gathering, analyzing, storing, and transmitting elevated, high-resolution information from clinical devices with doctors or at medical facilities are increasingly concerned with confidentiality, cost, and velocity concerns. Consequently, fog administrators will be in charge of regulating data flow among fog and cloud storage devices.

7.7.4 Standardization, Interoperability, and Regulatory Affairs

In general, the Internet of Things has raised questions over standardization. Manufacturers, service providers, and end consumers are also looking for specifications for interoperability inside and between the realms targeted by the applications of IoT. The challenge of standardization arises from the fact that the Internet of Things tends to include a broad variety of disciplines that are, in general, governed by various regulatory bodies. The difficulty of IoT eHealth is exacerbated by the stringent regulations imposed by medical guidelines. Before IoT eHealth goods are there in the market, IoT eHealth would have to negotiate a dynamic multi-agency regulatory framework.

7.7.5 Security and Heterogeneity

Fog computing security is a research topic due to the location of fog nodes. Working at the network edge exposes you to risks that would not be present in a well-organized cloud architecture. The most frequent type of assault is the man in the middle, in which an attacker relays and alters communication between two people. If the perpetrator tampered with the data being stored, this may have serious implications for the patients' wellbeing.

Heterogeneity, or the ability of various devices to interact with one another, is another problem that fog computing can face. Multiple gadgets, such as smartphones, self-driving vehicles, and other IoT smart things, make up the bottom layer of the IoT paradigm. The storage of data, its formatting, and the capacity to process the data are all issues of heterogeneity in IoT end devices. Allowing the network to connect with a wide variety of sensors to enable patient tracking is one example of how this may be a problem in healthcare. When data is sent to another computer to be processed or analyzed, heterogeneity must be present for this to happen. When travelling up to the next layer—which is the fog layer—nodes, clusters, switches, and other components that have processing and networking capabilities are included. As a result, heterogeneity plays an important role in architecture design, particularly when it comes to having various measurement instruments to communicate with the patient.

7.8 Conclusion

The increase in the number of Internet of Things devices that gather the rising data and use services related to cloud has put a strain on network and cloud infrastructure. Several information technology providers have adopted multiple tactics for providing robust parallel computing positioned near to the end user to overcome the issues related to data transmission to the cloud. Fog computing can deliver less response time, geographical distribution, and timely data support since it is deployed at the network edge. Research efforts in this area are still underway. Relevant depictions and limitations, on the other hand, remain ambiguous. The introduction to fog computing, the general architecture and features of fog computing, are presented in this chapter. The healthcare use cases of fog computing are also discussed. The chapter gives detailed information about the services provided by the fog layer, such as data management, event management, resource efficiency, etc. A new architecture for Internet of Medical Things with fog computing is proposed as well as a discussion about the daily monitoring and healthcare service provisioning is included. The chapter concludes with a list of issues that need to be addressed to improve the Internet of Things applications by extending the functionality of emerging fog computing.

References

Atzori, L., Iera, A., & Morabito, G. (2010). The Internet of Things: A survey. *Computer Networks, 54*(15), 2787–2805. https://doi.org/10.1016/J.COMNET.2010.05.010

Bonomi, F. (2011). Connected vehicles, the internet of things, and fog computing. *The Eighth ACM International Workshop on Vehicular Inter-Networking (VANET)*, ACM, 13–15.

Bonomi, F., Milito, R., Zhu, J., & Addepalli, S. (2012). Fog computing and its role in the Internet of Things. *Proceedings of the First Edition of the MCC Workshop on Mobile Cloud Computing—MCC '12.* ACM. https://doi.org/10.1145/2342509

Botta, A., de Donato, W., Persico, V., & Pescapé, A. (2016). Integration of Cloud computing and Internet of Things: A survey. *Future Generation Computer Systems, 56*, 684–700. https://doi.org/10.1016/J.FUTURE.2015.09.021

Cisco Global Cloud Index: Forecast and Methodology, 2015–2020. (2016). *Cisco Visual Networking Index: Forecast and Methodology*, https://www.iotjournaal.nl/wp-content/uploads/2017/02/white-paper-c11-738085.pdf

Durrant-Whyte, H. F. (2016). Sensor models and multisensor integration. *The International Journal of Robotics Research, 7*(6), 97–113. https://doi.org/10.1177/027836498800700608

eCall: Time Saved = Lives Saved " Europe Direct Aldershot. (2016). Retrieved June 20, 2021, from www.aldershotenterprisecentre.co.uk/ecall-time-saved-lives-saved/

Fog Computing and the Internet of Things: Extend the Cloud to Where the Things Are What You Will Learn. (2015). CISCO White Paper.

Gubbi, J., Buyya, R., Marusic, S., & Palaniswami, M. (2013). Internet of Things (IoT): A vision, architectural elements, and future directions. *Future Generation Computer Systems, 29*(7), 1645–1660. https://doi.org/10.1016/J.FUTURE.2013.01.010

Hosseini, M. P., Hajisami, A., & Pompili, D. (2016). Real-time epileptic seizure detection from EEG signals via random subspace ensemble learning. *Proceedings—2016 IEEE International Conference on Autonomic Computing, ICAC 2016*, 209–218. IEEE. https://doi.org/10.1109/ICAC.2016.57

Katal, A., Sethi, V., Lamba, S., & Choudhury, T. (2021). Fog computing: Issues, challenges and tools. *Emerging Technologies in Data Mining and Information Security*, 971–982. https://doi.org/10.1007/978-981-15-9927-9_92

López, G., Custodio, V., & Moreno, J. I. (2010). LOBIN: E-textile and wireless-sensor-network-based platform for healthcare monitoring in future hospital environments. *IEEE Transactions on Information Technology in Biomedicine, 14*(6), 1446–1458. https://doi.org/10.1109/TITB.2010.2058812

Lu, Z., Kim, D. Y., & Pearlman, W. A. (2000). Wavelet compression of ECG signals by the set partitioning in hierarchical trees algorithm. *IEEE Transactions on Biomedical Engineering, 47*(7), 849–856. https://doi.org/10.1109/10.846678

Mell, P. M., & Grance, T. (2011). *The NIST Definition of Cloud Computing. Information Technology Laboratory COMPUTER SECURITY RESOURCE CENTER.* https://doi.org/10.6028/NIST.SP.800-145

Miorandi, D., Sicari, S., de Pellegrini, F., & Chlamtac, I. (2012). Internet of Things: Vision, applications and research challenges. *Ad Hoc Networks, 10*(7), 1497–1516. https://doi.org/10.1016/J.ADHOC.2012.02.016

Monteiro, A., Dubey, H., Mahler, L., Yang, Q., & Mankodiya, K. (2016). Fit: A Fog computing device for speech tele-treatments. *2016 IEEE International Conference on Smart Computing*, SMARTCOMP 2016. https://doi.org/10.1109/SMARTCOMP.2016.7501692

Negash, B., Gia, T. N., Anzanpour, A., Azimi, I., Jiang, M., Westerlund, T., Rahmani, A. M., Liljeberg, P., & Tenhunen, H. (2018). Leveraging Fog computing for healthcare IoT. *Fog Computing in the Internet of Things: Intelligence at the Edge*, 145–169. https://doi.org/10.1007/978-3-319-57639-8_8

Oladimeji, E. A., Chung, L., Jung, H. T., & Kim, J. (2011). Managing security and privacy in ubiquitous eHealth information interchange. *Proceedings of the 5th International Conference on Ubiquitous Information Management and Communication, ICUIMC 2011*, ACM. https://doi.org/10.1145/1968613.1968645

Sarkar, S., Chatterjee, S., & Misra, S. (2018). Assessment of the suitability of Fog computing in the context of Internet of Things. *IEEE Transactions on Cloud Computing, 6*(1), 46–59. https://doi.org/10.1109/TCC.2015.2485206

Sarkar, S., & Misra, S. (2016). Theoretical modeling of fog computing: A green computing paradigm to support IoT applications. *IET Networks, 5*(2), 23–29.

Yi, S., Li, C., & Li, Q. (2015, June). A survey of fog computing: Concepts, applications and issues. *Proceedings of the 2015 Workshop on Mobile Big Data* 37–42. https://doi.org/10.1145/2757384.2757397

8

A Single-Point Control System for Consumer Devices Using Edge-Fog Computing

Karan Verma

Department of Computer Science
National Institute of Technology Delhi
Delhi, India

Prashant Kumar

Department of Computer Science
National Institute of Technology Delhi
Delhi, India

Ajay K. Sharma

Department of Computer Science
National Institute of Technology Delhi
Delhi, India

Ashok Kumar

Department of Computer Science
Government Women Engineering College
Ajmer, Rajasthan

CONTENTS

8.1 Introduction

8.1.1 Background

Human-computer interaction (HCI) is one of the growing areas of research that involves multiple computer science-related disciplines like image processing, computer vision, programming language as well as human science discipline [1]. These disciplines are

DOI: 10.1201/9781003188230-8

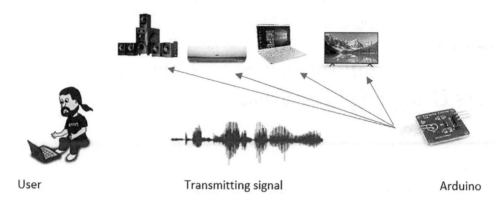

User   Transmitting signal   Arduino

FIGURE 8.1
An example scenario of single-point control system.

concerned with the design, evaluation, and implementation of interactive computing systems for human use for improving the interaction between humans and machines. The consumer devices, such as television or laptop, are attracting researchers to develop a single-point control system that can control the devices using hand movements of a user. Gesture recognition, an emerging field in HCI, enables humans to communicate with the machine and interact naturally without the use of any mechanical devices.

A gesture is a form of non-verbal communication or non-vocal communication in which visible bodily actions communicate particular messages. Gestures include movement of the hands, face or other parts of the body [2]–[4]. Gesture recognition systems (GRS) can identify the gestures of users to identify the function using initial sensors [5]. A GRS is supposed to be Range Set GRS (RSGRS) of a function and sets the magnitude of range of the identified function that is recognized by the system [5].

The sensors like gyroscopes and accelerometers depend on the posture of users that creates a posture dependency for users. By using only real-time image capturing and speech recognition, we can palm off from posture dependency. A system that provides the desired response by controlling the output using the user inputs is known as control system [6]. A single-point control system means controlling the different functions of different devices from a single device. This chapter is used for controlling four devices: AC, TV, sound system, and laptop (using camera and microphone of edge device). The example scenario of the work is shown in Figure 8.1. All the computation is done on fog devices that may be the same laptop or some other laptop. We can add more devices that can be operated on an infrared signal.

8.1.2 Motivation

The convenience of any consumer device relies upon the effortlessness of its utilization and the experience of the client [5] [7]. This work is roused by the accompanying perceptions in the current writing as follows:

1. Additional resources: In existing work a lot of additional resources like gloves with sensors, cameras, other sensor-containing devices like a wristwatch, smartphone and so on are required. Using extra resources is cost-inefficient and not convenient for the user.

2. Network connectivity: In some literature the author uploads all the data on cloud. Uploading and retrieving the data from cloud needs a good connectivity that is not suitable in all conditions.

3. Comfortability: Most of the existing work depends on posture of users that is inconvenient for user. The usability of any device depends on the convenience of the user.

4. Range set GRS: Until now hardly any papers worked on range set GRS, but even those papers depend on sensor data that is fully dependent on the posture of the user. In this chapter, we are trying to implement an RSGRS model, which is independent of user posture.

   Most of the range set GRS model is not convenient for all users. Handicapped persons who can speak or have use of their hands can also control their electronic devices using this.

This chapter gives a way for controlling all consumers' devices using gestures and the voice of the user. The model first identifies the consumer devices and their function and later controls the range of that function. It uses a laptop camera to identify the consumer device to be operated using CNN model and its microphone for recognizing the function of that device. This model employs an edge-fog computing paradigm where an image is captured in an edge device and computation is done at the edge or on a fog device.

The rest of the chapter is organized as follows. In Section 8.2, related work regarding hand gesture control systems is described in detail. In Section 8.3, the methodology for single-point control system is described in detail. Section 4 describes the result of ours. Section 5 presents the conclusion and future works.

8.2 Related Work

The work done in this field until now suffered from many issues like posture dependency, dependence on extra devices, higher network connectivity, and so on. This chapter tries to remove the issues that happened previously. The previous work, with positive and negative feedback, is discussed in Table 8.1.

TABLE 8.1

Differences between Related Work and the Proposed Work

Related Work	Strengthens	Weakness	Proposed Work
By D. Arsenault [2]	It reduces the learning rate of the model. About 72 gestures can be recognized to control the different functions of a device.	It uses extra sensor-able devices for sending or controlling functions of other devices. Response time delay is high.	Adapt so it uses fog computing to reduce the learning rate of the model.
By H. S. Chudgar [3]	It didn't use extra devices like gloves or other devices containing sensors, which led to cost savings too.	Power consumption is too high as the device is always in ready mode to send the data. Posture dependency and accuracy are major drawbacks in this paper.	Adapt so it uses mobile phone sensors to control the function that leads to cost savings.
By H. P. Gupta [5]	It gives posture independency and real-time application to user.	Few functions can be recognized by the model, and users are able to control only one device.	Adapt so it uses an incremental learning model to give posture independency to the user.

(Data from D. Arsenault and A. D. Whitehead, 2015; Gupta, H.P., Chudgar, H.S., Mukherjee, S., Dutta, T. and Sharma, K., 2016; Saraswat, S., Gupta, A., Gupta, H.P. and Dutta, T., 2019)

8.3 Proposed Methodology

The user performs three actions to control a consumer device. At first, users select the device and the function of that device in first phase. In second phase the user needs to control the range of that selected function. This research work purposed a model for operating the consumer device using gesture-capturing through the camera and audio using the microphone of an edge device (i.e., laptop). This approach has two major phases: (1) function selection, and the device using gesture and audio recognition; and (2) controlling the magnitude of that function using an image captured by a camera. Both phases are executed at the edge device. The block diagram of proposed methodology is shown in Figure 8.2.

8.3.1 Phase 1: Function and Device Selection Using Camera and Microphone

In this phase, an image is collected by using the camera of an edge device (laptop) then preprocessing that image to extract the features. After that, a classification model is built for identifying the gesture using those extracted features as shown in Figure 8.3. After identifying the gesture, identify the voice for function selection for that device that is selected by identifying gesture. The sensors like gyroscope and accelerometers depends on the posture of user that create a posture dependency for users. By using only real time image capturing and speed recognition we can able to palm off from posture dependency.

1. Data acquisition: This model uses a laptop embedded with camera for data acquisition. Images are selected because they are independent of posture of users. For distinguishing different hand gesture, we use CNN classification models for better accuracy. This work consists of six gestures for device selection. After device selection, the user voice is captured with the microphone of the laptop using

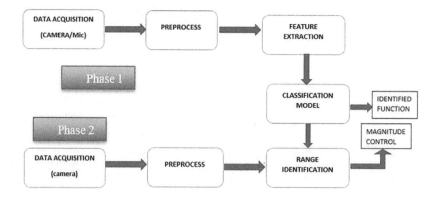

FIGURE 8.2
Block diagram of proposed methodology.

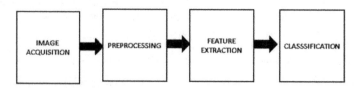

FIGURE 8.3
Steps for hand gesture recognition.

Pyttsx3 and speech-recognition Python packages. These packages are used for converting text to audio or vice-versa.

2. Data preprocess: The original image used for hand gesture recognition includes noise and background. For this, first crop the image containing only the hand from the whole frame. It will reduce the data size and training time also. After that, subtract the background and convert it into binary images for a better classification result. For function selection, audio is converted into text and saved in a variable using a speech-recognition package.

3. Feature extraction: This is an important step in which different algorithms and techniques compute representation that facilitates downstream task. Here the model is used to detect the shape and edge of a digital image or video by dividing it, pooling and stacking small areas of image to process them. Audio text is used to detect the function if some part of the text matched with a word that is relevant to a function of that device.

4. Classification model: A model is built using a neural network technique known as convolution neural network (CNN) [8] [9]. Figure 8.4 shows the 2D CNN model used in this work. The learning phase (i.e., training of model) is supervised, where with every image labels are required; but in the testing phase, the model is unsupervised. For function identification, audio is classified using the object-oriented programming language of Python. For this there's no need of any classification model.

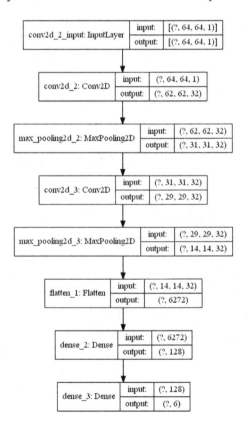

FIGURE 8.4
2D CNN model for hand-gesture recognition.

Source: Based on Mathe, E., Mitsou, A., Spyrou, E. and Mylonas, P., 2018

8.3.2 Phase 2: Magnitude Controlling

This research works using a camera to control the range of that function, which is selected in previous phase. The software used for this is Python and Open CV [10]. Python is used for object-oriented programming, and Open CV is a computer vision library for real-time image processing. The magnitude of function is controlled by the count of convexity defects [10] [11]. If the number of convexity defects is more than two, range of the function is increased or decreased. The original frame at the time of processing is shown as in Figure 8.5.

1) Algorithm for controlling the magnitude of function:

a. Extract a frame (i.e., hand image) from video stream.
b. Remove the background from input colored image frame, which was obtained by using webcam.
c. Set the threshold value according to the surrounding light.
d. Convert the colored image to a binary image.
e. Contour the binary image and draw this on another blank image.
f. Draw the convex hull with convexity defects.
g. Set certain points that are used in range set.

From obtained color image, binary of that image is derived with the help of segmentation followed by extracting the contour of binary image. Later it is used for drawing convex hull and finding the convexity defects. Convexity defects are those angles that are less than 90 degrees. After identifying all these functions and range operations, the model sends it to the infrared (IR) signal mapping device to control the home appliances as shown in Figure 8.6. Table 8.2 shows different simulated parameters that are used during work.

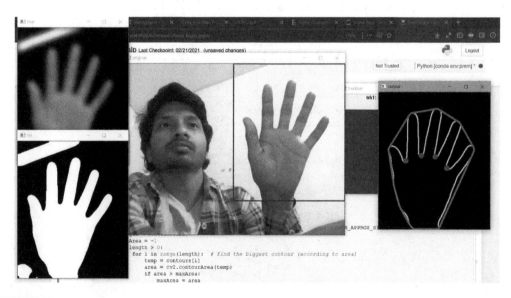

FIGURE 8.5
Magnitude controlling phase.

TABLE 8.2

Simulated Parameters

Parameter	Value	Description
Set Val (threshold)	60	Minimum value for pixel intensity
Set Val (no. of epoch)	15	Dataset division
Set Val (learning rate)	0	Hyper parameter for training the model
Set Val (iteration)	1	Repetition of process
Set Val (batch size)	12	No. of learning image
Set Val (no. of test sample)	177	No. of testing image

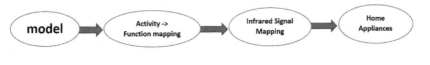

FIGURE 8.6
Sending IR signal to consumer devices.

8.4 Result and Discussion

Figure 8.7 shows the simulated accuracy of the model in phase 1 for identifying the hand gesture. The maximum simulated accuracy that we are able to reach is about 60% in the testing phase and about 99% in the training phase. Figure 8.8 shows the function loss in the training and testing phases.

Confusion matrix in Figure 8.9 shows the predicted and actual labels of different gestures obtained during the testing phase.

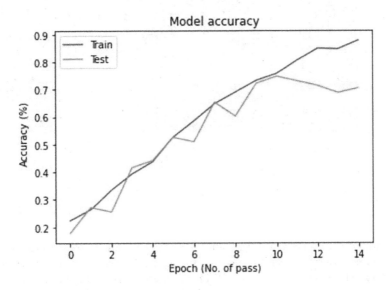

FIGURE 8.7
Accuracy of model in phase 1.

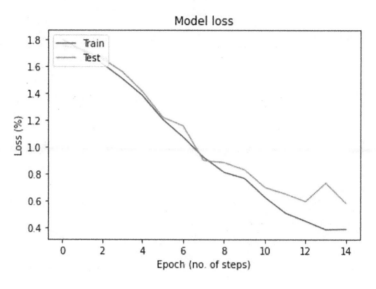

FIGURE 8.8
Model loss in phase 1.

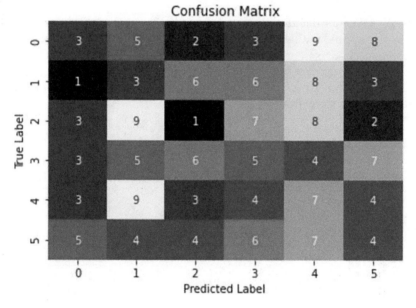

FIGURE 8.9
Shows the confusion matrix.

Figure 8.5 shows the convex hull (i.e., outer line of hand) and convexity defects where the angle is less than 90 degrees, with real-time images captured from the webcam of an edge device for phase 2 that is used for controlling the range of the selected device function. The red line shown in Figure 8.8 shows convex hull, and the blue dots are convexity defects. The convexity defect points are used for increasing and decreasing the magnitude of the function. Converxity defects were those angles that is less than 90 degrees. After identifying all these function, and range operation, the model sends it to the Infrared (IR) signal mapping devices to control the home appliances as show in Figure 8.9.

8.5 Conclusion

The research work proposed a CNN model for selecting the device and controlling the consumer device function using a laptop acting as an edge device. It uses the camera and microphone of the laptop for selecting the device and its function, unlike earlier work using sensors or other wearable devices. It uses real-time image processing for controlling the range of function that wasn't performed before. The proposed model can be used for complex, natural voice-recognition functions. We believe that this methodology helps other researchers in the area of single-point control systems.

References

1. Rautaray, S. S. and Agrawal, A., 2015. Vision based hand gesture recognition for human computer interaction: A survey. *Artificial Intelligence Review*, 43(1), pp. 1–54.
2. Arsenault, D. and Whitehead, A. D., 2015. Gesture recognition using Markov systems and wearable wireless inertial sensors. *IEEE Transactions on Consumer Electronics*, 61(4), pp. 429–437.
3. Gupta, H. P., Chudgar, H. S., Mukherjee, S., Dutta, T. and Sharma, K., 2016. A continuous hand gestures recognition technique for human-machine interaction using accelerometer and gyroscope sensors. *IEEE Sensors Journal*, 16(16), pp. 6425–6432.
4. Alladi, T., Chamola, V., Sikdar, B. and Choo, K. K. R., 2020. Consumer IoT: Security vulnerability case studies and solutions. *IEEE Consumer Electronics Magazine*, 9(2), pp. 17–25.
5. Saraswat, S., Gupta, A., Gupta, H. P. and Dutta, T., 2019. An incremental learning based gesture recognition system for consumer devices using edge-fog computing. *IEEE Transactions on Consumer Electronics*, 66(1), pp. 51–60.
6. Liacco, T. E. D., 1967. The adaptive reliability control system. *IEEE Transactions on Power Apparatus and Systems*, 5, pp. 517–531.
7. Ahlawat, S., Batra, V., Banerjee, S., Saha, J. and Garg, A. K., 2019. Hand gesture recognition using convolutional neural network. In *International Conference on Innovative Computing and Communications* (pp. 179–186). Springer, Singapore.
8. Mathe, E., Mitsou, A., Spyrou, E. and Mylonas, P., 2018. September. Arm gesture recognition using a convolutional neural network. In *2018 13th International Workshop on Semantic and Social Media Adaptation and Personalization (SMAP)* (pp. 37–42). IEEE.
9. Pradhan, A. and Deepak, B. B. V. L., 2015, May. Obtaining hand gesture parameters using image processing. In *2015 International Conference on Smart Technologies and Management for Computing, Communication, Controls, Energy and Materials (ICSTM)* (pp. 168–170). IEEE.
10. Jinda-Apiraksa, A., Pongstiensak, W. and Kondo, T., 2010, May. A simple shape-based approach to hand gesture recognition. In *ECTI-CON2010: The 2010 ECTI International Confernce on Electrical Engineering/Electronics, Computer, Telecommunications and Information Technology* (pp. 851–855). IEEE.
11. Liacco, T. E. D., 1967. The adaptive reliability control system. *IEEE Transactions on Power Apparatus and Systems*, (5), pp. 517–531.

9

Fog Computing: A Peek into Communication Security

Parminder Singh Sethi

Dell Technologies
Banglore, India

Ravi Tomar

School of Computer Science
University of Petroleum and Energy Studies
Dehradun, India

CONTENTS

9.1 Introduction to Fog Computing

As fog computing serves on a large scale, authentication, authorization, and trust become some of the most concerning issues in fog computing implementation. Because of these concerns, roughness is introduced in the fog computing distributed environment, which easily hampers privacy and causes data leakage by manipulating the signals shared among different layers of the fog framework.

The fog framework is distributed among multiple layers over the network, where different devices with different IP addresses are communicating with various layers at the same time, and tons of data is being shared among those various layers.

This architecture leads to various security attacks at different layers. Different attacks are possible [1] based on the context, capability, and responsibility of that specific layer. Some of the attacks concerning the different layers are mentioned in Figure 9.1.

This chapter aims to bring awareness by discussing the various challenges in implementation regards to security and privacy in fog computing like trust, authentication, and authorization. We will also learn how the devices work together in a distributed fog computing environment.

DOI: 10.1201/9781003188230-9

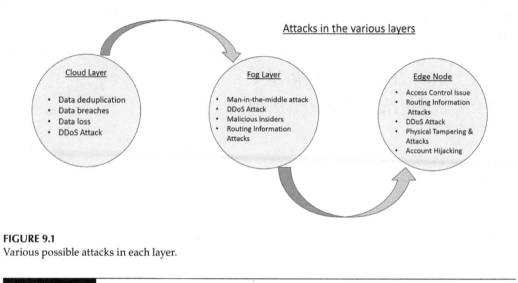

FIGURE 9.1
Various possible attacks in each layer.

9.2 Fog Computing and Cloud Computing

Fog computing is highly related to cloud computing and its services. Therefore, before we understand what fog computing is, let's try to understand and learn about cloud computing first. At a high level, cloud computing is an on-demand service that can be accessed via the Internet. This service is used to access the application, computation power, development tools, storage, high processing power, and so on. Data can be stored, processed, and retrieved from the cloud on-demand at any point in time. With the rise of IoT devices across various business verticals and a huge amount of data generated from them on daily basis, there is a requirement for a cost-effective, efficient, faster mode of data access. That is where fog computing comes into the picture. Fog computing was introduced by network giant, Cisco. Sometimes, [2] it is also called fog-networking or fogging. It is an architecture that can manage various devices, applications, or data at the edge of a network. The biggest advantage of fog computing is left-shift cloud intelligence, and now this intelligence of data processing would be closer to the devices.

This approach was focused on solving two major challenges:

- Handling the rapid increase in IoT devices, and data generated by the devices, by bringing the left-shift processing power closer to the devices.
- Providing an efficient way to access data and process the same in a cost-effective way.

Typically, most of the data is generated by IoT devices or sensors. This data is uploaded to fog for quick processing on-the-edge, instead of directly going to the cloud layer.

Here, fog would be considered as a middle layer between the cloud devices and application/sensors. Devices would be able to talk to the fog layer, which is closer to the device as compared to the cloud layer. Fog will compute, process, and analyze the data on the edge and if further analysis is required, the data is transported to the cloud.

9.3 Real-Time Distributed Architecture of Fog Computing

The real-time distributed architecture of fog computing is implemented by various organizations today. There are multiple variances of the fog computing implementation, and

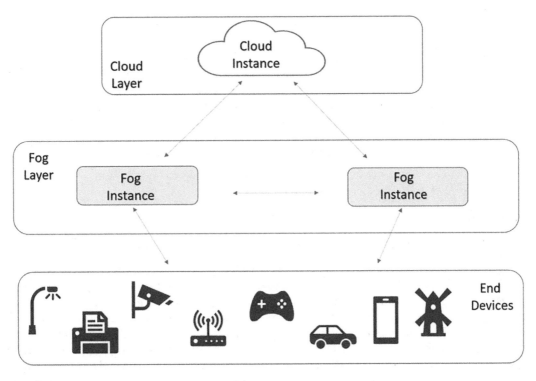

FIGURE 9.2
Three-tier architecture for fog computing.

here we will be learning about the 3-tier variance, which is also the most-used variance in the industry.

Before the evolution of fog computing, all devices would talk to the cloud layer directly using the Internet. As the devices were in direct contact with the last layer of the system, the turnaround time of this type of communication between the devices and cloud was always high. To save these multiple round-trips to the cloud, a middle layer called the fog layer was introduced.

As described in [3], the 3-tier architecture (Figure 9.2) consists of layers distributed over the network. All these layers execute independent tasks but also work together as a single end-to-end framework to serve the customers (in this case, end devices).

- End Device [4]: End devices are the ones that capture the data from various end points and forward it to the next layer for further processing, for example, sensors, smart cards, smartwatches, phones, systems, and so on.

- These devices can be on different geo-locations but might be communicating with the same fog instance or same logical fog instance.

- For example, all the smartwatches in a state might be communicating with the same fog instance. All these watches are at different geo-locations, but they are sensing and capturing the data and sending it for further analysis on the same fog instance.

- Fog Layer: [4] Fog layer is the middleman between the end device and cloud layer (data center). It consists of gateways, routers, or sometimes even fog servers that are sometimes called fog nodes. These nodes can be static or mobile—placed in a static building or part of some moving vehicle. These nodes can compute, transfer, and store the data (temporarily).

- Cloud Layer: [4] The third and last layer is the cloud layer. In most instances, this layer is a data center that is deployed and managed by the vendor. This layer would have high computational power and high storage for quick processing of the data. Because of its high storage capability, this layer stores all the information for long-term use and acts as a source of historical data for further processing like machine learning and AI use-cases.

9.4 Trust, Authentication, and Authorization in Fog Computing

Trust, authentication, and authorization are important security challenges of fog computing.

As we are aware that fog computing is inherited from cloud computing, the security and privacy issues of the cloud are also inherited, and on top of that, there are additional issues that are introduced in the fog computing implementation [5]. In this section of the chapter, we will be talking more about the challenges of trust, authentication, and authorization. Although these three terms are interrelated in the case of fog computing, let's understand how trust, authentication, and authorization work together in a distributed network of fog computing and what are the challenges and security concerns. Figure 9.3 is one variant of fog computing implementation:

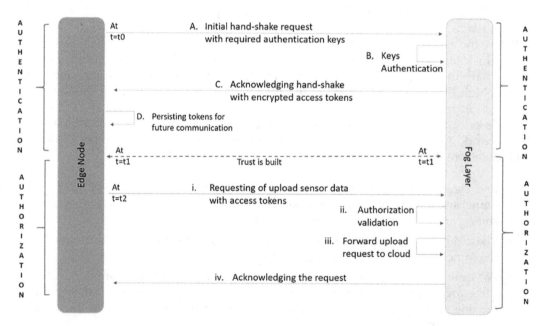

FIGURE 9.3
Working of authentication, authorization, and trust.

First, for simplicity, let's understand this concept between two layers: edge nodes and fog layers. The communication always starts from the edge node and is received and acknowledged by the fog layer. Following is the sequence of steps that happens between these two layers (see Figure 9.3):

- Authentication:
  - At t=t0, edge node devices try to authenticate themselves with the fog layer.
  - As part of step 'A', a handshake is initialized with the required and appropriate authentication keys.
    - The authentication keys are shared by the fog layer provider to the edge node through some other means, for example, offline communication, emails, etc. These keys can be thought of as something like the product keys which are different for different customers of the fog computing layer.
    - These keys are always encrypted to avoid the middleman replaying the transactions.
  - At step 'B', the fog layer receives the authentication request and validates the authentication keys by decrypting and validating the same. In this case, the request is from a genuine consumer. Therefore, a pair of keys are generated for this consumer. Every consumer receives a different set of keys specific to their transaction, even though they exist in the same edge network.
    - This variance of implementation is called the OAuth authentication implementation. As described in [6], OAuth is an open-standard authorization protocol that defines how an unrelated service can safely allow access (authentication) to the other entity without sharing the logon credentials.
    - These pairs of keys are also known as access keys (access token) and refresh keys (refresh tokens) [7]. The access token generally has a validity of a day, but the refresh token has a validity of nearly 1 year, approximately.
    - The access tokens are used for further authorization and if the access token is invalid, then the consumer's refresh token would be used to generate a new access token.
  - At step 'C', the handshake is acknowledged with the set of encrypted keys/ tokens. This is followed by step 'D', where the edge device would be persisting the tokens in their environment.
  - After these steps, authentication is complete, and therefore trust is built. This means that the authentication keys are validated, and specific access tokens are generated for each edge device for further communication.
- Authorization:
  - Authentication and authorization sound similar [8], but they are very different. Authentication confirms the identity, so users are who they say they are. On other hand, authorization talks more about permission and access to various roles/resources or actions of an authentic user only.
  - At t=t2, step 'i', an authentic edge-device sends a request to upload sensor data to the cloud storage. The access token is also sent, along with the request, to the fog layer.
  - As part of step 'ii', the fog layer validates the access token, and using the access token, the fog layer recognizes who the customer is (another type of authentication).

- After validation, the device authorization is performed. This includes questions such as: Is the device allowed to send the sensor data? Is the device allowed to send the request for upload? and many others, as per the use-cases and implementation.

- If the request is authentic, and the device is authorized to send this request, the fog layer takes appropriate action on that request.

9.5 Security Challenges in Communication and Data Privacy

Although cloud computing does have heavily protected solutions/algorithms and methods for various security challenges, all these solutions/methods are not robust enough to be directly applied to fog computing because of its diverse architecture and because of the responsibility and operations allowed in the fog-distributed environment [9].

Fog computing has more touchpoints, and more distributed interactions can happen over the network compared to cloud computing. Therefore, for fog computing, the list of challenges is long, but we will discuss some of the most common and high-priority challenges, for example, trust (authentication and authorization), secure communication, privacy, request-replay, data privacy, and so on.

- Trust—Authentication and Authorization:

    In an earlier section of this chapter, we learned about the working of trust, authentication, and authorization in a distributed network. Here, let's try to understand the security challenges for the same.

    Implementing trustworthy communication is a bit tricky [9] in the case of fog computing because of its two-way openness—that is, communication with the edge devices and at the same time communication with the cloud layer, as shown in Figure 9.4. The two-way openness leads to high-security vulnerability, as the security design should be robust enough to handle two-way communication with the least resources and by not compromising on the security.

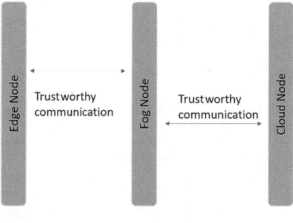

FIGURE 9.4
Trustworthy communication.

- Rogue Fog Node Attack—Privacy and Data Breach:

  This is one of the most commons attacks that happen in the customer environment, and this attack may lead to data loss, privacy issues, data breaches, information routing attacks, and so on.

  In this attack, another fog node is introduced by the attacker, which acts as a legitimate one in terms of behavior and service. This is done to steal the data coming from either side of the fog instance, that is edge nodes or cloud layer.

  Currently, various access-control algorithms and methods are applied to enable various protection points to the fog node and to help in detecting fake or rogue nodes in the fog environment, but it is still a big challenge as the hackers are coming up with stronger rogue techniques, with time [10].

  This may be considered as one of the sub-categories of man-in-middle attack and insider attack as shown in Figure 9.5.

- Insider attack:

  An insider attack [11] is a form of a malicious attack perpetrated on a network or computer system with the aid of using someone with legal gadget access. In this fog layer/instance, the admin who is the authentic and authorized person of the fog instance might initiate one rogue fog node/instance instead of the legitimate one [12].

- Man-in-middle:

  In this attack [13], a hacker or an unauthentic/unauthorized person would try to position himself in between the communication of an edge device with a fog instance. Here, the perpetrator would try to act as a fog node (rogue one) and

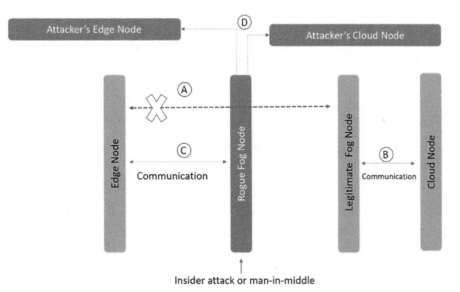

FIGURE 9.5
Placement of rogue layer by an attacker.

would give assurance to the edge node that the rogue fog instance is the legitimate one. [14] have established the feasibility of a man-in-the-middle attack in fog computing, earlier than which the gateway needs to be both compromised or changed with the aid of using a fake one.

In the rogue fog-node attack, another (rogue) fog node is introduced, and the attacker will make sure that the edge node and cloud node start trusting this rogue fog node for trusted communications.

By introducing this rogue node, an attacker can investigate the data flowing through either side of the network. He can manipulate the data flow with unexpected scripts, or he can even perform the replay request attack to get the information stored on either side of the fog node.

As we can see in Figure 9.5, before the introduction of the rogue fog attack, the edge node was communicating with the legitimate fog node using path 'A', and the legitimate fog node was communicating with the cloud node using path 'B'.

But, the attacker has introduced the rogue fog node in the environment by mocking the behavior of the legitimate fog node. The edge node is not aware of this activity, as the rogue fog node is behaving in the same way as the legitimate node. Therefore, the edge node continuously sends data to the rogue node without any interruptions.

Now, the attacker can also introduce a rogue cloud and rogue edge node to cascade the damage to the other endpoints. A rogue fog node has two options to perform various attacks and misuse the data, which are as follows:

- A rogue fog node, after creating the trust with the senders on both sides, that is cloud layer and edge node, can route the traffic/data coming from either of the ends to his own created instance (attacker's cloud and attacker's edge). This helps him understand the behavior of the legitimate layer and train his rogue layer to the best of their versions. In addition, the attacker can re-route all the data coming from the edge to his cloud instance and misuse the data, which can also lead to data breaches or privacy concerns.

  These are just a few things an attacker can perform, but there are possibilities of introducing more attacks to gain:

- Access in terms of authority
- Knowledge on legitimate behavior and re-train the attacker's layer
- More insights on the data that resides in the different segments of the layers

Other critical attacks are replay transaction attacks and DDoS attacks. A DDoS attack [15] is a distributed, large-scale coordinated attempt to flood the network with a substantial quantity of packets, which is tough for the victim network to handle, leaving the victim unable to offer the required and committed services.

For example, let's suppose the edge node is sending data to the fog instance with the required valid tokens and keys. Now the rogue node [16] can investigate the request sent by the edge and can capture the various authentication or authorization tokens sent as part of the request. The attacker can use these tokens for sending another request, or the same request might be replayed from a rogue fog node to the cloud.

Using this, an attacker can get access to data for which he is not authorized, and this leads to data breaches and privacy issues.

9.6 Summary

Fog networking/computing is known as a decentralized and distributed computing infrastructure in which various endpoints are sending and receiving data and storing them. The various responsibilities are scattered in the most logical and efficient layer in this distributed system, which makes it more effective in terms of the serviceability to the end-user as compared to traditional models like cloud computing.

Since it is more robust than the cloud, it has more doors for security loopholes and challenges when it comes to implementation. As fog is an emerging framework, the algorithms and methods to handle the security challenges (explained earlier in the chapter) are also emerging with time.

This doesn't mean that the solutions or methods we have today are not strong enough. There are some strong solutions, for example, context-driven authentication keys, rotating key mechanisms, and so on. These methods are quite strong but not very generic in terms of implementation. In fog, different situations might need different solutions in a single implementation, which makes it challenging overall.

References

[1] Y. I. Alzoubi, V. H. Osmanaj, A. Jaradat, and A. Al-Ahmad, "Fog computing security and privacy for the Internet of Thing applications: State-of-the-art," *Security and Privacy*, vol. 4, no. 2, p. e145, March 2021, doi:10.1002/spy2.145.

[2] "Introduction to Fog computing | by Patrick Gichini | Decode_ke | Medium." https://medium.com/decode-ke/introduction-to-fog-computing-ec477aa919cf (accessed May 18, 2021).

[3] T. Yu, X. Wang, and A. Shami, "A novel Fog computing enabled temporal data reduction scheme in iot systems," *2017 IEEE Global Communications Conference. GLOBECOM 2017 – Procedure*, vol. 2018, January, pp. 1–5, July 2017, doi:10.1109/GLOCOM.2017.8253941.

[4] "Fog computing architecture | Hierarchical & layered Fog architecture." www.educba.com/fog-computing-architecture/ (accessed May 04, 2021).

[5] A. Al-Noman Patwary et al., "Authentication, access control, privacy, threats and trust management towards securing Fog computing environments: A review," *arXiv:2003.00395*.

[6] "What is OAuth? How the open authorization framework works | CSO Online." www.csoonline.com/article/3216404/what-is-oauth-how-the-open-authorization-framework-works.html (accessed May 16, 2021).

[7] "Understanding refresh tokens—Auth0." https://auth0.com/learn/refresh-tokens/ (accessed May 16, 2021).

[8] "Authentication vs. Authorization | Okta." www.okta.com/identity-101/authentication-vs-authorization/ (accessed May 06, 2021).

[9] M. Mukherjee et al., "Security and privacy in Fog computing: Challenges," *IEEE Access*, vol. 5, pp. 19293–19304, September 2017, doi:10.1109/ACCESS.2017.2749422.

[10] A. A. Patwary, R. K. Naha, S. Garg, S. K. Battula, and M. Gong, "Towards secure Fog computing: A survey on trust management, privacy, authentication, threats and access control," *Electronics*, vol. 10, no. 10, p. 1171, 2021.

[11] "What is an insider attack?—Definition from techopedia." www.techopedia.com/definition/26217/insider-attack (accessed May 16, 2021).

[12] K. Munir and L. A. Mohammed, "Biometric smartcard authentication for Fog computing," *International Journal of Network Security & Its Applications*, vol. 10, no. 6, pp. 35–45, 2018, doi:10.5121/ijnsa.2018.10604.

[13] "What is MITM (Man in the Middle) attack | Imperva." www.imperva.com/learn/application-security/man-in-the-middle-attack-mitm/ (accessed May 16, 2021).

[14] I. Stojmenovic and S. Wen, "The Fog computing paradigm: Scenarios and security issues," *2014 Federated Conference on Computer Science and Information Systems*, IEEE, 2014, doi:10.15439/2014F503.

[15] K. A. Kumar, C. Santhosh, and S. Shanmugapriya, "EDAA – An efficient DDoS association analysis using hypergraph clustering in Fog computing," *International Journal of Computer Science and Engineering (IJCSE)*, pp. 75–80, 2019. www.internationaljournalssrg.org (accessed May 16, 2021).

[16] K. Zaidi, M. Milojevic, V. Rakocevic, and M. Rajarajan, "Data-centric rogue node detection in VANETs," *2014 IEEE 13th International Conference on Trust, Security and Privacy in Computing and Communications*, 2014, pp. 398–405, doi:10.1109/TRUSTCOM.2014.51. https://ieeexplore.ieee.org/abstract/document/7011275

10

Fog Computing and Machine Learning

Kaustubh Lohani

School of Computer Science
University of Petroleum and Energy Studies
Dehradun, India

Prajwal Bhardwaj

School of Computer Science
University of Petroleum and Energy Studies, Dehradun
Uttrakhand, India

Ravi Tomar

School of Computer Science
University of Petroleum and Energy Studies
Dehradun, India

CONTENTS

DOI: 10.1201/9781003188230-10

133

10.1 Introduction

Cloud as a concept was around since the 1960s, since the introduction of ARPANET. In 2006, Amazon launched Elastic Compute Cloud (EC2), arguably the first cloud-based service model. Not long after, NIST formally defined cloud in 2011. Soon, cloud computing picked up, gaining popularity as organizations started migrating to the cloud because of its benefits like low operational cost, low operational maintenance from their side, better flexibility, and scalability. Soon after, data collected on every device was sent to the cloud to get stored, processed, and analyzed.

Meanwhile, in the 1980s, a group of students from Carnegie Mellon University created a way to get an on-campus cola machine to report its contents to know when it is empty. Around the same time, in 1999, Kevin Ashton coined the term *Internet of Things*. During 2008–2009, adoption of IoT picked up as smartphones were mainstream, and the world's population increased to 6.8 billion in 2010. This boom of smartphones and the world population ensured that there were more Internet-connected devices than people worldwide. Essentially, there were more than 1 (1.84 to be exact) Internet-connected devices per person in the world for the first time in history [1].

A large chunk of data generated in those devices was sent to the cloud to get stored or processed. Then, machine learning algorithms were deployed to analyze the data and take out critical points based on which business decisions were made.

Now, all was going well until IoT started to show up in time-critical systems. For example, an automated intrusion detection system. Now, data analysis from data generated inside time-critical systems started getting delayed. This was happening due to centralized ML processing systems that were placed in the cloud. This centralized system posed a set of challenges; one of them was that data was getting delayed in transfer to the central system. On top of that, there were times when the central system was overloaded, delaying the results. The automated system relied on these results to function effectively and efficiently.

To counter this delay in transfer, fog computing is introduced as an extension of cloud computing. Furthermore, to nullify the delay in processing, fog nodes are armed with machine learning algorithms in place, such as anomaly detection, among others. Integration with machine learning resulted in faster decision-making, thus increasing the overall system's effectiveness and efficiency.

Fog computing paired with machine learning can solve several problems while using cloud computing or fog computing alone. As a result of ML algorithms deployed on the fog nodes, they can intelligently classify what data needs to be stored in the cloud, thus saving bandwidth and protecting privacy at the same time. Further, delays in transfer and processing are reduced as fog nodes are part of the same network, and time-critical data is passed through ML algorithms deployed on the fog nodes, thereby detecting potential problems before they can cause any severe damage to the overall operation.

The chapter is organized as follows. In the second section, we introduce the fog computing paradigm, explain its need, and list its features, advantages, and disadvantages along with the architecture. The third section focuses on introducing Machine Learning and its various techniques commonly used with fog computing. Finally, the fourth section delves deep into coalescing the previously defined fog computing technology, with ML learning algorithms defined in section 10.3, and gives several real-world scenarios that can benefit by utilizing fog computing with ML.

10.2 Introduction to Fog Computing

10.2.1 Definition

Fog computing is a layered model that puts processing and resources at the edge of a network rather than establishing cloud storage and usage channels. The model facilitates applications and services to be processed in fog nodes between intelligent devices and centralized cloud services [2].

Fog nodes are often programmed intelligently while also supporting standard data management and communication protocols. The primary function of these nodes is to provide local computational resources for the data collected via edge devices while also providing on-demand connectivity to centralized resources [2].

10.2.2 Evolution of Fog Computing

In 2011, the existing cloud computing paradigm was extended to give birth to fog computing. Fog computing was mainly born out of the need to real-time process and analyze vast amounts of data collected by the IoT sensors in low-latency applications [3].

In November of 2015, Cisco Systems, along with other leading vendors in infrastructure and cloud domains, founded the OpenFog Consortium to advance the development of fog computing.

10.2.3 Fog Computing Architecture and Positioning of Fog Nodes

The whole purpose of fog computing is to bring computational resources closer to the edge, where data is generated. Fog nodes are a highly virtualized implementation that is mainly responsible for providing computational resources and short-term storage to the data generated in the edge layer [4].

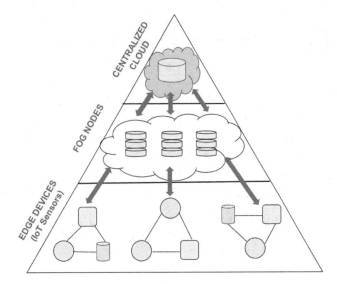

FIGURE 10.1
Fog computing architecture.

The holistic architecture of fog computing, as depicted in Figure 10.1, includes three layers. The first layer contains the edge devices like sensors and mobile devices and IoT networks. The second layer consists of fog nodes that connect wirelessly with the edge layer and provide a staging area for data collected at the edge nodes. The fog layer is responsible for processing and analyzing the data collected by the edge devices in the first layer. The second layer further connects edge devices on-demand to the third layer, the cloud layer; fog nodes do this by constant feedback from the devices in the edge layer, ensuring better utilization of resources in the cloud [4].

The fog layer can be further broken into sub-layers, as depicted in Figure 10.2. First, the physical and virtualization layer comprises all the physical devices and sensors present in the network. The primary function of this layer is to collect data and send them to further layers for processing. A node in this layer can be a standalone device like mobile phones or IoT sensors like light or temperature sensors. The second layer is the monitoring layer, where the physical nodes are monitored for performance, efficiency, and energy consumption, among other properties. Next is the pre-processing layer, which deals with data analysis-related tasks. This is the layer where intelligent ML algorithms are deployed to process and analyze the data. Next is the temporary storage layer, which deals with data duplication and replication. Data stored here is removed from this layer once it gets transferred to the cloud. Next comes the security layer, which deals with data encryption and decryption, data privacy, and integration measures. The final layer is the transport layer, which deals with sending the processed and refined data secured by the security layer to the cloud.

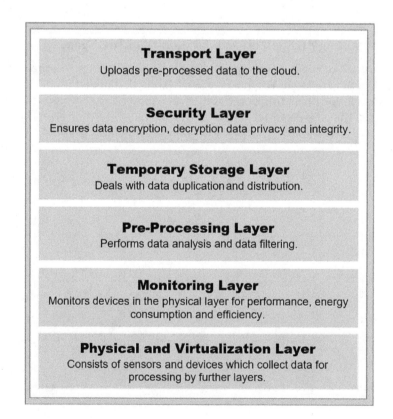

FIGURE 10.2
Layered architecture of fog computing.

10.2.4 Need for Fog Computing over Traditional Cloud Computing

In the cloud computing model, the devices at the edge send all the collected data back to the cloud to get processed, analyzed, and stored. However, when the system demands low-latency real-time analysis, sending data back to the cloud to get processed poses specific problems.

The first major issue is high latency. Cloud cannot guarantee real-time response due to the distance between edge nodes and data-processing stations. Second, almost all Internet-based networks suffer from downtime, and the cloud is no different. This might lead to a hiatus in data processing and analysis, affecting decision-making and proving detrimental in fully automated IoT systems. Finally, fog computing ensures that only specific data leave the network and travel to the cloud, increasing data privacy and lowering the risk of data leakage if the cloud is compromised.

10.2.5 Difference between Cloud Computing and Fog Computing

Cloud computing follows a centralized architecture approach. In contrast, fog computing by design is distributed in nature. Cloud connects from a more considerable distance with the edge nodes, while fog nodes are directly connected with the edge devices over a shorter distance, as they are part of the same network in many cases. Generally, the number of cloud nodes in an IoT system's overall implementation is significantly less than the fog nodes. Furthermore, data processing and analysis are carried out far from the collection source in the case of the cloud, whereas fog nodes process and analyze the data while remaining in the same local network as the data collection source. Table 10.1 shows the Differences between Cloud Computing and Fog Computing.

Furthermore, cloud computing provides higher computational capabilities than fog computing. Data privacy and security are better in fog computing because most data never leaves the local network. Data that gets transferred to the cloud is utilized for long-term analysis and, in some cases, to train ML models; whereas, data processed in fog nodes are utilized to provide instant actionable decisions for the optimal functioning of the IoT

TABLE 10.1

Summarizing the Differences between Cloud Computing and Fog Computing

Parameter	Cloud Computing	Fog Computing
Distribution architecture	*Centralized*	*Distributed*
Communication with edge devices	From a larger distance	From a shorter distance
Number of nodes	Low	High
Data processing and analysis	Far from the source of data collection	Close to the source of data collection
Computational capabilities	High	Low
Type of analysis	Long-term	Short-term
Latency	High	Low
Geographical coverage	Global	Local (building or a city-wide)
Data received is generated by	Mainly humans	Devices and sensors
Data storage (duration)	As much as required (days, years)	Short-term
Main use case	To process, analyze, and store data	To process and analyze data
Operational costs	High	Low

system. In many cases, models trained at the cloud layer are deployed at the fog nodes to facilitate instant automated decision-making. Latency is higher in cloud computing when compared with fog computing. Operating expenses are higher in the case of the cloud. Cloud computing offers global geographical coverage, while fog computing is primarily local to a city or a building.

In most cases, data received in the cloud for processing are generated by humans, whereas fog nodes receive data generated via devices and sensors. Data transferred to the cloud can be stored for as much time as required, but storage in fog nodes offers ephemeral storage. Cloud is mainly used to process, analyze, and store data for more extended periods. In contrast, the primary use case for fog computing includes processing and analysis of data rather than long-term data storage.

10.2.6 Advantages of Fog Computing

- *Low latency*: Fog computing processes data locally without sending it to the centralized cloud system, reducing the distance that the data needs to travel to start getting processed. Further, the faster the processing of data can start, the faster the results can be delivered. Thus, faster data processing in fog computing ensures low latency in time-sensitive services. Moreover, low latency reduces the overall response time, which improves the overall user experience [5] [6].

- *Increased compliance with local laws*: Several data security and privacy laws and frameworks require sensitive data to be processed locally without involving a third party. Fog computing is designed to keep the data processing and analysis local without sending it to the cloud, ensuring that the business is compliant with the local laws.

- *Security*: Data security is another aspect that mandates businesses to use the best approach to handle their data. The longer the data is en route, the greater the potential for it to get compromised. Fog computing reduces the travel of the data, making it less prone to leakage through cyber-attacks. Furthermore, fog computing systems are distributed, making denial of service (DoS) attacks challenging to execute. To successfully execute a DoS attack to affect the system's availability, it is imperative to attack all the fog nodes near the client system. Executing such a coordinated attack can be computationally expensive for the attacker, making the fog system less prone to DoS attacks [7].

- *Better data privacy*: Fog computing is designed to handle sensitive data locally without sending it to the centralized cloud, eliminating the need for a third party and increasing data privacy.

- *Less bandwidth usage*: In fog computing, data travels to just the edge of the network, minimizing bandwidth usage.

- *Better service for remote locations*: Internet connectivity can be unreliable at remote places, which reduces the accessibility to cloud systems. Low accessibility can hamper operations, further causing a total service interruption. Fog computing can process the data locally without the computational resources of the cloud, requiring less network bandwidth, benefitting systems placed in geographically remote locations around the world.

10.2.7 Challenges of Fog Computing

- *Increased complexity*: In fog infrastructure, an additional layer called the fog layer contains fog nodes that process and analyze the data. The additional layer of fog nodes incorporated into the network increases the overall complexity of the network. Furthermore, each node can be processing different datasets, managing all the nodes located in different locations, and coalescing the data analyzed by many fog nodes to produce actionable results that can significantly increase the system's complexity.

- *Ensuring security*: Many fog nodes are involved in fog computing, which provides computational resources and storage to data collected by the edge devices. Since each node is involved in data processing or storage, all the nodes must be adequately secured via data encryption techniques. Moreover, even if one node is not appropriately secured, it could be the inlet for cyber-attacks [8] [9].

- *High maintenance*: Unlike cloud architecture, which is generally centralized, fog systems are distributed and decentralized, making computational servers and storage systems distributed across different geographical locations. Different locations mean that each node has to be fully functional to ensure no interruption, and fog networks having such a high number of nodes increases the required maintenance to minimize the downtime of the whole system.

- *Increased costs*: There are many fog nodes present in a fog infrastructure. All these nodes operate on electricity, which increases the cost of overall infrastructure deployment.

Fog computing collects vast amounts of data that are a pre-requisite for a machine learning model. A machine learning model can be trained on the data collected by the fog nodes and deployed back to make data-oriented decisions in real-time. Thus, before proceeding further, we would like to introduce machine learning.

10.3 Introduction to Machine Learning

A subset of artificial intelligence, machine learning (ML) is the study of computing algorithms that enable computers to predict outcomes by learning and improving user data without being explicitly programmed.

Machine learning algorithms build a "model" based on "training data" to predict outcomes without being explicitly programmed to do so. Instead, ML algorithms use computational statistics and mathematical optimization theory to train the model based on sample training data and to further predict outcomes using the trained model.

Machine learning uses statistical and mathematical approaches to teach computers and develop specialized algorithms for a particular task. There needs to be a training dataset to model a use case like object detection using ML algorithms. This dataset can have correctly labeled values fed to the chosen ML algorithm for constructing a model unique to that particular use case. For example, to train a system to predict stock prices, a dataset containing historical stock prices can be used as training data for a regression algorithm in machine learning.

10.3.1 Machine Learning Implementation Strategies

Machine learning can be implemented in several ways. There are 4 categories of machine learning algorithms: supervised learning, unsupervised learning, semi-supervised learning, and reinforcement learning. These approaches are broadly classified based on the training data and desired outcomes.

- *Supervised learning*: Supervised machine learning uses a labeled training set to train ML models. The training data is correctly labeled with input and output pairs. This training data is then fed to the model, which adjusts its weight to fit the training data correctly. The algorithm uses a cost function minimized using optimization algorithms like gradient descent and stochastic gradient descent to adjust the weights appropriately and achieve the least error between the given value and predicted value. Once the cost is minimized, the model is fitted to the training data. Then this model is evaluated using a test set, which is separated from the initial data before training. The model's accuracy on a test set measures how well the model will perform on unseen real-world data.

  Supervised learning can be used to address two types of problems. First is the classification problem; second is the regression problem.

  - *Classification problem*: This problem involves using a supervised learning algorithm to assign data accurately to predefined categories. For example, categorizing an image of an animal into a cat or a dog is a classification problem. Classification can be binary or multi-class classification. In binary classification, the algorithm outputs discrete values 0 and 1, denoting the two different categories in the data. In contrast, multi-class classification algorithms deal with data having more than 2 categories.

    Popular classification algorithms include K-Nearest-Neighbors (KNN), Support Vector Machines (SVM), Random Forests Classification, Neural Networks, Logistic Regression, Naïve Bayes, and Decision Trees.

  - *Regression problem*: Regression is a supervised learning problem that involves predicting output with continuous values instead of discrete values like in the classification problem. For example, stock prices are a continuous variable that can range from 1 to infinity and everything in between. So, to design a stock price predictor, the choice of supervised learning algorithm should be regression.

    Standard regression algorithms include Linear Regression, Lasso Regression, Polynomial Regression, and Support Vector Regression.

- *Unsupervised learning*: Unsupervised learning algorithms use unlabeled datasets as training input. These algorithms search for patterns and groupings in the dataset to segregate the data into different categories without human assistance. In contrast with supervised learning, unsupervised learning does not need labels to categorize the data, which means input data is available but not output results. Instead, unsupervised learning aims to find the underlying similarities in the dataset group and present the data according to those similarities. This makes unsupervised learning ideal for exploratory data analysis, which data analysts use to understand the data before modelling.

Unsupervised learning algorithms are mainly used for clustering, dimensionality reduction, and association.

- *Clustering*: This is an exploratory data analysis technique used to divide the dataset into several clusters. Multiple data points in the same cluster should have similar characteristics, and points located in different clusters should have little in common. Standard clustering algorithms include K-Means Clustering, DBSCAN, Hierarchical-DBSCAN, Hierarchical Clustering, and Fuzzy Clustering.

- *Dimensionality reduction*: Data is essential in machine learning, but too much data can cause problems like overfitting, which makes data more specific to the training set, making its predictions on the unseen data considerably worse. Furthermore, a massive number of features in a dataset can make it difficult to visualize. Dimensionality reduction can be used on such a dataset where there are large numbers of features or dimensions. Dimensionality reduction can reduce the features in the dataset while retaining most of the meaningful properties of the original data.

  Principal component analysis (PCA) is an example of a commonly used dimensionality reduction algorithm.

- *Association*: Association is a method used to identify relationships between different variables in the dataset. Association rule can determine the likelihood of one item based on other items. Association is generally used for market-based analysis where it is used to determine that if a customer has purchased item A, what other items he is likely to buy.

- *Semi-supervised learning*: This learning approach falls in between supervised and unsupervised approaches. Acquiring labeled data is expensive and time-consuming since labeling is done via a domain expert. Semi-supervised learning utilizes a large amount of unlabeled data as a training set, while a much smaller set is used for model evaluation, reducing the dependence on labeled data, which lowers the time taken and the cost for model implementation.

- *Reinforcement learning*: This learning approach gives the system constant feedback to adjust itself until the model can solve the given problem with the desired accuracy. The model is given rewards for performing as expected or penalties for failing to achieve the potential outcome. The system is designed to maximize the rewards or minimize the penalties. This approach differs from supervised learning. In supervised learning, the model is trained with the correct label itself, whereas in reinforcement learning, there is no correct way the model decides its way (and there can be multiple). One of them is finalized based on maximum reward.

10.3.2 Steps for Machine Learning Implementation

The steps involved in implementing machine learning algorithms start from data collection. Once the problem is defined, data collection is started. Data can be sourced from structured databases like the organization's own database or extracted from unstructured mediums like log files and clickstreams. Further data can be purchased through data providers. If sufficient data cannot be sourced from databases or files, it can be manually collected via sensors or cameras, just like in an IoT system. Figure 10.3 shows the Steps to implement machine learning.

The data collected will not necessarily be provided in a machine learning friendly format. Therefore, the second step in the lifecycle deals with data pre-processing to make data compatible with machine learning algorithms. Moreover, before any ML algorithm is trained on the collected data, data scientists need to understand the available information in the data. Exploratory data analysis (EDA) is performed to fully understand the data, including constructing visualizations to understand the information presented. Furthermore, the data pre-processing step also deals with missing and inaccurate data via replacing them or removing them. After cleansing the incomplete or inaccurate values, data scientists extract the most critical features via the feature selection process. These selected features contain the information on which the ML algorithm will build its model [10].

The third step involves building the model and training it. The data scientist must choose the best machine learning algorithm for a specific problem statement in this step. The dataset prepared in the earlier step is split into a training set and a test set for training the model. Then, the training set is fed to the algorithm so that it can learn from it. In contrast, the test set is used to evaluate the model performance. Moreover, this step also includes hyperparameter tuning that is done to fine-tune the model results.

After training the model, it is evaluated on performance. Although several evaluation metrics like the AUC-ROC curve, accuracy, confusion matrix are available to evaluate ML models, the data scientist must choose which fits the business purpose best. For example, a cancer detection model with an accuracy of 95 percent sounds excellent according to the accuracy metric. However, a closer look at the model results reveals that 10 percent of the results are false negatives, which means that the model is incorrectly classifying the people who have cancer and labeling their condition as benign, which might prove detrimental to the patient's well-being. So, a better metric for this use case would be precision.

Finally, after training and evaluation are completed, the model is deployed to predict outcomes on incoming data. Model deployment is essentially the process of utilizing the predictions generated by the trained model. First, the trained models are saved using specialized formats like pickle. Next, a process workflow is created to feed incoming data to the pickle file to generate predictions in real-time.

After model deployment, it is necessary to monitor it. Monitoring the model helps the organization decide when to pull back the model from deployment for retraining.

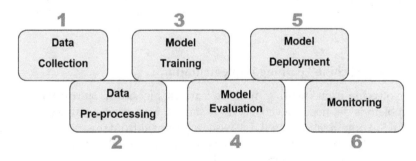

FIGURE 10.3
Steps to implement machine learning.

10.3.3 Advantages of Machine Learning

A critical feature of machine learning is to crunch large volumes of data and identify patterns and trends unique to the data that are not readily perceivable to humans. These patterns and trends can help businesses make correct data-driven decisions that will help increase their product or service adaptability in the market. Furthermore, these patterns and trends can help find out the relationship among variables explaining a particular phenomenon.

Another advantage of using ML algorithms is the scope for continuous improvement. Conventional algorithms lack this feature. Once programmed, conventional algorithms will deliver the same level of accuracy throughout their life. Furthermore, conventional algorithms are susceptible to the same errors. In contrast, ML algorithms can improve via tweaking the hyperparameters or supplying more data. ML algorithms can improve themselves upon further training, increasing the efficiency and accuracy of the model.

Furthermore, machine learning can automate everything, saving time and reducing costs, as ML models require little to no human intervention. Automation allows data scientists and analysts to devote their time elsewhere after successfully deploying a trained ML model. Moreover, automation allows ML systems to be available 24/7, which is impossible for a human doing the same task.

Furthermore, ML can solve various problems ranging from tuning recommendations and customizing each customer's experience in e-commerce to complex applications like driverless cars. In addition, ML models can predict outcomes, reduce expenses via automation, predict the future, or analyze past data, provided there is enough training data available. ML models can also handle massive multi-dimensional data, which can be intimidating for a human analyst.

10.3.4 Challenges of Machine Learning

A primary requirement and the first step in ML modelling is data collection. Data collection is a cumbersome process resulting in low accuracy, inconsistency, and bias in model predictions if done incorrectly. Data collection is complex, as the data requirement is huge for training and testing models. Furthermore, data collected should not be biased; for example, if modelling anything based on gender, all genders should have equal data points across all the features. Moreover, there can be times when data is not readily available; in that case, a data scientist needs to wait for it to become available, which can take anywhere from hours to years, depending on usage and complexity. Surveys are another avenue of data collection, but surveys generally contain incorrect data, leading to low accuracy for unseen real-world data models.

Furthermore, in supervised and semi-supervised learning methodology, the data should be labeled correctly before being fed into the algorithm. However, this labeling often requires the services of domain experts, which increases the overall time and cost of implementation. Essentially, data acquisition is a complicated process to get right. Moreover, data collection often consumes time and drives up the total cost of ML modelling.

Machine learning models are designed to function independently without the need for human assistance. Unfortunately, this independent nature sometimes gives rise to undesirable errors or unexpected outcomes, making ML models prone to errors. These errors are often caused because of incorrect or biased data used during training the model. For example, customers can get bogus recommendations not based on their search history or past purchases, or an object can be wrongly classified as something else. Getting to the bottom of these unexpected behaviors can be a tedious task that requires examining the data and its source in detail; even then, it might not be entirely possible to determine the cause of the unexpected behavior.

Furthermore, training complex models like face detection using deep learning can require substantially more computational resources, which is often expensive and difficult to acquire in some cases. Moreover, a larger dataset increases the required time for training. Having less computing power can increase the modelling time, further increasing the implementation cost of the machine learning algorithm.

Lastly, creating an intelligent system using machine learning has many advantages, but correct decisions must be taken according to the use case to reap these benefits. These decisions include data collection, algorithm selection, and evaluation metric selection, among others. Therefore, to correctly implement the life cycle of the ML model, a highly specialized team comprised of domain experts, data scientists, data analysts, and machine learning engineers are required. This team will label the collected data, analyze the data, manually run different algorithms on the data, and choose the best model based on evaluation metrics. However, finding and maintaining such a skilled team can be time-consuming and expensive.

10.4 Machine Learning in Fog Computing

With IoT gaining more relevance in everyday applications, massive amounts of data are generated. However, processing the generated data is traditionally done in the cloud, which causes latency issues in time sensitive IoT applications. To counter this, data processing can be done on the edge and fog layers, and the cloud can be reserved for training intelligent models and long-time storage of selected data.

Fog and edge nodes are incredibly high in number, and they deal with a large variety of data. For example, fog nodes in a smart home can deal with temperature data, data regarding various appliances, and data about the outside environment. Processing all this variety of data and making decisions in real-time can be challenging for a centralized system like a cloud. Furthermore, processing such a large variety of data can be challenging without intelligent algorithms, as conventional pre-programmed algorithms cannot be designed to deal with infinite possibilities in real-world scenarios [11].

An algorithm must determine on its own whether a situation requires attention and alert the administrator of the same. For example, if a break-in is in progress in a building equipped with a smart lock, the algorithm must detect an anomaly, an unfamiliar face in this case, and alert the homeowner. Moreover, this should happen in real-time without delay so authorities can be alerted, and the perpetrator can be caught. This combination of low latency and intelligent automation can be achieved by combining fog computing with machine learning [12].

In fog computing, machine learning can allocate resources effectively and increase the security and accuracy of fog systems and data processing tasks [13].

10.4.1 Resource Allocation in Fog Using Machine Learning

There are several computing devices and sensors in an IoT system; all of these produce a variety of data that require processing. Some of these data should be processed ahead of others due to latency requirements. In such heterogeneous IoT environments with different latency needs and limited computational power, the fog nodes should wisely allocate their limited resources to accommodate varied latency needs. This heterogeneous composition of fog computing makes resource allocation in fog computing extremely important [14].

Implementing resource allocation via pre-programmed methods can be inefficient, as it is not possible to account for infinite possibilities that might happen in real-world scenarios. Moreover, dynamic latency demands can further increase the complexity of pre-programmed rules. This leaves implementing intelligence to automate resource allocation in the fog paradigm [15].

One part of resource allocation is delay prediction and provisioning of computational resources in the fog layer. Machine learning algorithms can accurately predict the completion time and resources required for a given task. Moreover, a task is assigned a priority based on the latency requirements. After priority assignment, the task can be scheduled to the available fog node. Furthermore, based on the predicted task completion time, the availability of the fog nodes is calculated, and subsequent tasks can be scheduled to the suitable fog nodes ahead of the completion of the previous task. To train ML models for resource allocation, supervised learning algorithms, reinforcement learning, and deep learning approaches can be used Hong et al. proposed a multimedia fog computing platform, which uses a set of ML algorithms to predict job completion time, manage idle computational resources, and schedule available jobs to fog devices based on predicted completion time [16].

Another aspect of resource allocation is decision-making. For example, ML models can be trained to decide which data will be processed in the fog nodes and which data should be uploaded to the cloud. These trained models require low computational resources and can be deployed on edge devices.

Moreover, many data processing tasks like object detection can demand high resources and consume much time if not assigned to a suitable fog node. This can be solved by reassigning them to a more computationally capable node. However, several problems arise when reassigning is attempted, including which task to reassign and where to reassign it. These problems become complicated when factors like latency and Quality of Service (QoS) requirements are considered. ML models trained on past task reassignment data can help solve these issues.

Moreover, intelligent resource allocation algorithms can optimize latency, network bandwidth, energy consumption, resource consumption, and availability.

10.4.2 Data Pre-Processing in Fog Using Machine Learning

IoT sensors and devices generate vast amounts of data that need to be processed. Fog computing can help with real-time low latency processing but is more computationally expensive, and tasks with no latency barrier should be processed in the centralized cloud. Furthermore, data analysis often uses data aggregated from multiple sources, making analysis in fog nodes more cumbersome due to the distributed nature of data. However, data collected by IoT sensors is raw and large, which means that sending it directly to the cloud can take up a lot of network bandwidth and increase operational costs. Compressing or aggregating the data in the fog layer before sending it to the cloud can lower the bandwidth usage during transfer [17].

Using conventional data compression methods works fine for a single data type like image or video, but IoT sensors capture various data, and designing compression rules for each is not practical. There is a need for intelligent data compression methods that can take raw data as input and give out compressed data as output to overcome this limitation. Furthermore, data compression also reduces the space required for storing large amounts of data generated by IoT sensors.

Unsupervised machine learning algorithms that deal with dimensionality reduction can be utilized for data compression before sending it to the cloud. Examples of such algorithms include principle component analysis (PCA). Moreover, neural network auto-encoders can compress various data that can be decoded on arrival via a matching decoder.

In [18], the author has proposed a lossy data compression technique using machine learning for industrial IoT applications using the neural network regression technique. Moreover, for efficiency, they have utilized a "divide and conquer method."

10.4.3 Security in Fog Using Machine Learning

Fog nodes collect and process various sensitive data, ensuring the security and privacy of this data is of paramount importance. Fog nodes are decentralized and closer to the edge. This decentralized behavior poses specific problems; one node cannot know whether other nodes in the network are compromised. This makes fog nodes vulnerable to forgery and man-in-the-middle attacks [19]. Furthermore, sophisticated distributed denial of service (DDoS) attacks can affect the fog nodes by consuming network bandwidth, thus impacting latency and performance as the resources are limited in fog systems. Fog computing, like any digital paradigm, is also vulnerable to malware attacks. A malware can remotely access a colossal amount of data that comes to the fog nodes for processing or storage, compromising user privacy. Data collected on the fog layer is raw, which comes directly from the source; due to this, many private user identifiers like IP and MAC addresses are present in the data. If fog nodes get compromised, private user data could get leaked, leading to compromised user privacy [20].

Protection against malware in fog nodes can be accomplished via fixed systems, matching suspicious file signatures with a master database. If there is a match, the suspicious file can be quarantined. Another fixed approach would be to quarantine the suspicious file, run it in a virtual environment, and monitor possible predefined malware-like traits. Finally, a static firewall approach would block the IP address that crosses the threshold request limit allowed in a specific time to prevent DoS attacks. These rule-based approaches may seem reasonable, but there is a high error susceptibility. These conventional systems might miss a sophistically designed malware that is not yet in the master database. Moreover, a static firewall can block a genuine request that might affect the whole system's performance.

Trained ML models can be deployed on the fog layer to monitor traffic and analyze patterns to detect potential intrusion. Sophisticated ML models can automate the prevention and detection of threats in the fog nodes by using ML algorithms such as artificial neural networks (ANN), Naïve Bayes, and K-Nearest Neighbor (KNN). Furthermore, ML workflows can be set up to flag suspicious behavior and alert the system administrator for further action.

Moreover, unsupervised feature extraction algorithms like PCA can extract relevant data points that carry much of the information captured by the edge devices except the personal user and device data. This extracted data can be shared with the centralized cloud for long-term storage or computationally expensive analysis. Thus, single ML-based feature extraction can be used to safeguard user privacy for a large variety of collected data without being explicitly programmed. In contrast, a rule-based system must be designed specifically for each type of collected data.

10.4.4 Advantages of Using Fog Computing with Machine Learning

- *Efficient energy consumption*: Fog computing involves an extra layer of devices that process and analyze data, increasing the total number of devices present in the network. All devices in the extra layer consume energy, which increases the overall energy consumption. Deploying trained machine learning models can intelligently and efficiently distribute available computational resources to optimize energy consumption [21].

Prakash et al. proposed an intelligent machine learning model that reduces the demand for energy in the fog computing paradigm in IoT services [22]. The authors have simulated the trained reinforcement learning (RL) model with 100 virtual machines on various performance metrics and have found out that the proposed RL model reduces energy consumption and outperforms all other mentioned algorithms.

Moreover, implementing ML in fog computing saves the human energy required to deliver and maintain the IoT services because ML models can perform with little to no human intervention. Moreover, they can detect or predict any potential malfunction and alert the system administrator before the malfunction can affect any services.

- *Ability to perform tasks without explicit programming*: Fog nodes collect a large variety of data; useful information needs to be extracted from all the data. Extraction reduces the data size as storage, and network bandwidth is limited in a fog system. A rule-based feature extraction system can be implemented to discard features that are not relevant in analysis. However, given the variety of data collected in an IoT system, a customized rule engine for each type of collected data must be designed to filter out the valuable information from the data.

On the other hand, PCA—an unsupervised ML technique—can be used for dimensionality reduction of collected data. PCA constructs a set of new features called principal components (PC). Usually, a small subset of principal components are required to explain a large amount of variance in the original data. Moreover, PCA can do feature extraction without being explicitly programmed, unlike the rule-based method.

Fog systems deployed with ML algorithms offer a unique advantage. There is no need for explicitly programming instructions in the system. Instead, given enough data, they can learn to perform any operation on their own.

- *Reduced delay*: Data processing and analysis, when carried out in the cloud, increase latency in time-sensitive applications such as virtual reality and object detection, where there are strict latency constraints for ensuring QoS requirements. Implementing data analytics using machine learning at the edge instead of the cloud can aid in faster response times for latency-critical applications.

Shukla et al. proposed a novel three-tier fog computing architecture that uses fuzzy methodology and reinforcement learning techniques to reduce network latency in healthcare IoT systems [23].

- *Decreased bandwidth usage*: Fog nodes capture unprocessed raw data. Sometimes captured data is needed to be transferred to the cloud for processing, and sending unprocessed raw data takes up more network bandwidth. However, intelligent machine learning algorithms can extract valuable information from the raw data, reducing the data size that needs to be transferred. Moreover, pre-processing can be done on the fog nodes themselves, which organizes and reduces raw data size.

Memon et al. proposed a bandwidth and latency reduction system using predictive analytics for fog-to-cloud communications [24]. Marquesone et al. proposed a filtering, aggregation, compression, and extraction (FACE) approach that shifts data pre-processing at the edge, reducing the data traffic from end-user to the centralized cloud, effectively saving network bandwidth [25].

- *Room for continuous improvement*: ML models deployed on the fog can be monitored continuously for the possibility of improvement. The accuracy or performance of the deployed models can be improved further by tuning the hyperparameters or retraining them with more data. In contrast, the performance of the rule-based engine is set in stone; it can only be improved if the rules are tweaked, which is often a significant change, and implementing it will require many simulations on real-world data.

- *Wide range of possible applications*: IoT sensors capture a massive amount of data. Without analysis, captured data is of no value. Machine learning algorithms are very versatile and can aid in identifying and analyzing trends and patterns in the data collected by the edge sensors. Furthermore, combining fog and machine learning provides low latency real-time data processing. A wide range of possible areas can benefit from this combination, such as healthcare, smart cities, and driverless cars [26]. Basumatary et al. proposed a "healthcare as a fog service" model that uses Ensemble Deep Learning deployed on edge to automate the diagnosis of heart diseases [27].

10.4.5 Challenges of Using Fog Computing with Machine Learning

- *Increased deployment time and cost:* There are many devices present in the fog node. All the extra hardware adds to the overall system cost. Furthermore, some machine learning tasks require significantly more computational power, which adds to the cost further. However, these tasks can be shifted to the cloud, but that will cause latency issues in real-time applications. Moreover, training machine learning algorithms is also a time-consuming process, as there are several steps involved in it, starting from data collection, training, evaluation, and finally deployment.

- *Difficult to diagnose errors*: Machine learning as technology is highly susceptible to errors if training data is biased or the model's hyperparameters are not tuned properly. If a trained ML model deployed on the fog behaves unexpectedly, pinpointing the cause of that error becomes very difficult due to the size of the training sample. However, there are several ways to find out the overall dataset issue, including checking for high bias or high variance. Solving high bias or high variance problems can ultimately increase the accuracy of the model on unseen data.

- *Requires more computational power*: Some applications of ML on fog like speech recognition and object detection can be computationally costly. Moreover, deep learning models require even more computational power than machine learning models based on supervised or unsupervised approaches—one approach to solving more computational resources is to shift the processing to the cloud. However, shifting data analysis and processing to the cloud might affect applications that require real-time low latency processing. Essentially, this boils down to choosing between minimizing the operational costs associated with computationally powerful hardware or reducing latency and maximizing performance by driving the costs up [28].

- *Increased deployment time due to data collection and model training*: Machine learning models require large amounts of data to be trained. A biased or skewed dataset that does not mimic the real-world scenario is not ideal for model training and evaluation. Collecting data for training a model is a cumbersome process that could take anywhere from days to years. Moreover, model training also consumes time depending on the complexity of the model and algorithm utilized.

10.4.6 Fog Computing with Machine Learning Use Cases

Smart cities: IoT sensors are deployed in large numbers in smart cities. They collect vast amounts of data from all over the city. As automation is incorporated in every aspect of smart cities, IoT sensors are increasing in number, making analysis and processing of vast amounts of data a significant challenge that smart cities face. Fog computing makes it possible to reduce the amount of data needed to be sent to the cloud and reduce the latency for real-time applications. ML deployed on the fog nodes aid in data analysis and automated decision-making in smart cities. In addition, ML models can be used to secure smart cities by detecting hazardous events like fire in a building and automatically alerting the fire services [29].

Driverless cars: Autonomous vehicles are the future of transport. Driverless cars can reduce the accidents that happen on the road and make transport safer and more efficient. To accomplish safe movement without a human driver, intelligent algorithms need to be deployed to drive the cars or guide the human drivers. Moreover, data analysis for autonomous cars needs real-time analysis with low latency to ensure fast decision-making, which rules out deploying driving algorithms on the cloud. Machine learning deployed on the fog nodes can ensure low-latency, real-time analysis of the data collected by the car sensors.

10.5 Conclusion

In this chapter, we have talked about fog computing and how it can be paired with machine learning to enhance the fog technology and expand the possible use cases. We have explained fog computing and the differences between cloud computing and fog computing. Moreover, we have also talked about machine learning, its pros and cons, implementation strategies, and implementation steps. Finally, we have discussed the application of machine learning in fog computing, its benefits and challenges, and described popular examples of how it is utilized with machine learning.

Machine learning combined with fog computing can prove a potent combination in the IoT ecosystem. We have tried to shed light on the usage of machine learning in enhancing the functionality of time-critical fog computing applications in IoT. However, additional research is still required to utilize the power of ML in fog computing fully. As discussed, machine learning in fog can make fog more energy- and bandwidth-efficient while maintaining the users' data privacy. Moreover, various applications like smart cities and autonomous vehicles can be enhanced using machine learning in fog. Furthermore, we have discussed some cons of deploying machine learning models in fog.

References

1. M. Keertikumar, M. Shubham, and R. M. Banakar, "Evolution of IoT in Smart Vehicles: An Overview," *2015 International Conference on Green Computing and Internet of Things (ICGCIoT)* (pp. 804–809). IEEE, October 2015.
2. M. Iorga, L. Feldman, R. Barton, M. J. Martin, N. Goren, and C. Mahmoudi, *Fog Computing Conceptual Model*, NIST, 2018.
3. "Fog Computing," *Wikipedia*, 28-Jun-2021 [Online]. Available: https://en.wikipedia.org/wiki/Fog_computing [Accessed: 30-Jun-2021].
4. M. Aazam, S. Zeadally, and K. A. Harras, "Fog Computing Architecture, Evaluation, and Future Research Directions," *IEEE Communications Magazine*, vol. 56, no. 5, pp. 46–52, 2018.
5. A. Radford, "Edge and Fog Computing: Overview and Benefits," *Securus Communications Ltd*, 23-Mar-2021 [Online]. Available: www.securuscomms.co.uk/edge-and-Fog-computingoverview-and-benefits/ [Accessed: 30-Jun-2021].
6. M. Al-khafajiy, T. Baker, H. Al-Libawy, Z. Maamar, M. Aloqaily, and Y. Jararweh, "Improving Fog Computing Performance via Fog-2-Fog Collaboration," *Future Generation Computer Systems*, vol. 100, pp. 266–280, 2019.
7. M. Firdhous, O. Ghazali, and S. Hassan, "Fog Computing: Will It be the Future of Cloud Computing?," *Proceedings of the Third International Conference on Informatics & Applications*, Kuala Terengganu, Malaysia, 2014.
8. K. H. Abdulkareem, M. A. Mohammed, S. S. Gunasekaran, M. N. Al-Mhiqani, A. A. Mutlag, S. A. Mostafa, N. S. Ali, and D. A. Ibrahim, "A Review of Fog Computing and Machine Learning: Concepts, Applications, Challenges, and Open Issues," *IEEE Access*, vol. 7, pp. 153123–153140, 2019.
9. M. Mukherjee, R. Matam, L. Shu, L. Maglaras, M. A. Ferrag, N. Choudhury, and V. Kumar, "Security and Privacy in Fog Computing: Challenges," *IEEE Access*, vol. 5, pp. 19293–19304, 2017.
10. "Lifecycle of Machine Learning Models," *Oracle* [Online]. Available: www.oracle.com/a/ocom/docs/data-science-lifecycle-ebook.pdf [Accessed: 30-Jun-2021].
11. A. Salis, "Machine Learning and Fog-to-cloud Computing," *mF2C project*, 26-Jun-2018 [Online]. Available: www.mf2c-project.eu/index.html@p=2746.html# [Accessed: 30-Jun-2021].
12. Q. D. La, M. V. Ngo, T. Q. Dinh, T. Q. S. Quek, and H. Shin, "Enabling Intelligence in Fog Computing to Achieve Energy and Latency Reduction," *Digital Communications and Networks*, vol. 5, no. 1, pp. 3–9, 2019.
13. S. Dey and A. Mukherjee, "Implementing Deep Learning and Inferencing on Fog and Edge Computing Systems," *2018 IEEE International Conference on Pervasive Computing and Communications Workshops (PerCom Workshops)*, 2018, pp. 818–823, doi: 10.1109/PERCOMW.2018.8480168.
14. A. S. Gowri and S. Bala, "Fog Resource Allocation Through Machine Learning Algorithm," *Advances in Computer and Electrical Engineering*, pp. 1–41, 2020.
15. A. Nassar and Y. Yilmaz, "Resource Allocation in Fog RAN for Heterogeneous IoT Environments Based on Reinforcement Learning," *ICC 2019–2019 IEEE International Conference on Communications (ICC)*, (pp. 1–6). IEEE, May 2019.
16. H. J. Hong, J. C. Chuang, and C. H. Hsu, "Animation Rendering on Multimedia Fog Computing Platforms," *2016 IEEE International Conference on Cloud Computing Technology and Science (CloudCom)* (pp. 336–343). IEEE, December 2016.
17. T. Pfandzelter and D. Bermbach, "IoT Data Processing in the Fog: Functions, Streams, or Batch Processing?," *2019 IEEE International Conference on Fog Computing (ICFC)* (pp. 201–206). IEEE, June 2019.

18. J. Park, H. Park, and Y. J. Choi, "Data Compression and Prediction Using Machine Learning for Industrial IoT," *2018 International Conference on Information Networking (ICOIN)* (pp. 818–820). IEEE, January 2018.

19. A. Aljumah and T. A. Ahanger, "Fog Computing and Security Issues: A Review," *2018 7th International Conference on Computers Communications and Control (ICCCC)* (pp. 237–239). IEEE, May 2018.

20. M. Farhadi, J. L. Lanet, G. Pierre, and D. Miorandi, "A Systematic Approach Toward Security in Fog Computing: Assets, Vulnerabilities, Possible Countermeasures," *Software: Practice and Experience*, vol. 50, no. 6, pp. 973–997, 2020.

21. Q. D. La, M. V. Ngo, T. Q. Dinh, T. Q. S. Quek, and H. Shin, "Enabling Intelligence in Fog Computing to Achieve Energy and Latency Reduction," *Digital Communications and Networks*, vol. 5, no. 1, pp. 3–9, 2019.

22. M. V. Prakash, V. Porkodi, S. Rajanarayanan, M. Khan, B. F. Ibrahim, and M. Sivaram, "Improved Conservation of Energy in Fog IOT Services Using Machine Learning Model," *2020 International Conference on Computing and Information Technology (ICCIT-1441)* (pp. 1–4). IEEE, September 2020.

23. S. Shukla, M. F. Hassan, L. T. Jung, A. Awang, and M. K. Khan, "A 3-Tier Architecture for Network Latency Reduction in Healthcare Internet-of-things Using Fog Computing and Machine Learning," *Proceedings of the 2019 8th International Conference on Software and Computer Applications* (pp. 522–528), February 2019.

24. S. Memon and M. Maheswaran, "Optimizing Data Transfers for Bandwidth Usage and End-to-End Latency between Fogs and Cloud," *2019 IEEE International Conference on Fog Computing (ICFC)* (pp. 107–114). IEEE, June 2019.

25. R. D. F. P. Marquesone, E. A. da Silva, N. M. Gonzalez, K. Langona, W. A. Goya, F. F. Redígolo, F. F., T. C. M. de Brito Carvalho, J.-E. Mangs and A. Sefidcon, "Towards Bandwidth Optimization in Fog Computing using FACE Framework," *International Conference on Cloud Computing and Services Science*, vol. 2, pp. 491–498. SCITEPRESS, April 2017.

26. J. He, J. Wei, K. Chen, Z. Tang, Y. Zhou, and Y. Zhang, "Multitier Fog Computing with Large-Scale IoT Data Analytics for Smart Cities," *IEEE Internet of Things Journal*, vol. 5, no. 2, pp. 677–686, 2018.

27. S. Tuli, N. Basumatary, S. S. Gill, M. Kahani, R. C. Arya, G. S. Wander, and R. Buyya, "HealthFog: An Ensemble Deep Learning Based Smart Healthcare System for Automatic Diagnosis of Heart Diseases in Integrated IoT and Fog Computing Environments," *Future Generation Computer Systems*, vol. 104, pp. 187–200, 2020.

28. X. Q. Pham, N. D. Man, N. D. Tri, N. Q. Thai, and E.-N. Huh, "A Cost- and Performance-effective Approach for Task Scheduling Based on Collaboration Between Cloud and Fog Computing," *International Journal of Distributed Sensor Networks*, vol. 13, no. 11, p. 155014771774207, 2017.

29. B. Tang, Z. Chen, G. Hefferman, S. Pei, T. Wei, H. He, and Q. Yang, "Incorporating Intelligence in Fog Computing for Big Data Analysis in Smart Cities," *IEEE Transactions on Industrial Informatics*, vol. 13, no. 5, pp. 2140–2150, 2017.

11

Communication Protocols in Fog Computing: A Survey and Challenges

Avita Katal

School of Computer Science
University of Petroleum and Energy Studies
Dehradun, India

Vitesh Sethi

School of Computer Science
University of Petroleum and Energy Studies
Dehradun, India

CONTENTS

DOI: 10.1201/9781003188230-11

TABLE 11.1

Abbreviations Used

Abbreviations	Full form
CC	Cloud Computing
FC	Fog Computing
FL	Fog Layer
CP	Communication Protocols
QoS	Quality of Service
HTTP	HyperText Transport Protocol
MQTT	Message Queuing Telemetry Transport
CoAP	Constrained Application Protocol
XMPP	Extensible Messaging and Presence Protocol
DDS	Data Distribution Service
AMQP	Advanced Message Queuing Protocol
D2D	Device to Device
D2C	Device to Cloud
C2C	Cloud to Cloud

11.1 Introduction to Fog Computing

In general, fog nodes are presently close to the sensors and extend the cloud computing. Fog computing is a distributed computing paradigm that acts as a link between cloud data centers and Internet of Things (IoT) devices. It enables cloud-based services to be provided closer to IoT devices/sensors by providing compute, networking, and storage capabilities (Katal et al., 2021). In 2012, Cisco introduced the concept of fog computing to address the constraints of IoT systems in standard cloud computing. Near the network's edge, IoT devices/sensors, as well as real-time and latency-sensitive service requirements, are widely spread. Fog computing includes cloud-based application components along with the edge devices between cloud and the sensors. Fog computing provides mobility, computer resources, communication protocols, interface heterogeneity, and cloud integration to satisfy the needs of applications that are delay-sensitive across a large and dense geographical distribution. Since cloud data centres are widely dispersed, they typically fail to fulfil the memory and networking requirements of billions of globally scattered IoT devices/sensors. As a result, there is network congestion, excessive service delivery delay, and poor Quality of Service (QoS) (Sarkar & Misra, 2016). Fog computing is capable of constructing enormous geographical dispersion of cloud services due to its networking components. In addition, fog computing assists in location awareness, mobility aid, actual communications, flexibility, and compatibility (Bonomi et al., 2012). As a result, fog computing can be more efficient in terms of service delay, energy usage, network activity, and other factors (Sarkar et al., 2018).

The rest of the chapter is structured as follows: section 11.2 describes the architecture of fog computing; section 11.3 describes the services provided by fog computing; section 11.4 describes the various communication protocols, followed by sections 11.5 and 11.6 that cover the comparison of protocols and the research challenges in this domain respectively.

Table 11.1 shows the abbreviations used in this chapter.

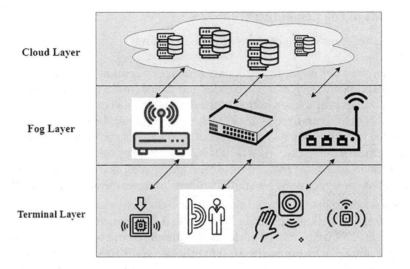

FIGURE 11.1
Three-level architecture of fog computing.

11.2 Architecture of Fog Computing

An important research subject is the reference model of fog computing architecture. In recent years, several fog computing approaches have been presented. Figure 11.1 depicts the architecture of the FC.

- Terminal Layer—This is the layer that is closest to the user and the physical environment. It is made up of different Internet of Things devices such as sensors, mobile phones, smart cars, smart cards, etc. In general, these devices are extensively spread geographically. They sense physical objects or event feature data and transfer it to the top layer for processing and storage.

- Fog Layer—This layer is located at the network's perimeter. The fog computing layer consists of several fog nodes such as routers, gateways, switchers, and so on. They might be fixed in one location or mobile on a moving carriage. To obtain services, end devices may easily connect to fog nodes. They can transmit, compute, and store the detected data temporarily that has been received. The applications that are delay sensitive and require actual analysis are possible in the fog layer. Also, the fog chains are interconnected to the data center through an IP core network and are responsible for communicating and collaborating with the cloud to obtain more robust processing capabilities.

- Cloud Computing Layer—The CC layer is made up of several large servers and devices for storage that provide a variety of services like smart transportation, smart homes, smart factories, etc. It features significant processing and provides facilities for storage that allow for comprehensive calculations and long-term storing of massive amounts of data. However, unlike typical cloud computing architecture, not all computational and operations related to storage are done in cloud layer. The cloud core modules are efficiently controlled and planned based on demand by certain control techniques to optimize cloud resource usage.

11.2.1 Benefits of Fog Computing

The following are some of the benefits of fog computing:

- *Reduction of network traffic:* The billions of mobile devices now utilized to create, receive, and transport data, such as smartphones and tablets, make the case for bringing computing abilities near to the location of the devices, instead of sending all data through the networks to centralized data centres. Sensors gather data every second, depending on the frequency set. As a result, sending entire, not computed data to the cloud is neither efficient nor logical. As a result, FC helps here by offering a platform for filtering and analyzing data provided by these edge devices, as well as for the development of local data perspectives. This significantly minimizes the amount of traffic.

- *Efficient for queries and tasks of IoT:* With the increasing variety of technical devices on the market, the bulk of demands involve the device's surroundings. Consequently, these sorts of requests may be performed without relying on the cloud's information dissemination. For example, the aforementioned sports tracker program Edomondo lets a user find individuals nearby who are participating in a similar sport. Because the usual requests made by this application are local in nature, it executes the queries in fog network instead of cloud. A smart connected car, for example, must detect events that are only 100 metres away. The FC helps in minimizing the distance of communication by doing the computation near to the devices.

- *Low latency requirement:* For mission-critical operations, actual data processing is essential. Cloud bots, fly-by-wire aircraft control, and anti-lock brakes on an automobile are some of the most notable instances of such implementations. Motion control for a robot is determined by data acquired by sensors and input from the control system. Because of communication issues, the sense-process-actuate loop may be slowed or missing if the system that is used to control sensors runs on the cloud network. This is where FC comes in, since it does the computations that are important to the control system relatively close to the robots, allowing for real-time reaction.

- *Scalability:* If all processing data created by end devices is transmitted forever to the cloud, also with almost limitless storage, it may create a hurdle. Because fog computing tries to process incoming data closer to the source of data, it minimizes the strain on the cloud, alleviating scalability concerns caused by a growing percentage of terminals.

11.2.2 Comparison of Fog Computing and Cloud Computing

The fundamental difference between FC and CC is that the cloud is a centralized system, whereas the fog is a distributed decentralized architecture. FC acts as a connection point between devices and remote servers. It defines which information will be sent to the

TABLE 11.2

Differences between Cloud Computing and Fog Computing

Parameters	Cloud Computing	Fog Computing
Latency	High	Low
Mobility	Limited	Supported
Location awareness	Partially supported	Supported
Energy consumption	High	Low
Bandwidth costs	High	Low
Geographical distribution	Centralized	Decentralized

client and which should be processed locally. In this respect, fog acts as an intelligent gateway, offloading clouds and enabling more efficient data storage, processing, and analysis. Table 11.2 shows the differences between CC and FC based on different parameters.

11.3 Services Provided by Fog Computing

11.3.1 Communication Services

Wireless nodes dominate communication in the Internet of Things. Because of resource restrictions in the perception layer, many wireless protocols are optimized to use less power for functioning, limited communication, or extended coverage range. Now, the industry provides a multitude of different methods. The fog layer is ideally positioned to integrate these many wireless protocols and streamline its interaction with the cloud layer. This aids in the management of sensor and actuator subnetworks, providing security, routing communications between devices, and improving system dependability. Furthermore, by identifying and understanding the representation format, this layer provides the interoperability of various protocols. The fog layer allows non-IP-based devices to be visible and accessible through the Internet (Rahmani et al., 2015).

11.3.2 Computing Services

Remote monitoring approaches have been established because of the restrictions in the processing power of the devices in the perception layer. The computations at the FL are motivated not just by the limitation of processing capability at sensor network, but also by the need to better meet specifications while conserving energy. Previously cloud-based computation shifted to FL for local analysis and fast response (Datta et al., 2015; Hu et al., 2017). In this way, numerous configurations of spreading the computational burden across the several layers in the systems that are based on IoT are possible, and the computational needs changes depending on the activity.

11.3.3 Storage Services

Sensor nodes may create massive amounts of data, and there are billions of these devices in the world. Given the velocity of data production, the storage capacity in the devices at the perception layer is frequently insufficient to retain even a single day's worth of data. As previously mentioned, moving all the information to the cloud without pre-processing it is not beneficial, especially where there is irrelevance or redundancy. In such circumstances, it is prudent to segregate and temporarily store information in the FL (Sarkar et al., 2018). When merged with the model of computing, the data collected may be filtered, processed, and reduced for transmission purposes or for gaining local knowledge about the system's behaviour. In such cases, it is recommended to filter the data and temporarily store it in the interim fog layer.

11.4 Communication Protocols: An Overview

In general, the interaction models of the potential CP, namely request-response and publish-subscribe, vary. One of the most fundamental communication paradigms is the request-response model. It denotes a message exchange pattern that is particularly frequent in the architectures of clients. It enables clients to request data from a server, which gets the request message, analyzes it, and provides a reply message. This type of data is often maintained and transferred at a centralized level. REST HTTP and CoAP are the most-used protocols based on the request/response technique. AMQP, MQTT, and CoAP protocols offer extremely minimal QoS support for message delivery. MQTT and AMQP use three distinct QoS levels, but CoAP only allows for two request and reply messages. The underlying transport protocols enable QoS in REST, HTTP, and XMPP. Apart from this, DDS offers a comprehensive set of QoS rules, including over twenty distinct QoS choices defined by the standard (Foster, 2014.).

11.4.1 HyperText Transport Protocol (HTTP)

This is the primary CS model protocol for the web, which is highly compatible with the existing architecture. Nowadays, HTTP/1.1 is the most widely used version of this protocol. Request/response messaging is used to communicate between a client and a server, with the client submitting an HTTP request message and the server delivering a reply containing the resource that was requested if the request was accepted. The integration of HTTP protocol with REST is notable because gadgets can render its status data easily available. Since the statistical analysis is not standardized, the format is flexible, with JSON and XML being most used. Most IoT standards revolve around JSON via HTTP. TCP is the transport protocol utilized by HTTP. TCP allows dependable transmission of huge volumes of data, which is advantageous in connections with no stringent delay needs (Shang et al., 2016). The most common issue is that restricted nodes mostly communicate tiny quantities of data infrequently, and establishing a TCP connection takes time and adds needless cost. HTTP does not give any extra choices for QoS, instead relying on TCP as long as the link is not disrupted; this ensures successful delivery. HTTPS, or a secure version of HTTP, is created by utilizing the well-known TLS (Dierks & Rescorla, 2008) to provide a safe encrypted communication channel. A TLS handshake is the first stage in safeguarding client-server data transfer. The client/server sides then transfer credentials that use the agreed-upon key exchange mechanism. The information is encrypted so that no one can listen to or comprehend it. While HTTP is among the most dependable choices, it still faces some issues that have prompted the research of other connection options, including HTTP complexities, long fields of header, and energy consumption. Moreover, HTTP uses the request/reply model, which is inconsistent with alerts, in which the server provides messages to the user before even requesting them. As HTTP doesn't explicitly describe QoS levels, further assistance is required. It has led in HTTP modifications and expansions, significantly HTTP/2.0 (Peon & Belshe, 2015), which introduced many innovations that are particularly related to IoT. HTTP/2.0 makes better use of network services and reduces delay by including compacted parameters. It uses a very quick and economical memory compaction technique and also allows many simultaneous transfers on the same connection (Stenberg, 2014). These properties are especially appealing for IoT since they reduce packet size substantially, making it a more suitable alternative. Figure 11.2 shows the different HTTP versions.

11.4.2 Constrained Application Protocol (CoAP)

CoAP has been the most often-used protocol in IoT systems due to benefits like programmer ease, simple design in terms of energy consumption and transmission, scalability,

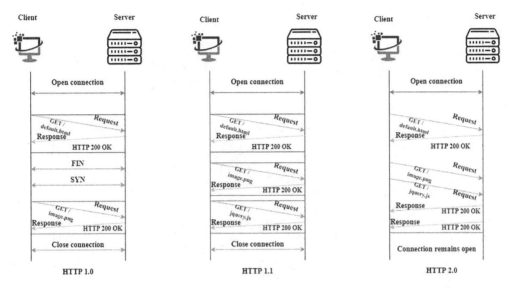

FIGURE 11.2
Different HTTP versions.

Source: Based on Al-Masri et al., 2020

adaptability, and having adequate ways to enhance data integrity and security (Iglesias-Urkia et al., 2017; Thangavel et al., 2014; de Caro et al., 2013). Islam et al. (2019) presented harmonization of IoT based on the cloud by utilizing the CoAP protocol, and their evaluation tests indicated that the CoAP protocol is superior than MQTT for integrating sensor interaction in a cloud computing system. Furthermore, CoAP has quickly received adoption and support from big corporations, and researchers have presented it to be utilized in a variety of domains. CoAP employs the UDP protocol that is utilized by reduced networks and machines with little computing capability. CoAP makes use of the EXI format that is smaller than the XML/HTML binary format (Bilal et al., 2018). This protocol is stateless and uses the request-response model for message exchange. It is based on a client-server infrastructure. Figure 11.3 shows the message flow in CoAP.

CoAP, like HTTP, employs the REST model, in which the resources of the server are addressed by URIs. CoAP is built on a framework separated into two conceptually distinct levels. In other words, clients can control URI-identified network resources via GET, PUT, POST, or DELETE techniques. The second layer distinguishes CoAP from HTTP. CoAP depends on a secondary structural layer, called the message layer, to transfer data lost packets since UDP doesn't really ensure reliable communication. This layer differentiates the four kinds of messages: NON, CON, REST, and ACK.

CON messages are intended to ensure trustworthy connection, and they need an acknowledgement from the receiver side in the form of an ACK message. By adding an observer option to a GET request, CoAP can enhance the request/response paradigm with allowing customers to keep providing changes from the server on a requested resource. CoAP utilizes DTLS as a security layer. It works on the TLS protocol, but with modifications that allow it to operate on an unstable network. Because of this, the CoAPS protocol has been developed, which is secure. The bulk of the differences between TLS and SSL are characteristics that prevent the termination of connection with missing or out-of-sequence packets. Figure 11.4 shows the layers of CoAP.

FIGURE 11.3
Message flow in CoAP.

Source: Based on Al-Masri et al., 2020

FIGURE 11.4
Layers of CoAP.

Source: Based on Shelby et al., 2014

11.4.3 Message Queuing Telemetry Transport (MQTT)

MQTT is a protocol that runs on the application layer developed for lightweight M2M (machine to machine) communications that is simple, easy to build, and quick. MQTT is appropriate for the devices that are constrained to the resources, low-bandwidth, low-latency networks, and dependable networks. MQTT is an Organization for the Advancement of Structured Information Standards (OASIS) protocol that operates over TCP/IP. It is a topic-based publish/subscribe paradigm with three components: two types of clients (publisher or subscriber) and one server (called a broker). Publishers transmit messages inside a given topic, and subscriber clients receive these messages, which relate to the same topic to which they subscribed through a broker. Furthermore, the publisher does not require the subscribers' addresses. MQTT has a smaller overhead, is synchronous and dependable, and offers several degrees of service quality. There are three forms of QoS utilized between client and server for delivery assurance that are as follows (Banks & Gupta, 2014):

- *QoS Level 0:* The publisher delivers the message to the subscriber via the broker, and the subscriber receives it just once. Furthermore, the broker never sends an acknowledgement letter to the publisher.
- *QoS Level 1:* The publisher sends the message to the clients at least once, and the brokers give an acknowledgement if the message is lost.
- *QoS Level 2:* When a message is lost or duplicated, the publisher utilizes level 2, which needs a four-way handshake to send the message precisely once, causing an increase in overhead.

A helpful MQTT feature is its ability to store specific data for new clients by using a 'retain' flag in a broadcast message. If no one is interested in a topic of which the publisher publishes updates, the brokerage will delete the posted communications, particularly when the program's membership is not updated on a regular basis. In the usual case, active users would have to wait for status to change without getting a subject notification. Adding the 'retain' flag directs the broker to store the uploaded message so that prospective customers can get it. MQTT makes use of TCP, which is crucial for devices with limited resources. A MQTT-SN version that utilizes UDP and includes subject term searching has been proposed to do this (Stanford-Clark & Truong, 2013). This approach does not rely on TCP, but rather on UDP. Figure 11.5 shows the MQTT message flow.

The size of the payloads is reduced by assigning numeric topic IDs to data packets rather than lengthy subject names. The most significant drawback is that MQTT-SN is presently compatible with much fewer platforms, and the only free broker version is RSMB. MQTT does not provide encryption since it was meant to be lightweight, transmitting data in plain text. As a result, encryption should be joined as a distinct feature, such as using TLS, which increases overhead. Many MQTT brokers provide authentication using CONNECT. Brokers need clients to define a username/password combination when delivering the CONNECT message before verifying the connection or denying it if authentication fails. Overall, security is a continuous endeavour for MQTT. In comparison to other alternative options, resolving the security problem would provide a significant benefit for MQTT. Figure 11.6 shows the stack of MQTT.

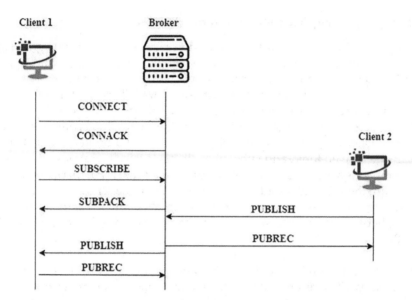

FIGURE 11.5
Message flow in MQTT.

Source: Based on Al-Masri et al., 2020

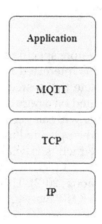

FIGURE 11.6
Stack of MQTT.

Source: Based on Al-Masri et al., 2020

11.4.4 Data Distribution Service (DDS)

The DDS is a middleware component that is intimately connected to data-intensive applications where service quality is critical. It is a data-centric, publish-subscribe programming approach, and its distributed design is used to build high-performance power applications in industries including the military, banking, automobiles, and modelling. Because of its brokerless design, DDS is excellent for M2M connectivity. The DDS communications paradigm is divided into two parts: DCPS and DLRL. The DCPS layer is mainly accountable in associating the contents of data items in an app throughout the publish/subscribe process. In other words, it allows a publishing program to connect data items with values that must be published. Subscribing programs can also discover data items and get their values. DDS, like AMQP and MQTT, allows you to create interesting topics. DDS also allows subscribers and publishers to attach QoS policies via the DCPS interface layer (*About the Data Distribution Service Specification Version 1.4*, 2015). DDS's data model is based on the relational data paradigm. When data is requested, the DDS middleware protocol processes it like a database system; it manages both the queries and content filters and the scheme. DDS allows producers and consumers to find each other automatically without the necessity of computers, allowing them to manage the flow of data among different entities. It is also capable of triggering patterns for keeping subscription material up to date. Furthermore, it facilitates interoperability across different vendor applications using the RTPS wired interface (*About the DDS Interoperability Wire Protocol Specification Version 2.3*, 2019). A security policy strengthens the security characteristics of DDS that are implemented via service plugin interfaces (SPIs). It gives support to the plugins of security and adapters that allow SPI-based interaction across multiple DDS applications. Its support for application interconnection makes it an ideal solution for applications related to IoT that require actual communication. DDS's default protocol is UDP, although it may also handle TCP. RTPS (Sonck Thiebaut et al., 2002) wire protocol, a DDS compatibility solution, enables information to be accessed across manufacturer applications. One of the benefits of utilizing DDS is the large number of QoS rules that are accessible. When transmitting data, the QoS policies of each subject, data writers, and publishers determine how and when data is transmitted to the middleware. Policies regulate a wide variety of characteristics of DDS, such as identifying the entities that are located remotely, data transfer, and availability of data. DDS implements a variety of security mechanisms. If TCP is the transport protocol of choice, then TLS is used; or DTLS if UDP is the transport protocol of choice. DTLS, like TLS, introduces too much cost in restricted settings, for which better techniques needs to be presented. DDS is also working on safety standards, and more features are expected to be added in the future. As Pradhan et al. (2014) describe, the enhancements planned will create a secure system for discovery that is capable of protected transport flows among applications that are based on DDS. Because of its decentralized publish-subscribe architecture and flexibility in both powerful and limited devices, DDS is an essential option for IoT-based settings. Figure 11.7 shows the DDS data centric model.

11.4.5 Advanced Message Queuing Protocol (AMQP)

AMQP is another lightweight yet flexible messaging protocol developed for M2M communications that is both an ISO and OASIS standard (*CloudAMQP—RabbitMQ as a Service*, n.d.). AMQP is commonly used in business settings. It is a binary protocol that runs on the application layer that allows for a variety of implementations related to messaging or patterns of communication. AMQP 0.9.1 employs a publish-subscribe model that is centered on two key AMQP entities that are both parts of an AMQP broker: message queues and exchanges. AMQP supports both the request-response and publish subscribe formats for overcoming interoperability concerns when utilizing message-oriented middleware (MOM). It enables topic-based publish-subscribe communications, like MQTT. AMQP also enables flexible routing and business operations. AMQP features two modes of communication engagement: consume and browse. In the browser mode, a customer may look for messages in a line that has been determined; but in the consumer mode, a customer can burn through messages from a line that has been characterized. AMQP message distribution is divided into three

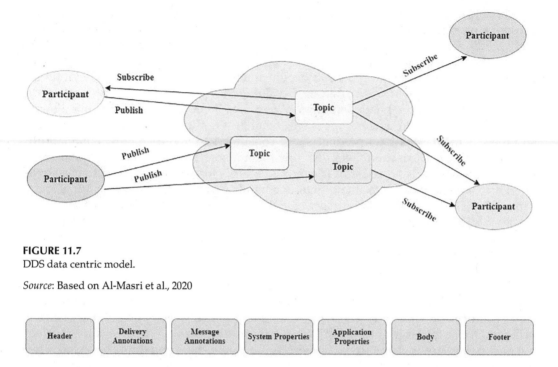

FIGURE 11.7
DDS data centric model.

Source: Based on Al-Masri et al., 2020

Header	Delivery Annotations	Message Annotations	System Properties	Application Properties	Body	Footer

FIGURE 11.8
Message structure AMQP.

Source: Based on Al-Masri et al., 2020

parts: queue, binding, and exchange. AMQP, like MQTT, employs TCP for reliable transmission and offers three distinct degrees of QoS. AMQP standard provides extra security features such as TLS encryption for data security and Simple Authentication and Security Layer (SASL) identification. AMQP uses many levels to exchange and transmit knowledge. A routing agent running on a virtual host on a broker's server represents an exchange. An exchange type has its own set of match criteria and mechanisms. Depending on the permissions provided, such programs can, for example, generate, distribute, utilize, or delete messages. Bindings represent information exchange and message queues. Bindings, for instance, transport data across exchanges to the correct queues based on the kind of message exchange. Permanent and temporary exchanges are the two types of exchanges. Durable message exchanges are permanent and continue to operate even if a broker is restarted, whereas transient exchanges are just transitory. After a broker restarts, transitory exchanges must be resumed. In general, there are four forms of message exchange: direct, subject, fan out, and header. With all its capabilities, AMQP requires a lot of energy, computation, and storage. This protocol is used for system parts with higher processing capability that are not limited by bandwidth or latency. Figure 11.8 shows the message structure of AMQP.

11.4.6 Extensible Messaging and Presence Protocol (XMPP)

XMPP is an open platform communication system developed by the Internet Engineering Task Force (Saint-Andre, 2004) and was initially meant for instant messenger and app-to-app message exchange. It supports client-server as well as publish-subscribe interaction.

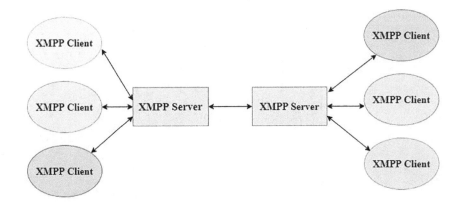

FIGURE 11.9
XMPP message transfer flow.

Source: Based on Lee, n.d.

This client/server architecture, formerly known as Jabber, was created to allow programs to provide instant messaging features. XMPP allows the customer-server communications, but recent additions allow for the usage of a general publish-subscribe mechanism as well. Those additions allow XMPP organizations to create topics and publish data, during which an incident notice is issued to all organizations grouped in a particular node. This implementation is essential in fog IoT cloud scenarios since it acts as the basis for a variety of applications that need automatic updates. XMPP works via TCP/IP and utilizes XML. XMPP includes a set of basic services known as XMPP core services, as well as extensible services known as XEPs that expand BOSH, which is a feature of XEPs that enables HTTP binding for XMPP traffic. The XEP series presently comprises over 350 IETF-governed features that build on the foundation of XMPP. The PubSub XEP is a major XMPP extension protocol that allows XMPP to implement the publish-subscribe architecture. Then, using PubSub XEP, XMPP may be used as a communication protocol for IoT systems. The XMPP standards currently include TLS techniques, giving a reliable way to ensure secrecy and data integration. The XMPP standards have also been enhanced in levels of protection, identification, confidentiality, and authentication. In addition to TLS, XMPP features SASL, which provides client verification by XMPP-specific configuration. Because XMPP was originally developed for instant chat, it has certain noteworthy potential flaws. The size of the messages when utilizing XML makes it problematic on networks that have less bandwidth. Another disadvantage is the lack of dependable QoS assurances. Nevertheless, a lot of work has lately been made into making XMPP more appropriate for IoT. A publish-subscribe technique that is lightweight for the IoT devices with fewer resources was proposed by Wang et al. (2017), thereby enhancing and optimizing the current version of the same protocol. Figure 11.9 shows the XMPP message transfer flow.

11.5 Comparison

Table 11.3 shows the comparison of the different protocols on the basis of different features.

TABLE 11.3

Comparison of Different Protocols Based on Different Features

Feature	HTTP	CoAP	MQTT	AMQP	DDS	XMPP
Year	1991	2013	1999	2003	2001	2002
Transport	TCP	UDP	TCP	TCP	UDP or TCP	TCP
Network Layer	IPv4 or IPv6	IPv6	IPv4 or IPv6	IPv4 or IPv6	IPv6	IPv4 or IPv6
Extensibility	No	No	No	Yes	Yes	Yes
QoS Support	No	Yes	Yes	Yes	Yes	No
QoS Levels	On the basis of TCP	2	3	3	23	None
Communication Scope	D2C, C2C	D2D	D2C	D2D, D2C, C2C	D2D, D2C, C2C	D2C, C2C
Filtering	Resource Identifier	Resource Identifier	Topic	Queue	topic, time, content	type, iq, present packets
Fault Tolerance	Server is SPOF	Decentralized	Broker is SPOF	Broker is SPOF	Decentralized	Server is SPOF
Architecture	Client server	Tree	Tree		Bus	Client server
Messaging	Request/Response	Request/Response	Pub/Subsrb; Request/Response	Pub/Subsrb; Request/Response	Pub/Subsrb; Request/Response	Pub/Subsrb; Request/Response

11.6 Research Challenges

11.6.1 HTTP

- Communications involve a lot of back and forth, connections must be kept up, and plain text results in bigger message sizes. All of this needs more electricity.
- HTTP consumes more system resources, resulting in higher power usage. Because IoT devices now include wireless sensor networks, HTTP is not appropriate.
- Due to the significant network latency, the protocol is unsuitable for real-time or mission-critical IoT applications.
- Another issue that arises with an HTTP connection is privacy. If a hacker succeeds in intercepting the request, they will be able to access all of the content on the web page. Aside from that, they can get sensitive information such as the login and password.
- Since HTTP does not use an encryption strategy, any changes to the content are possible. Because of this, HTTP is seen as an insecure technique prone to data integrity.

11.6.2 CoAP

- UDP does not ensure datagram delivery. CoAP provides a mechanism for requesting a confirmation acknowledgment, which confirms that the message was received. This does not guarantee that it was received in its entirety and correctly decoded.
- An endpoint in a restricted network can freely read and write messages; protocol is vulnerable to spoof and phishing software.
- It is a device-to-device protocol. It does not offer broadcasting capabilities, and it is not readily scalable or extendable.
- In business networks and cloud settings, network address translation (NAT) devices are widely utilized. Because IP addresses might change over time, CoAP may have difficulty connecting with devices behind a NAT.
- Since UDP, the protocol has a restricted amount of encryption.

11.6.3 MQTT

- MQTT is an unencrypted protocol. TLS/SSL is used instead for security encryption.
- MQTT clients must support TCP; connections with brokers must be kept open (always on). For restricted devices, there is a limited sleep mode.
- Protocol is incompatible with D2D communication.
- The topic names are sometimes lengthy, which is inconvenient for LR-WPANs.
- It is not appropriate for the multimedia transfer of the IoT devices.

11.6.4 DDS

- The size of implementation libraries is enormous (sometimes over 2GB).
- Events are generated in real-time by a single source rather than from numerous sources.
- It is not appropriate for IoT devices that are based on edge, with limited processing and computational power.
- It is very complex, which is why it is difficult to implement.

11.6.5 AMQP

- The standard does not include facilities for extending other protocols.
- The standard was created in the banking sector and is not suitable for IoT or M2M.
- The AMQP protocol requires higher bandwidth.
- There is no multicast.
- Reliability is restricted to what the transport protocol provides.

11.6.6 XMPP

- On the basis of the communication and computations of IoT devices, the XML message format adds significant overhead.
- Binary data transfers are not feasible since XMPP transmits data in an XML format. As a result, other protocols such as HTTP are utilized to circumvent this restriction.
- With more than 70% of the XMPP protocol's server data traffic present and almost 60% being sent again, the XMPP protocol now has significant overhead data to deliver to numerous receivers.

11.7 Conclusion

The growing number of Internet of Things devices that collect data and use cloud-related services has put a pressure on network and cloud infrastructure. To address the problems associated with data transfer to the cloud, some information technology companies have implemented a variety of strategies for offering strong parallel computing close to the end user. Because fog computing is implemented at the network edge, it may provide faster reaction time, geographical dispersion, and timely data support. Efforts to do research in this area are currently ongoing. On the other hand, relevant representations and restrictions remain unclear. This chapter introduces FC as well as its overall architecture and benefits. The services provided by fog computing are also discussed in this chapter. The chapter gives detailed information about the various communication protocols like HTTP, MQTT, CoAP, etc. along with the comparison of different protocols based on different parameters. The chapter concludes with a list of research challenges in each protocol.

References

About the Data Distribution Service Specification Version 1.4. (2015). Retrieved June 20, 2021, from www. omg.org/spec/DDS/1.4/About-DDS/

About the DDS Interoperability Wire Protocol Specification Version 2.3. (2019). Retrieved June 20, 2021, from www.omg.org/spec/DDSI-RTPS/2.3/About-DDSI-RTPS/

Al-Masri, E., Kalyanam, K. R., Batts, J., Kim, J., Singh, S., Vo, T., & Yan, C. (2020). Investigating Messaging Protocols for the Internet of Things (IoT). *IEEE Access, 8*, 94880–94911. https://doi. org/10.1109/ACCESS.2020.2993363

Banks, A., & Gupta, R. (2014). MQTT Version 3.1.1. *OASIS Standard*. Retrieved from http://docs.oasis-open.org/mqtt/mqtt/v3.1.1/os/mqtt-v3.1.1-os.html

Bilal, D., Rehman, A.-U., & Ali, R. (2018). Internet of Things (IoT) Protocols: A Brief Exploration of MQTT and CoAP. *International Journal of Computer Applications, 179*(27), 9–14. https://doi. org/10.5120/IJCA2018916438

Bonomi, F., Milito, R., Zhu, J., & Addepalli, S. (2012). Fog Computing and Its Role in the Internet of Things. *Proceedings of the First Edition of the MCC Workshop on Mobile Cloud Computing—MCC '12*. ACM, https://doi.org/10.1145/2342509

CloudAMQP—RabbitMQ as a Service. (n.d.). Retrieved June 20, 2021, from www.cloudamqp.com/

Datta, S. K., Bonnet, C., & Haerri, J. (2015). Fog Computing Architecture to Enable Consumer Centric Internet of Things Services. *Proceedings of the International Symposium on Consumer Electronics, ISCE, 2015-August*. IEEE, https://doi.org/10.1109/ISCE.2015.7177778

de Caro, N., Colitti, W., Steenhaut, K., Mangino, G., & Reali, G. (2013). Comparison of Two Lightweight Protocols for Smartphone-based Sensing. *IEEE SCVT 2013—Proceedings of 20th IEEE Symposium on Communications and Vehicular Technology in the BeNeLux*, IEEE. https://doi. org/10.1109/SCVT.2013.6735994

Dierks, T., & Rescorla, E. (2008). *The Transport Layer Security (TLS) Protocol Version 1.2*. Draft-Ietf-Tls-Rfc4346-Bis-10. https://datatracker.ietf.org/doc/html/rfc5246

Hu, P., Ning, H., Qiu, T., Zhang, Y., & Luo, X. (2017). Fog Computing Based Face Identification and Resolution Scheme in Internet of Things. *IEEE Transactions on Industrial Informatics, 13*(4), 1910–1920. https://doi.org/10.1109/TII.2016.2607178

Iglesias-Urkia, M., Orive, A., & Urbieta, A. (2017). Analysis of CoAP Implementations for Industrial Internet of Things: A Survey. *Procedia Computer Science, 109*, 188–195. https://doi.org/10.1016/J. PROCS.2017.05.323

Islam, Md. M., Khan, Z., & Alsaawy, Y. (2019). A Framework for Harmonizing Internet of Things (IoT) in Cloud: Analyses and Implementation. *Wireless Networks, 27*(6), 4331–4342. https://doi. org/10.1007/S11276-019-01943-6

Katal, A., Sethi, V., Lamba, S., & Choudhury, T. (2021). Fog Computing: Issues, Challenges and Tools. *Emerging Technologies in Data Mining and Information Security*, 971–982. https://doi.org/ 10.1007/978-981-15-9927-9_92

Lee, H. D. (n.d.). *XMPP: A Communication Protocol for the IoT*. Retrieved June 20, 2021, from https:// medium.com/@danny_54172/xmpp-a-communication-protocol-for-the-iot-2e8fbb0fe327

Foster, A. (2014). *Messaging Technologies for the Industrial Internet and the Internet of Things Whitepaper*. Retrieved June 20, 2021, from www.smartindustry.com/whitepapers/2015/ messaging-technologies-for-the-industrial-internet-and-the-internet-of-things/

Peon, R., & Belshe, M. (2015). Hypertext Transfer Protocol Version 2 (HTTP/2). *Draft-ietf-httpbis-http2–17*. Internet Engineering Task Force (IETF), https://doi.org/10.17487/RFC7541

Pradhan, S., Emfinger, W., Dubey, A., Otte, W. R., Balasubramanian, D., Gokhale, A., Karsai, G., & Coglio, A. (2014). Establishing Secure Interactions Across Distributed Applications in Satellite Clusters. *Proceedings—5th IEEE International Conference on Space Mission Challenges for Information Technology, SMC-IT 2014*, 67–74. IEEE. https://doi.org/10.1109/SMC-IT.2014.17

Rahmani, A. M., Thanigaivelan, N. K., Gia, T. N., Granados, J., Negash, B., Liljeberg, P., & Tenhunen, H. (2015). Smart e-Health Gateway: Bringing Intelligence to Internet-of-Things Based Ubiquitous Healthcare Systems. *2015 12th Annual IEEE Consumer Communications and Networking Conference, CCNC 2015*, 826–834. IEEE. https://doi.org/10.1109/CCNC.2015.7158084

Saint-Andre, P. (2004). *Extensible Messaging and Presence Protocol (XMPP): Core.* Core. RFC 3920, RFC Editor. Retrieved from https://xmpp.org/rfcs/rfc3920.html

Sarkar, S., Chatterjee, S., & Misra, S. (2018). Assessment of the Suitability of Fog Computing in the Context of Internet of Things. *IEEE Transactions on Cloud Computing, 6*(1), 46–59. https://doi.org/10.1109/TCC.2015.2485206

Sarkar, S., & Misra, S. (2016). Theoretical Modelling of Fog Computing: A Green Computing Paradigm to Support IoT Applications. *IET Networks, 5*(2), 23–29. https://doi.org/10.1049/iet-net.2015.0034

Shang, W., Yu, Y., Droms, R., & Zhang, L. (2016). Challenges in IoT Networking via TCP/IP Architecture. *NDN, Technical Report NDN-0038.* NDN Project.

Shelby, Z., Hartke, K., & Bormann, K. (2014). *The Constrained Application Protocol (CoAP).* Retrieved from https://datatracker.ietf.org/doc/html/rfc7252

Sonck Thiebaut, S., Pardo-Castellote, G., Hamilton, M., Choi, H., Rhee, S., Subramanian, G., Dai, Y., Sin, E., & Bose, A. (2002). Real-Time Publish Subscribe (RTPS) Wire Protocol Specification. *Draft-Thiebaut-Rtps-Wps-00.Txt.* Retrieved from https://datatracker.ietf.org/doc/html/draft-thiebaut-rtps-wps-00

Stanford-Clark, A., & Truong, H. L. (2013). *MQTT For Sensor Networks (MQTT-SN) Protocol Specification Version 1.2.* International Business Machines Corporation (IBM).

Stenberg, D. (2014). HTTP2 Explained. *ACM SIGCOMM Computer Communication Review, 44*(3), 120–128. https://doi.org/10.1145/2656877.2656896

Thangavel, D., Ma, X., Valera, A., Tan, H. X., & Tan, C. K. Y. (2014). Performance Evaluation of MQTT and CoAP via a Common Middleware. *IEEE ISSNIP 2014–2014 IEEE 9th International Conference on Intelligent Sensors, Sensor Networks and Information Processing, Conference Proceedings.* IEEE. https://doi.org/10.1109/ISSNIP.2014.6827678

Wang, H., Xiong, D., Wang, P., & Liu, Y. (2017). A Lightweight XMPP Publish/Subscribe Scheme for Resource-Constrained IoT Devices. *IEEE Access, 5,* 16393–16405. https://doi.org/10.1109/ACCESS.2017.2742020

12

Fog Computing, Today and in the Future with IoT

Hitesh Kumar Sharma

School of Computer Science
University of Petroleum and Energy Studies
Dehradun, India

Anurag Mor

School of Computer Science and Engineering
University of Petroleum and Energy Studies
Dehradun, India

Shlok Mohanty

School of Computer Science
University of Petroleum and Energy Studies
Dehradun, India

CONTENTS

12.1 Introduction

Fog creation manages to advance the management and establishment, as well as the chiefs over the web spine switching on all those that are often integrated into the LTE association [1] [2], instead of the specific significant control only via network doors. We can ease the processing framework such as a virtualised computer company, which offers the specific help of advantageous workplaces to various workplaces. These fog centre kinds manage the wide applications in particular plus firms to look for the special ingredient inside the customer-related proximity. Fog and edge processing include both pushing the arrangement and knowledge in the region where the information normally starts. The key areas for speculation will be organising IoT gadgets in excursions between March and June 2017 (checking manufacturing undertakings, transport, keen network ignites, sharp constructions, plus dynamically, customer IoT [3] [4], and splendid house robotization). The present scenario begins a collection of further developments and frameworks to address the quickly increasing proportion of information and

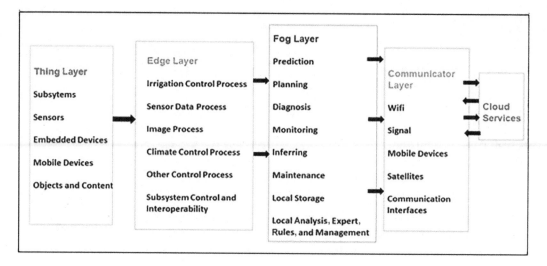

FIGURE 12.1
Communication using fog computing.

data at the core of IoT, including the collecting and creation involved. With this creation, we can say that Fog computing is a unique solution provided by IoT for future oragnization works for automation. We will also explain how large IoT data evaluation is suited for current progress and how the Internet of Things can deal with this company [5]. This core feature complements our attempt to provide the excellent things regarding fog calculation that are imminent in specific instances, just like capacity and low lack of activity. In this unique formula, the fog computing design offers the basic format to learn the specific concentration of IoT programme space on the edge from the particular fog processing construction. The fog computing structure provides the essential point stated by numerous detector variants, which is typically that IoT improvement is rising in particular. In addition to the shortcoming related to the limit and the obvious information option for the control of various kinds of created details, unbelievable data examination may offend you in this very rapid rise in the particular dimension of information. This problem may be resolved by fog computing, which consists of keen devices that take care of the forces arranged near the client to help the use of frameworks, to prepare and to shut the edge [6], evaluation, monitoring, appropriateness and also improvement of the show. The combination of IoT and fog computing gives us noticeable chances where the specialised group in different geographical locations may prove useful in various fog centres, as well as being the owner of numerous residents across distinct vertical sectors. The deployable environment and requirements of fog processing are generally the major questions contained in the fog computing regulation [7]. This is truly the clarification, because generally in the fog computing zone, the processing plans are unpredictable [7]. (See Figure 12.1.)

12.2 Fog Computing: An Overview

The programme of fog main partnerships at the edge is essential for this security of a sharp and rash future, to perform clever assessments, extensive data assessment for the better orchestration and the identification of explicit and dangerous occurrences. In this growing phase of the fog computing structure, a fog computing definition must be cleared. Definitions from a comprehensive view of fog computing cannot yet increase the

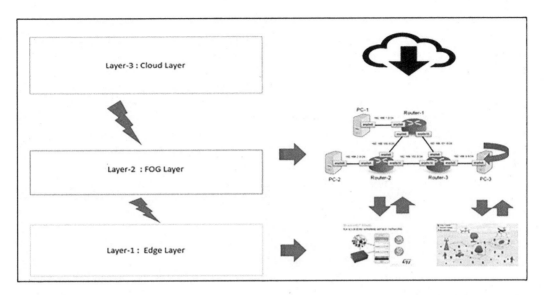

FIGURE 12.2
Three-layered architecture of fog computing.

incredible cloud resemblance. The great definition of fog and earlier events is necessary for portraying and isolating all functionality, and that is our definition [8]. Fog computing is a computer development progress with a resource pool in which in any occasion an unavoidable plus decentralized node(s) is usually secure in comparison to cloud planning. In addition to computer versatility, better conversation and collection limits, fog center services measure efforts without pariah impedances. Moreover they offer an increased number of contraptions, clients and end customers in a changing environment [9].

Fog is without question a better cloud processing plan in order to provide regularity in the partnership. Fog processing is an excellent partner for IoT devices in order to combat the unique problems connected with the conventional closed signal [10]. Fog processing is a good partner. Medium concentrations close to the benefit are generally used to perceive, request and regulate IoT gadget-associated specific natural data collecting. In order to prevent air pollution plus declaration protection, this design allows the edge-level centres to be operated in milliseconds. In design, impair degree centres often focus on information stress, separating, testing and alteration. About all of this could work, and the physical could be an impaired model. These kinds are more modest than the regular cloud allows, so that they can provide some required border-level study about main unexpected mental controls. In the level system, information and data can be transformed directly into information on a pleasant occasion. Fog-related linking facilitators also give fog computer connections with IaaS, PaaS or SaaS in order to make efforts via the development of a relationship between the cable connection or cell tower. Fog is a key element for linking facilitators (Figure 12.2).

12.3 The Layered Architecture of Fog Computing

The guidance to fog computing would be to complement the less unexpected inactivity about the typically time-fragile IoT constraints. Different scientists have created distinct analytical structures of fog. These versions have been explored and are organized in distinct geologies expressly for consumers and businesses.

Reference design for fog computing, comprising the seven different layers, is normally structured to be explicit. These forms of quantity fog structure depend on various uses. The significance of each level is highlighted, and the quantity used is typically described in various applications. The aim of these runs is to work together to press a task in terms of performance by using good IoT to buy fog installations [11] [12] (Figure 12.3). The primary information generator of fog computing is the different forms of information provided by the sensors. The information can be transmitted from different contents as wise houses and equipment, surveillance systems, automated motor vehicles, tenacity and time-sensors. The fog specialist, fog device or the front entry might be an IoT or even a free gadget. Moreover, since the fog worker manages distinct fog contraptions, it is recognisable that a finest plan is required inside for entrance and devices. Different elements such as equipment arrangement, network accessibility and gadgets that it may provide are included in making business. The specific section of the fog worker in the IoT sector is referred to. The fog devices are controlled by a collection of virtual sensors and authentic sensors. Fog specialists will also be organized for several fog gadgets. The fog worker should be carefully evaluated and limited with fog instruments. It should also be advanced and like the fog device restriction. A specific meeting of fog counter-positions related to the indefinite worker can, if necessary, talk to one another. In a skilled automobile use case, just additional interpersonal fog situations might restrict any application calculation. If a request is, for instance, typically counted if data from various interpersonal fog devices or if *messfühler* get-togethers are needed to look through a fuel-surprising method. The estimate must be done on diverse laboratories and fog equipment to close a sensitive decision. The programme notification will thereafter be able to pick these. It includes several portions of this level with the data analysis of basic and sophisticated data. During this stage, the data must be analyzed, blocked, monitored and replicated when necessary. When data is ready, the section called the data stream guidance, in which data should be utilised to ensure that regional care is taken whether it is at the fog or in the cloud. The insane problem in fog handling is that it is advantageous to arrange the information and to take care of the lower portion of the information. The key concept is to supply the information that is frequently utilised by fog staff and the data that is used just occasionally or not for the attracted people to the cloud. Data are produced from different detectors in the use of wonderful transport. These details are finally reviewed and processed for specifics. This has not been useful for creating details. In fact, some scenarios are everything but optimal to keep this data. In this case, the particular facts are transmitted by the sensor each second, depending on the application form, where the value of the specific data is generally looked after inside the two and a half hours. Data are generally monitored and a great number of restrictions are maintained in this way. In other circumstances, if the information in question does not change in a given time, the specific display will surely decrease your quantity of information gathered. A large amount of information might thus eventually be altered. The accuracy attained may not exactly be high, but the needs would be met. A further element of this level will be the pleasure of information that regulates the age of information, which is broken by the specific sensors. This component also requires therapy to modify the information dependent on a certain data plan if one of its sensors does not reveal the specific mark and prevents aggravation of application plus other interferences. The information aid module is reliable to alter the information support plan sometimes. Leader resource includes portions that will determine resources and then solve and oversee energy saving problems. There is a part called work quality, which generally maintains the consistency connected with programme planning and resource allocation. Just when the resource eye is high in the last several hours, fog resource is assured total versatility. The cloud phase is fostered in terms of total flexibility to get vertical as well as level versatility. The relevant resources when the required pattern is incorporated as a threshold are part of a dispersed resource game plan are an essential problem [13] [14]. The portion, decommissioning and reorganization of the vast number of issues are covered by the fragment of reference distribution. The fog environment is proposed as a utility approach exactly like an environment that is impaired. In a poor environment, the customer requires all cloud organizations, but in the fog environment the customers connect with the structure of the fog to those of the companies, whilst the middleware in the fog handles and preserves all communication connected with cloud. The customer who wants to relate to assistance should thus be supported. To provide assurance that everyone involved with absolute free styles in the fog will be necessary to have the approval. This is essential to maintain security, through encryption across different transactions, to minimise disturbances with malicious clients. The encryption element will definitely jumble different IoT and the specific cloud links. Most fog pieces are connected by a remote-control connection, which is important in terms of safety management. The specific facts relating to completely free designs must not be revealed throughout the fog environment, yet it is essential to safeguard client information. Most adroit town organizations or sharp homes have problems since client data are not to be revealed in their systems. Customers absolutely comprehend virtually any security strategy without providing them a genuine reading within the current conditions. It is therefore essential that these organizations, where the customer's safety relationship is vital, examine all apps that have lethargy as a problem and have used the fog atmosphere for all reasons. These are part of virtually any utility company that may aid fog to give greater assistance and cuts. A programme that employs more news can establish fog, as it will shift the globe today.

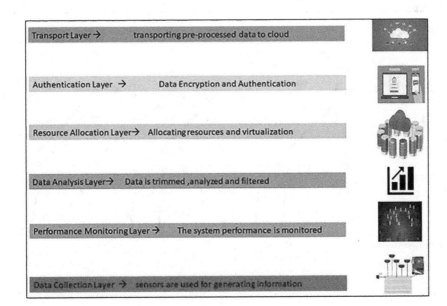

FIGURE 12.3
Layered architecture of fog computing.

12.4 The Role of Fog Nodes in Fog Computing

Usually this is a major distinction in edge processing. Near the end of the day, the fog IoT application may select what typically is the best data evaluation location, which can be used for the data assessment and send them there for a short amount of time afterwards. Fog centres might be either real or even virtual components; thus, the sharp contraptions or even access affiliations are very well combined.

For the unique opportunity that the data is often time-touchy at a sensitive level it is effectively sent out from the fog region that is normally closest to the data-assembling stage of the evaluation. The special chance that it's less time fragrant is nothing but a fog-acquiring centre, and if it isn't a general feeling, it may just go to the cloud for enormous information evaluation among others (Figure 12.4). Different forms might come from the unique fog local location. There is the cut-off equipment to accomplish what needs to be done at the specific edge, and it might be a fog nearby. A fog location point may also be found in several places: for example in the event of openness, a particular development line with an oil plant or in the vehicle. In case of a fog set criteria to accomplish in milliseconds or presumably within an timeframe, an efficient framework need to be set up.

12.5 Fog Computing with the IoT

Fog computing is concerned with these problems. It is anything other than a continuously virtualized paradigm in which cloud workers operate with, accumulate, and create resources. In addition, most of the information conveyed by these IoT contraptions should

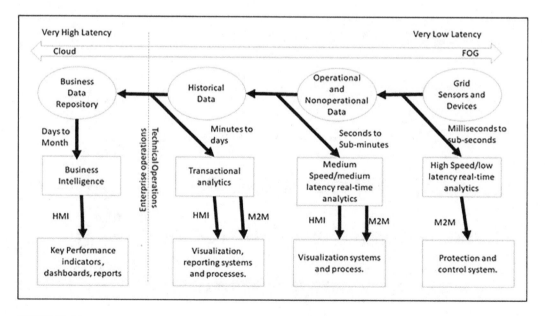

FIGURE 12.4
Analytics for fog computing.

be updated and rapidly decommissioned in order to increase the amplitude of IoT requests. Fog computing looks at and collects a smashing point and interference network up to a specific association edge to deal with the rapid issue of IoT and complete IoT warranty. Fog processing provides a complete licencing arrangement to various applications and firms. In the middle of a few IoTs that mention things such as linked cars, the fog can pass persuasive short tranny. The analysis of fog computing is the superior solution for applications with reduced time demands such as increased realism, fluctuating press streaming and game playback, etc. The integration of IoT with fog computing has several advantages to various IoT applications. Fog processing helps to reduce support times, particularly with IoT requests that are time fragile, by short contact amid IoT devices. Furthermore, the capacity to restore sensor connections of huge degree is often among the essential components connected with fog computing. Fog computing might give various IoT applications several advantages. This section highlights the distinctive research publications on the interconnection between IoT and fog computing. In this section we assess the current work that has been discussed in different applications regarding IoT and fog computing joints. The manufacturers have maintained an eye on the motive and characteristics of IoT applications. It displays data that can be handled by fog effortlessly by IoT devices. It also conveys the problems of holding up time and block, which can simply be driven by fog. Fog computing will also help in a wonderful way, regulating decentralised and quickly developing the IoT plans, enhancing new businesses inside the network and restricting the results of different programmes connected to network facilitator activity, as well as potential customers. The builders began by contemplating many challenges in the construction of IoT structures and that this is extremely difficult in order to pick issues along with current versions of the business and calculation frameworks. Then we talk about the advantages of the book plan for the structuring of frames, how to cope with them and the limit. Fog computing may be applied to create amazing possibilities for businesses using technical advancements. In this way, the unique framework analyzes the greatest characteristics of fog processing as enough benefits as well as many replies to a couple of IoT issues. The fog computing framework can push the new possibilities in business automation and it can help a traditional business processes to convert into advanced automation based business process.

This gives the cloud a middleware that foreshadows fog that acts without reservation. As a further alternative of fog cells, cloud-based middleware is investigated, tested and organized. Furthermore, the manufacturers suggested a structured fog framework. They passed on software with respect to a breeze farm with a shrewd, light-fitting visitor to look at the qualities of their style. Articles on the regulating causes of fog processing in research content are seldom truly investigated. The process employs the specific task and unambiguously determines resources for control sources and takes into consideration everything. These people stated that they could better regulate their own job to achieve much more specific research and development linked to one another so that they might use fog computing plus IoT to convert to grouped product sales associated with the special impairment of professions. The makers have defined a big improvement problem to prevent the reactivity of available nebulous care. They evaluated their specific design, sometimes simply by differentiating and active approaches, which results in a fall in inactivity. The manufacturers have evaluated the best way of restoring IoT devices, which are generally resource-focused barriers. In addition, three motivating situations with WSNs, clever automobiles, and clever organizations will be presented, showing that fog's activities may be used for a few useful purposes and organizations. The fog compact utilises a centre area process to create goods possibly integrated in a professional slave interface, where expert centres use the planning resources to record information from slave centres. Fog provides different advantages for using IoT, as they may collect and work near to the edge of the association. Fog movable rear load changes between the pro-centers to correlate the slave centre points with the stacking master, which updates the whole system's flexibility. The manufacturers have proposed a tonal decreasing approach for fog-related centres that often reduces IoT centre inactivity companies. They proposed a technique of just spreading the local store, which would build up fog-to-fog to convey corporate lethargy. Regarding unload calculations, the specific approach obviously represents simply not just the full line but also a few interest lessons, which otherwise have a distinct estimate time. The unique manufacturer has noticed the basic advances for the viewpoint of the fog. In addition, a flexible phase for tasks in fog computing is provided to provide a start to finalise operations of fog about the requirement that the cycle be determined. Furthermore, these folks presented a case for using IoT environmental factors to relax the prosperity problem by fog computing in confirmatory reversal data.

They also considered safety measures to be beneficial in ensuring that the IoT fog emphasises an interest in facilitating the provision of fog computing using diverse protective systems. There are scarcely any research publications considered regarding automobiles and fog computing. A car strategy reported since the transmission with handling business is known as automotive "fog digesting," they are simply recommended by physicians to increase the partnership with clients to finish the transmission and preparation, based on vehicle assets. They are optimistic in connection with this building.

Unused approaches are used by fog vehicles to influence fog computing. In the same vein, the manufacturers expect a cross-cutting design of the fog vehicles to depict the dimensions of policy-making and, for instance, the fog centres in different organizations (Figure 12.5).

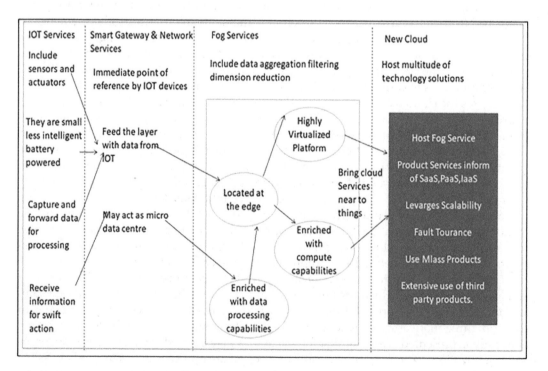

FIGURE 12.5
Fog computing services and components at each layer.

12.6 Integration of Cloud Computing and Fog Nodes IOT with Fog Computing

Fog computing, as shown earlier, promotes the specific CC value and enhances its imperative edge flexibility in conjunction with the principal grouping to make them expandable, non-trivial organizations of computation. Computing is also a key component. Some current updates are showing more massive fog processing. Nevertheless, for fog to operate with the clouds, numerous fogs and points or customers, fog's interfaces should work with versatile treatment and aggregate and manage limitations among these many sorts of substances and their dynamic immigration. This combined an outstanding amount of matching customer evaluation for fog processing organizations and permitted the specific pioneers to fit and maintain strong quality standards. The important thing to discover is to dynamically transmit data and relationships in nebula and cloud. Normality and granularity should determine how the fog or cloud may react to these data and data.

From fog to cloud, it's obvious that it is compulsory for nebula to help obscure and damage nebula support, which provides successive aid. Fog to fog, the focuses should accommodate pooled assets to aid each other and cope. For example, any transmitted fog community is able to share their information collection, computing and processing with an emphasis on focusing on some customer applications. Various fog community focuses can accordingly work closely together for each other's strongholds (Figure 12.6).

The distinctive and unmistakable affirmation of design clarified the interfaces between fog and cloud and IoT by means of an iteratively continual fog structure. The right half of

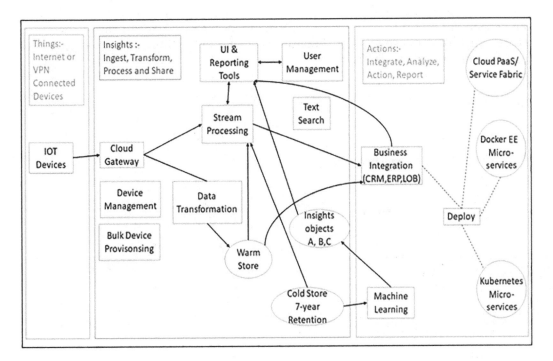

FIGURE 12.6
Component level workflow of fog nodes.

the picture shows an emerging time of progress from round computers to nearly sent fog computing. It also shows what kind of interface is also connected to different time kinds. Around the rest of the graphic, emphasis is drawn to why we have these pressing progressive degrees in solo and in fog computing. Finally, we requires more efforts to make fog computing a general technology that can be adapted by traditional applications also.

12.7 Fog and IoT Application: Smart Farming

IoT-enabled agriculture has executed current mechanical responses for reliable data. It has moreover overcome any hindrance among creation and quality and sum yield. With reliable beginning-to-end brilliant exercises and improved business measure execution, produce gets arranged faster and shows up at general stores in the quickest time possible. Aeris, the IoT establishment, gives precision agriculture associations the advancement to change separated things into related courses of action with significant encounters reliant upon examination to achieve ideal resource use and usefulness at any field, wherever in the world (Figure 12.7).

12.8 Conclusion

Fog computing offers progressively disseminated design that can assist to mix mechanical components and administrations, such as eager urban communities, smart network frameworks, cars linked and sophisticated houses, not so far in the future. The arrangement of fog-based organizations on the bright future is essential to make canny calculations, a

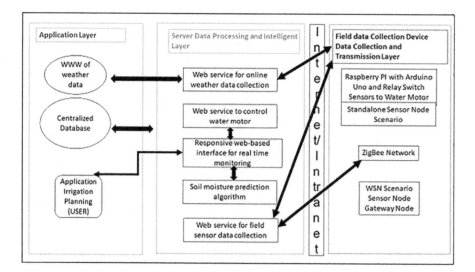

FIGURE 12.7
IoT-based irrigation architecture.

massive inquiry into improved preparations and the identification of strange and danger-ous occasions. Therefore, with the resulting period of the fog computing structure, the fog computing definition should be clarified. To describe and contrast all of fog's features with the previous framework, the fundamental description is required. Fog computing is a compositional development of computing with an asset pool where at least one universal, decentralised hub is reinforced for participation potentially and only excessively in edges in conversation or bunch transmission, rather than cloud preparation. With the implemen-tation of existing important advances, the management of fog systems might be shrewd. Notwithstanding various opportunities of fog computing for company consistency, capa-bilities, cost reductions and so on, there are still numerous challenges in the management phase of contemporary information. Some tonnes, of which the bulk were linked with fog treatment without questions in fundam, have been considered by IoT applications. However, the great majority of the examinations still operate in pause or uncertainty about the expansion and improvement of shrewd city areas, which may be done with mixtures of sophisticated construction.

References

1. Mohammad Aazam, Sherali Zeadally, Khaled A. Harras, Offloading in fog computing for IoT: Review, enabling technologies, and research opportunities, *Future Generation Computer Systems*, 87, pp. 278–289 (2018), ISSN 0167–739X, https://doi.org/10.1016/j.future.2018.04.057.
2. https://labs.sogeti.com/iot-vs-edge-vs-fog-computing.
3. www.embeddedcomputing.com/technology/iot/wireless-sensor-networks/how-fog-computing-can-solve-the-iot-challenges.
4. Hany F. Atlam et al., Fog computing and the Internet of Things: A review, *Big Data and Cognitive Computing*, 2(10) (2018), https://doi.org/10.3390/bdcc2020010.
5. www.rtinsights.com/what-is-fog-computing-open-consortium.
6. www.powersystemsdesign.com/articles/five-reasons-why-your-iot-application-needs-fog-computing/140/14857.
7. A. A. Alli, M. M. Alam, The fog cloud of things: A survey on concepts, architecture, standards, tools, and applications, *Internet Things*, 9, p. 100177 (2020).
8. https://labs.sogeti.com/iot-vs-edge-vs-fog-computing/.
9. J. C. Patni, P. Ahlawat, S.S. Biswas, Sensors based smart healthcare framework using Internet of Things (IoT), *International Journal of Scientific and Technology Research*, 9(2), pp. 1228–1234 (2020).
10. S. Taneja, E. Ahmed, J. C. Patni, I-Doctor: An IoT based self patient's health monitoring system, *2019 International Conference on Innovative Sustainable Computational Technologies*, CISCT 2019 (2019).
11. I. Khanchi, N. Agarwal, P. Seth, P. Ahlawat, Real time activity logger: A user activity detec-tion system, *International Journal of Engineering and Advanced Technology*, 9(1), pp. 1991–1994 (2019).
12. R. Tiwari, H. K. Sharma, S. Upadhyay, S. Sachan, A. Sharma, Automated parking system-cloud and IoT based technique, *International Journal of Engineering and Advanced Technology*, 8(4C), pp. 116–123 (2019).
13. K. Kshitiz, Shailendra, NLP and machine learning techniques for detecting insulting com-ments on social networking platforms, *Proceedings on 2018 International Conference on Advances in Computing and Communication Engineering*, ICACCE 2018, 2018, pp. 265–272, https://doi.org/10.1109/ICACCE.2018.8441728.
14. https://medium.com/yeello-digital-marketing-platform/what-is-fog-computing-why-fog-computing-trending-now-7a6bdfd73ef.

13

Integration and Application of Fog, IoT and Edge Computing

Mohammed Ali Shaik

School of Computer Science and Artifical Intelligence
SR University
Warangal Telangana, India

P. Praveen

SR University Warangal
Telangana, India

T. Sampath Kumar

SR University
Warangal Telangana, India

CONTENTS

13.1 Introduction

This chapter provides a detailed overview of fog, Internet of Things (IoT) and edge computing and their applications in domain of IoT. This chapter introduces edge computing and its applications.

In general, difficulties present in the IoT framework are system delay, network complexity and critical data handling. Fog computing enhances cloud computing and its management to the edge of the system, like cloud. Fog also affords data processing in application administration to end-clients, and stockpiling. Routing the data safely to fog from sensors

DOI: 10.1201/9781003188230-13

where all analytics are being performed at fog, there is no proper routing algorithm in place. Most of the routing algorithms in IoT are targeted at wireless sensor level upto sensor gateway or cluster head and not IoT. Sensors and other objects in IoT communicate to cloud, where a lot of IoT applications and communication methods are to be developed.

IoT protocols and applications do not take into consideration fog computing, as IoT was conceived with cloud as a source for performing analytics. IoT involves heterogeneous type of data which can be health, agriculture, energy, etc. Not a single standard routing mechanism has been developed so far for existing IoT. Handling such heterogeneous data from different sensors or end devices requires minimal levels of analytics for predicting the data pattern and autonomously coordinating among the fog routers for fast data processing and exchange among the objects.

The MQTT protocol is one of the widely accepted protocols in the IoT environment due to its simplicity and reliability features applied to embedded devices. The major advantage of this protocol is the 'publish/subscribe' method, so that clients can enroll in the topics they desire. This protocol is designed in a centralized broker architecture, which again increases latency. To overcome the limitation, a new modified publish/subscribe-based method for edge computing is proposed with a remote broker. In the traditional MQTT, the broker resides at the central place, and it is responsible for all the transactions.

The new upcoming changes in the fog computing require new hardware changes, which increase the system complexity. To overcome these issues, a novel software-defined, multi-tier fog computation model is proposed. In this software design method, the nodes are grouped into three different layers viz., sensing network as layer one, edge/fog level as layer two and data center as layer three. The first layer consists of the sensors and actuators and also the wireless connectivity to the second level of edge/fog level. The novelty of this proposed work is to bring in a systemized four-tier processing methodology in the edge/fog. This method processes each event in all the four tiers. The first tier is the 'publish/subscribe' broker to aggregate the messages from the end devices; the second tier is the critical sensing layer; the third tier is edge computing nodes to perform computing at edge level; and the final tier is intermediate nodes to perform the parallel computing among the available edge computing nodes. The final layer receives the preprocessed data for further processing.

Deep learning offers precise information when associated with further learning algorithms. Similarly, the rapid growth in the area of Internet of Things (IoT) has been taking place, which has many application areas. Moreover by 2025, there will be 60% of data generated by sensors. Edge/fog computing offers the solutions for these challenges.

13.2 Internet of Things (IoT)

Internet of Things is the system of substantial gadgets such as vehicles, home appliances and distinct devices that are associated with the Internet. These procedures are equipped with software, hardware, network, sensors and actuators, which allow these "things" to connect and exchange data [1]. This interconnection opens the door for more upfront coordination of the 'real world things' into computer-based frameworks. This binding improves proficiency changes, commercial advantages and reduced human efforts. A survey conducted in 2017 states that there were 8.4 billion IoT gadgets during that year, and it also appraises that there will be around 60 billion gadgets by the end of 2025 [2]. The worldwide market estimates that IoT is anticipated to be $9.3 trillion by 2025 [3] [4].

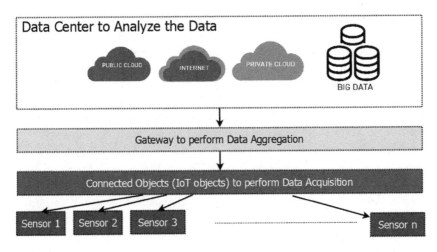

FIGURE 13.1
IoT architecture reference model.

13.2.1 IoT Architecture

Internet of Things shares the existing networking infrastructures along with minor modifications. The IoT allows multiple off-the-shelf products to connect with its network and accept almost all kind of communication protocols, i.e., RF, Bluetooth, Zig Bee, and IEEE 802.11. IoT consists of three different levels [5], which are shown in Figure 13.1, and these levels are explained next.

13.2.2 Technologies

IoT technology stack has been divided into data management and API cloud brokers. These technology stacks are elaborated below:

- **Communication:** This plays a significant role in the IoT by physically linking 'things' to the existing network. This part includes both wired and wireless communication methodologies viz., Ethernet, PLC, Fiber optics, 4G/LTE, IEEE 802.15.4, Wi-Fi, Z-Wave, RFID, Wi-Max, LoWRAN, ZigBee, etc. [6].

- **Backbone:** The backbone of the IoT is the combination of different kinds of networking things viz., IPv4, IPv6, UDP, TCP, and 6LoWPAN. IPv6 over Low Power Wireless Personal Area Networks is called 6LoWPAN. The 6LoWPAN offers header compressions and communicates among different routing techniques that enable IPv6 packets to be sent over IEEE 802.15.4 based network [7].

- **Hardware:** Heterogeneous types of hardware are available in the market. In general, these are classified as Wireless System on Chip (SoC), which are manufactured by Nordic Semiconductor, Gainspan, TI, Wiznet and other manufacturers making independent, RF module setup that has the option to connect using protocols on the chip [8].

- **Protocols:** A various number of IoT protocols exist for data communication in IoT. Among them, MQTT, CoAP, XAMPP, AMQP, DDS and RPL are major ones [9]. These are briefly discussed in the chapter.

- **Software:** In IoT, different kinds of software are coming up with the prototyping boards. The generic software is also available in the market, which will be configured and deployed based on specific operations. RIOT OS is an operating system (OS) for IoT gadgets. This OS is dependent on a microkernel and intended for vitality effectiveness, autonomous equipment improvement and a high level of particularity, which underpins the 6LoWPAN, IPv6, RPL, TCP and UDP. This product has worked for most extreme vitality proficiency and low resource necessities, i.e., Min RAM (~ 1.5kB) and Min ROM (~ 5kB). This OS can work on a few stages both in the installed gadgets and standard PCs. This product likewise focuses on standard programming in C or C++ and can be both 16- and 32-bit processors [10].

- **Cloud Platforms:** These cloud platforms are called data brokers, where the data from IoT end devices are collected and stored in the central storage for future purposes. A vast number of cloud service providers exist in the market, and amongst them, the ThingWorx platform gives polish application schemes, real-time and knowledge condition-enabling associations. Decisions are made by cloud service provider quickly in the M2M and interconnected smart things. 'EVERYTHNG Engine' gives high-scale, mechanical innovation to make and serve a large number of active digital identities (ADI) for an organization's items and different articles. These different online profiles createa constant, exceptional computerized nearness for any real-time interrogation on the web. Open Sense is another open platform for everyone who needs to envision, model and test new devices, installations, scenarios and applications. This is widely used for an immersive world of fashioners, engineers, tinkerers, understudies, specialists, R&D offices, artisans and self-quantifiers [11].

- **Machine Learning:** Machine learning plays a vital role in current generation systems. In the past, machine learning required a massive amount of computational resources, but recent growth in the hardware platforms and optimized machine learning algorithms make it possible to execute machine learning even in resource-constrained devices. The giants like Intel, Google, Microsoft, Nvidia and IBM are introducing small-scale embedded devices for IoT. These chips are powerful when compared to other regular computational devices. This technique enables the machine learning to perform magic in the 'things' [12].

13.2.3 IoT Protocols

- **Constrained Application Protocol:** *CoAP* stands for Constrained Application Protocol, which is built for the low-power networks in IoT. It is a software-based protocol that works on the application layer to use in the constrained Internet-connected devices [13]. CoAP runs over the UDP protocol and satisfies the Representational State Transfer full (RESTful) towards supporting Uniform Resource Identifier (URI) [14]. An overview of nodes connected using CoAP is shown in Figure 13.2. CoAP is a compressed version of the HTTP. In messaging, it supports four different kinds of messages: confirmable (CON), non-confirmable (NON), acknowledgement (ACK), reset (RST).

- **Message Queue Telemetry Transport (MQTT):** This targets gadget data-gathering. From its name, the essential role is telemetry or remote observing. This protocol will collect the information from the various gadgets and transmit this information to a centralized server. MQTT provides a realistic, considerable low-code print that is straightforward and different from the Quality of Services (QoS) level [15]. 'Publish/Subscribe' is the standard for MQTT, where each gadget is associated with a data server. To avoid the data misleading, the MQTT deals with

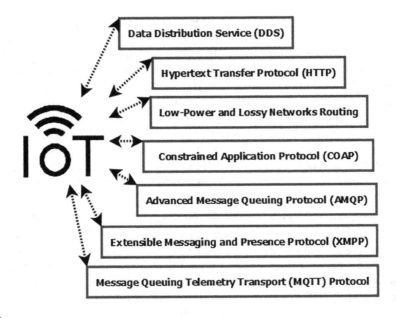

FIGURE 13.2
IoT protocols.

TCP, which gives an unmodified, reliable stream of data [16]. Since the centralized cloud utilizes the data, the whole framework is intended [17] to effortlessly transport data into significant business innovations like Endeavor Service Bus (ESBs) and ActiveMQ [5]. MQTT endows applications such as detecting holes or damages in enormous oil pipelines. The data from a huge volume of sensors deployed in pipelines should be moved into a separate space for further processing. When the application identifies an issue, it will transfer to redress these issues. Various utilization of the MQTT protocol incorporates power utilization monitoring, and even smart agriculture [18]. MQTT shares the demand for information from several sources thatare accessible to other customer applications.

- **Extensible Messaging and Presence Protocol (XMPP):** This was called at first 'Jabber.' It was produced for texting to associate individuals to other individuals using instant messages (IM). XMPP stands for Extensible Messaging and Presence Protocol [19]. This protocol is focused on utilizing the nearness, it implies, with which users are individually associated. XMPP employs the XML content group to exchange information among the entities. Like MQTT, it runs over TCP/HTTP [20]. It is an essential quality that *name@domain.com* plots the boundaries, which act as an indicator in the enormous Internet pile. XMPP provides a simplified operation to address a device in the IoT habitat. This XMPP protocol is particularly convenient and very flexible, which supports both synchronous and asynchronous protocols. It is not intended to be fast. This protocol is mostly utilized in surveying or monitoring for updates. Bidirectional-streams Over Synchronous HTTP (BOSH) offers a methodology to drive information from the customer end [13].

- **Advanced Message Queuing Protocol (AMQP):** This is used to exchange business information amongst various applications and organizations [12]. This protocol interconnects the various systems and then fetches the required information for the business processes and transmits reliable instructions to another end [17]. This evolved from the financial domain as message-driven middleware. This can offer many effective, robust queues of messages. AMQP is centralized, without dropping any messages. Correspondences from the distributors to trades and endorsers utilize TCP, which gives the entirely dependable point-to-point association. Further, endpoints must recognize the acknowledgment of every message [21]. AMQP protocol queues all messages and guarantees each message is conveyed as planned, paying heed to dropped messages and resent again. AMQP is mostly used in business communications. It, as a rule, characterizes 'devices' as handheld tools that exchange information with data centers. AMQP is most suitable for the control-level or server-based discovery capacities in the IoT atmosphere [22].

- **Data Distribution Service (DDS):** As a divergent from the protocols like XMPP and MQTT, the DDS targets gadgets that specifically utilize device information [23]. It circulates data to different gadgets. The DDS's primary role is to associate devices to different gadgets, as it is a message-driven middleware that strongly works on the principles of superior safeguards and modern and implanted applications [24]. DDS is very effective in imparting massive numbers of messages every second to an excessive number of synchronous collectors. Gadgets request different details from the infrastructure. 'Real time' is frequently valued in microseconds. Appliances must exchange information among numerous different appliances in complex ways [25]. Centered point-and-talk is entirely unseemly for gadget data to utilize. Instead, DDS executes guided gadget-to-gadget 'BUS' correspondence with social data demonstration. Real-time innovations (RTI) considers this as a 'data bus,' where it acts as a system administration to a database. This convention precisely does what some superior gadgets need to cooperate as a single framework [26]. Elite incorporated gadget frameworks utilize DDS. It is the main innovation that conveys the adaptability, dependability and speed essential to fabricate unpredictable, ongoing applications. Applications incorporate military frameworks, wind ranches, healing facility mix, medicinal imaging and resource-following frameworks, and car test and security [27].

- **Low-Power and Lossy Networks Routing:** Routing Protocol for Low-Power and Lossy Networks (6LoWPAN) face tremendous challenging issues in routing viz., resource constraints, frequent topology changes and multi-hop networking. Specific application requirements should be considered for both IPv6 and 6LoWPAN components [28]. A good amount of support is provided by RPL protocols for connection layers that are constrained, lossy, etc. RPL is predominantly used in host or switch gadgets with significant benefit in building/home automation and urban applications [29]. It can rapidly develop and organize routes, appropriately learn routes among hubs and adjust the topology in an extremely effective manner. In the most regular setting of RPL, the hubs of the system are connected to the root node or gadgets that are routed in a multi-hop manner. Also, the root node is responsible for data accumulation and coordination [30]. For every topology, a Destination Oriented Directed Acyclic Graph (DODAG) is made by representing join costs, hub qualities/status data and an objective function that maps the improvement of the actual situation. RPL can incorporate various types of activities, and the data exchanged among hubs are flagged that rely upon the prerequisites of the data streams [19]. Point-to-Point

TABLE 13.1

Comparison of IoT Protocols

Protocol	Transport	Messaging	Content Awareness	Applicable	Security	Fault Tolerance
CoAP [6]	UDP	Request/ Response	None	D2D	DTLS	Decentralized
MQTT [7]	TCP	Publish/ Subscribe	None	D2C	TLS	Implementation Specific
XMPP [8]	TCP	Request/ Response	As per sensor data	D2C, C2C	TLS	Centralized
AMQP [9]	TCP	Publish/ Subscribe	None	D2D, D2C, C2C	TLS	Implementation Specific
DDS [10]	UDP, TCP	Publish/ Subscribe	As per content query	D2D, D2C, C2C	TLS, DTLS	Decentralized
LPLNR [11]	UDP	Publish/ Subscribe	None	D2D, D2C, C2C	TLS	Decentralized
HTTP [12]	UDP, TCP	Request/ Response	None	D2C	DTLS	Implementation Specific

(P2P), Point-to-Multipoint (P2MP) and Multipoint-to-Point (MP2P) communications are supported in RPL. Comparison of these IoT protocols are presented in Table 13.1.

13.2.4 IoT Challenges

The most adaptable five factors that lead to growth and development as well as major concerns of the Internet of Things, which are to be overcome to generate everlasting productivity and prosperity through these incredible technologies, are:

- **Security:** Security attacks over IoT devices are penetrated by expanding the attack surface due to day-by-day increase in cybercriminals who penetrate a secured network to crack it and get access to the sensitive materials or information. The major concern lies with IoT devise users to fix the security issues that lead IoT devices towards potential security threats that are supposed to be patched or updated and protected when dealing with computers and smartphones.

- **Regulation:** Government regulation is one of the major characteristics in innovations, as it may lead to huge concerns if not followed, which may take a great deal of time to catch up with where present technology is concerned. Due to immense upgradation in the field of IoT, the required time in attaining the norms of government is also considered to be crucial information for handy decision-making.

- **Compatibility:** Most of the competitors are emerging in the field of IoT with no exception, as competition creates many choices for consumers, which leads to frustrating compatibility issues, though Bluetooth technology is more compatible with IoT device standards (such as home automation) and to be related to mesh networking, with many competitors to challenge it.

- **Bandwidth:** Connectivity is a major issue in any kind of technology, including IoT, due to an increase in end users of IoT and its applications. Similar to audio/video streaming, it is a considerable challenge to the present client-server model, which uses a central server to direct traffic by authenticating the requests received over IoT networks.

- **Customer expectations:** Most of the IoT startups are facing issues such as under-promise and over-deliver aspects with dynamic customers' expectations, which tend to change a lot. This may lead to complete system failure when the expectations are not met.

13.3 Edge/Fog Computing

Due to huge demand and usage in IoT devices that performs exchange of information and networking in the present cloud architecture which is not capable of handling the flood of data by offering any type of cloud extensively to perform computation or storage for performing the user connectivity process for accessing data on cloud efficiently and economically. These centralized resources are capable of creating remarkable delays that lead to lack of performance in the devices that are located far away from a centralized cloud, such as a data center or a data grid.

Edge computing, otherwise called merely "edge," does processing near the data source, and should not transmit to the remote cloud or other unified frameworks for handling. The time it requires to move data to the source is reduced, which enhances the speed and execution of data transmission [29].

Fog computing is a standard that characterizes how edge processing should function. It also encourages the task of figuring, stockpiling and system administration benefits between end-to-end devices, where data values are identified in the cloud. Furthermore, fog off-loading the cloud for edge processing [30] can resort to many applications.

There is a range of critical abilities that edge can provide for Industrial IoT (IIoT) applications considering the prerequisites of the current issues, as enunciated by the accompanying instances found in regular mechanical tasks [18]. With edge, PC and capacity frameworks dwell at the edge also, as close as conceivable to the segment, gadget and application or human that creates the data being handled. The objective is to minimize latency because the data need not be sent from the edge of the system to a central organizing framework and back to the edge [3].

13.4 Need for Edge Computing

Edge computing is the process of distributed computing foundation where processing of assets and application is administrated along with the correspondence of the basis of data to the cloud with computational necessities that can be fulfilled at the edge, where the data is gathered, or where the client performs specific activities. The advantages are recorded underneath.

13.5 Challenges in the Edge Computing/Fog Computing

- Data management is a critical challenge faced by fog/edge computing as data is generated from various data sources. Data management by the resource-constrained devices needs to be taken care of sensitively [14].

- Latency reduction is a vital feature of fog computing, but this makes some delay in the request processing when a massive number of requests happen [15].

- Heterogeneity is an unavoidable feature in the IoT environment, and most of the edge devices are designed for specific end devices and custom applications [5].

- Modification in the existing IoT protocols is required. The current IoT data communication protocols are designed for the IoT end devices that are directly communicating to the cloud servers and receiving responses from the cloud resources. So, this calls for modifications or the introduction of new protocols for edge/fog computing [16].

- The existing IoT application is deployed in an application-specific manner [18].

- Mobility is another major challenge in the edge computing environment because most of the end devices are resource-constrained and adhoc in nature [19].

- The QoS requirement varies for each application. Some applications require the highest priority, and even millisecond delays may cause massive damage, for example, automated self-driving cars [20].

- Security plays a vital role in the IoT devices when localized devices are introduced to the process. The safety of the processing device will be a questionable one. Previously these requests were processed in the centralized cloud environment [31].

- Scalability is an inescapable feature in edge computing due to adhoc function where the end devices are handled dynamically [32].

13.6 Applications of Fog and Edge Models

The following are some of the applications available and most often used in the present era of IoT devices with fog and edge computing.

- **Linked vehicles:** Most of the self-driven vehicles are presently available in the market and tend to produce significant volumes of data where the information has to be easily interpreted and processed based on traffic driving conditions over a specific environment in which to process data quickly with fog computing aid.

- **Smart grids and smart cities:** Energy networks comprise of most of the real-time data which is used to managing IoT process efficiently as the remote data located with multiple sensors that are closely associated for resolving all sorts of problems related to IoT using fog computing.

- **Real-time analytics:** Transfer of data using fog computing that is being deployed from any location with real-time analytics attained by financial institutions in a production network can be analyzed.

- **LiveMap:** One scalable mobile information system is LiveMap, which synthesizes vehicular update streams by performing fine-grain or deep-zoom details with conditions such as 'Dead cat in left lane at GPS location (x,y); here is a proof image' or 'Smoke detected at GPS location (x,y), visibility down to 30 feet' with video proof.

- **Traffic congestion management:** Fog computing provides government bodies a novel weapon in the fight against traffic congestion, as fog is capable of leveraging traffic-related big data in a flexible manner by enabling municipalities and police to take necessary measures.

- **Process manufacturing:** Based on the market supply and sales demand, most of the perishable goods must be capable of meeting the lifecycles of product without losing the products and decaying them. Fog computing provides us with the capability of enabling a digital dual process that tends to replicate most of the key functions by enabling the fog nodes to scale up or down as per the demand and supply by ensuring data privacy.

- **Smart buildings:** In the present era most of the smart buildings are leveraging improved business outcomes due to IoT implementation, such as better services with minimal operational costs. These buildings will be comprised of thousands of sensors generating data all the time, and fog nodes are to be kept at room level and floor level of the building to make it smarter.

- **Real-time subsurface imaging:** In the present era, detecting the minerals or water levels or detecting soil fertility can be performed by understanding subsurface structures by integrating IoT sensor networks with fog computing to perform geophysical imaging, as the scalability feature of fog will enable real-time computation in remote field locations, including support for complex compute algorithms.

13.7 Deployment Models of Fog and Edge

Based on the ownership we can easily classify fog models as per the guideline of fog infrastructure and underlying resources, and there exist four distinct types of fog and edge models. They are:

- **Private fog:** A private fog is created, then owned and further managed and operated by some organization or a third-party organization or some combination of them, and as per the deployment model, resources of private fog are offered for extensive use by a single business unit.

- **Public fog:** A public fog is created, then owned and further managed and operated by some government company or organization or an academic institute or some combination of them, as fog providers deploy by making use of public fog resources that are offered for open usage.

- **Community fog:** The name itself says that this fog is maintained by group of members of various organizations or a third party or a combination of both. This fog can be deployed on or off premises, and exclusive users are offered these resources who share common concerns.

- **Hybrid fog:** A hybrid fog is a combination of any of these fogs, with physical resources and limitations of fog as per the service provider rules that are imposed. In most of the cases the major advantage is that hybrid fog is scalable and can be updated as per the end-user requirement is concerned.

- **Privacy and security:** In the present era, almost all the applications are comprised of personal data, which can be a good input to unintended users, and by this there exists a huge risk. Hence there is a need of secured fog that has its own privacy and security rules and measures as per the trust level of the end user or the third party that provides this service.

13.8 Required Middleware

Due to day by day increase in fog computing applications and users' deployment of fog platforms must be facilitate all the requirements through number of middleware systems that supports flawless application for development of following middlewares:

- **Data stream:** Most of the processing systems were primarily established using the big data community [33]. Though most of the authors also identified that there exists huge interest and demand in fog computing environment by reducing data transfer rate between IoT devices and the cloud [34], as most of the systems have been developed and deployed with distinct variations over a specific provided feature [35].
- **Function-as-a-service:** This middleware supports the process of development that is event-driven, with server less applications that enable various functions or pieces of code to perform a specific task without provision or management of servers based on the adopted architecture by providing function as a service [36].
- **Message-oriented middleware (MOM):** This is a technique that performs communication processes in between software components and the distributed systems that aim to provide support for emitting messages between distributed and heterogeneous components [37].
- **Web application servers:** These are the providers of software frameworks that comprise applications that run at service layers for addressing distinct concerns [38]. In most of the cases, distributed requests over most of the physical servers to manage and develop fog-based tools that facilitate management and programmers for taking services between data centers and end users.

13.9 Conclusion

We introduced the concept of Internet of Things with various architectures evolved so far with technologies of IoT, fog and edge computing in the domain of IoT. Then IoT challenges were illustrated. Edge or fog computing was introduced, along with needs and challenges of edge computing. And further we discussed various applications evolved so far in fog, IoT and edge computing, and further we illustrated the deployment models of these applications in detail along with the required middleware.

References

1. A. Yousefpour, C. Fung, T. Nguyen, K. Kadiyala, F. Jalali, A. Niakanlahiji, J. Kong, and J. P. Jue, "All one needs to know about fog computing and related edge computing paradigms: Acomplete survey," *Journal of Systems Architecture*, vol. 98, 2019, pp. 289–330.

2. Flavio Bonomi, Rodolfo Milito, Jiang Zhu, and Sateesh Addepalli, "Fog computing and its role in the internet of things," *Proceedings of the First Edition of the MCC Workshop on Mobile Cloud Computing* (MCC '12). Association for Computing Machinery, New York, NY, 2012, pp. 13–16. https://doi.org/10.1145/2342509.2342513

3. L. Vaquero, "Finding your way in the fog: Towards a comprehensive definition of fog computing," *ACM SIGCOMM Computer Communication Review*, vol. 44, no. 5, 2014.

4. OpenFog Consortium, "OpenFog reference architecture for fog computing," 2017, www.openfogconsortium.org/ra/

5. R. Mahmud, R. Kotagiri, and R. Buyya, "Fog computing: A taxonomy, survey and future directions," in: Di Martino B., Li K. C., Yang L., and Esposito A. (eds) *Internet of Everything. Internet of Things (Technology, Communications and Computing)*. Springer, Singapore, 2018. https://doi.org/10.1007/978-981-10-5861-5_5

6. IEEE Standards Association, "IEEE 1934–2018—IEEE standard for adoption of OpenFog reference architecture for fog computing," 2018, https://standards.ieee.org/standard/1934-2018.html.

7. X. Chen, "Decentralized computation offloading game for mobile cloud computing," *IEEE Transactions on Parallel and Distributed Systems*, vol. 26, no. 4, 2014.

8. Mohammed Ali Shaik, T. Sampath Kumar, P. Praveen, and R. Vijayaprakash, "Research on multi-agent experiment in clustering," *International Journal of Recent Technology and Engineering IJRTE*, vol. 8, no. 1S4, June 2019, pp. 1126–1129.

9. H. Atlam, R. Walters, and G. Wills, "Fog computing and the Internet of Things: A review," *Big Data and Cognitive Computing*, vol. 2, no. 2, 2018.

10. P. Praveen, C. J. Babu, and B. Rama, "Big data environment for geospatial data analysis," *2016 International Conference on Communication and Electronics Systems (ICCES)*, Coimbatore, 2016, pp. 1–6, doi:10.1109/CESYS.2016.7889816.

11. P. Praveen, and Ch. Jayanth Babu, "Big data clustering: Applying conventional data mining techniques in big data environment," *Innovations in Computer Science and Engineering, Lecture Notes in Networks and Systems*, vol. 74, 2019, Springer, Singapore, ISSN 2367–3370, https://doi.org/10.1007/978-981-13-7082-3_58.

12. R. Ravi Kumar, M. Babu Reddy, and P. Praveen, "Text classification performance analysis on machine learning," *International Journal of Advanced Science and Technology*, vol. 28, no. 20, 2019, pp. 691–697, ISSN: 2005–4238.

13. Mohammed Ali Shaik, "Time series forecasting using vector quantization," *International Journal of Advanced Science and Technology IJAST*, vol. 29, no. 4, 2020, pp. 169–175.

14. R. Ravi Kumar, M. Babu Reddy, and P. Praveen, "An evaluation of feature selection algorithms in machine learning," *International Journal of Scientific & Technology Research*, vol. 8, no. 12, December 2019, pp. 2071–2074, ISSN 2277–8616.

15. P. Praveen, M. A. Shaik, T. S. Kumar, and T. Choudhury, "Smart farming: Securing farmers using block chain technology and IOT," in: Choudhury T., Khanna A., Toe T. T., Khurana M., and Gia Nhu N. (eds) *Blockchain Applications in IoT Ecosystem*. EAI/Springer Innovations in Communication and Computing, Springer, Cham, 2021. https://doi.org/10.1007/978-3-030-65691-1_15

16. P. Praveen, and B. Rama, "An empirical comparison of Clustering using hierarchical methods and K-means," *2016 2nd International Conference on Advances in Electrical, Electronics, Information, Communication and Bio-Informatics (AEEICB)*, Chennai, 2016, pp. 445–449, doi:10.1109/AEEICB.2016.7538328.

17. P. Praveen, C. J. Babu, and B. Rama, "Big data environment for geospatial data analysis," *2016 International Conference on Communication and Electronics Systems (ICCES)*, Coimbatore, 2016, pp. 1–6, doi:10.1109/CESYS.2016.7889816

18. R. K. Naha, S. K. Garg, D. Georgekopolous, P. P. Jayaraman, L. Gao, Y. Xiang, and R. Ranjan, "Fog computing: Survey of trends, architectures, requirements, and research directions," *CoRR*, vol. 6, 2018, http://arxiv.org/abs/1807.00976.

19. P. Praveen, and B. Rama, "An empirical comparison of Clustering using hierarchical methods and K-means," *2016 2nd International Conference on Advances in Electrical, Electronics, Information, Communication and Bio-Informatics (AEEICB)*, Chennai, 2016, pp. 445–449, doi:10.1109/AEEICB.2016.7538328.

20. Wenlu Hu, Ziqiang Feng, Zhuo Chen, Jan Harkes, Padmanabhan Pillai, and Mahadev Satyanarayanan, "Live synthesis of vehicle-sourced data over 4G LTE," *Proceedings of the 20th ACM International Conference on Modelling, Analysis and Simulation of Wireless and Mobile Systems (MSWiM'17)*, Association for Computing Machinery, New York, NY, USA, 2017, pp. 161–170. doi:https://doi.org/10.1145/3127540.3127543

21. P. Praveen, and B. Rama, "A novel approach to improve the performance of divisive clustering-BST," in: Satapathy S., Bhateja V., Raju K., and Janakiramaiah B. (eds) *Data Engineering and Intelligent Computing. Advances in Intelligent Systems and Computing*, vol. 542, Springer, Singapore, 2018.

22. Kiryong Ha, Zhuo Chen, Wenlu Hu, Wolfgang Richter, Padmanabhan Pillai, and Mahadev Satyanarayanan, "Towards wearable cognitive assistance," *Proceedings of the 12th Annual International Conference on Mobile Systems, Applications, and Services (MobiSys'14)*. Association for Computing Machinery, New York, NY, USA, pp. 68–81, 2014. doi:https://doi.org/10.1145/2594368.2594383

23. Mohammed Ali Shaik,"A survey on text classification methods through machine learning methods,"*International Journal of Control and Automation IJCA*, vol. 12, no. 6, 2019, pp. 390–396.

24. P. Praveen, and B. Rama, "An efficient smart search using R tree on spatial data," *Journal of Advanced Research in Dynamical and Control Systems*, no. 4, ISSN1943–023x.

25. OpenFog Consortium, "Out of the fog: Use case scenarios (live video broadcasting)," 2018, www.fogguru.eu/tmp/OpenFog-Use-Cases.zip.

26. Mohammed Ali Shaik, and Dhanraj Verma, "Enhanced ANN training model to smooth and time series forecast," *IOP Conference Series: Materials Science and Engineering*, vol. 981, 2020, p. 022038, https://doiorg/101088/1757-899X/981/2/022038.

27. P. Praveen, B. Rama, and T. Sampath Kumar, "An efficient clustering algorithm of minimum Spanning Tree," *2017 Third International Conference on Advances in Electrical, Electronics, Information, Communication and Bio-Informatics (AEEICB)*, Chennai, 2017, pp. 131–135, doi:10.1109/AEEICB.2017.7972398.

28. Swarnava Dey and Arijit Mukherjee, "Robotic SLAM: A review from fog computing and mobile edge computing perspective," *Adjunct Proceedings of the 13th International Conference on Mobile and Ubiquitous Systems: Computing Networking and Services (MOBIQUITOUS)*, Association for Computing Machinery, New York, NY, USA, pp. 153–158. 2016. doi:https://doi.org/10.1145/3004010.3004032

29. P. Praveen, B. Rama, and T. Sampath Kumar, "An efficient clustering algorithm of minimum Spanning Tree," *2017 Third International Conference on Advances in Electrical, Electronics, Information, Communication and Bio-Informatics (AEEICB)*, Chennai, 2017, pp. 131–135, doi:10.1109/AEEICB.2017.7972398.

30. Mohammed Ali Shaik, and Dhanraj Verma, "Deep learning time series to forecast COVID-19 active cases in INDIA: A comparative study," *IOP Conference Series: Materials Science and Engineering*, vol. 981, 2020, p. 022041, https://doi.org/101088/1757-899X/981/2/022041.

31. Cisco, "Enabling MaaS through a distributed IoT data fabric, fog computing and network protocols," *White Paper*, 2018, https://alln-extcloud-storage.cisco.com/ciscoblogs/5c0a6ea91edbb.pdf.

32. B. Thomas, B. Close, J. Donoghue, J. Squires, P. Bondi, M. Morris, and Wayne Piekarski, "ARQuake: An outdoor/indoor augmented reality first person application," *4th International Symposium on Wearable Computers*, 6, 2000, pp. 139–146. 10.1109/ISWC.2000.8884802000.

33. P. Hu, S. Dhelim, H. Ning, and T. Qiu, "Survey on fog computing: Architecture, key technologies, applications and open issues," *Journal of Network and Computer Applications*, vol. 98, November 2017.

34. S. Kyriazakos, M. Mihaylov, B. Anggorojati, A. Mihovska, R. Craciunescu, O. Fratu, and R. Prasad, "eWALL: An intelligent caring home environment offering personalized context-aware applications based on advanced sensing," *Wireless Personal Communications*, vol. 87, no. 3, 2016.

35. Mohammed Ali Shaik, and Dhanraj Verma, "Agent-MB-DivClues: Multi agent mean based divisive clustering," *Ilkogretim Online—Elementary Education*, vol. 20, no. 5, 2021, pp. 5597–5603, doi:10.17051/ilkonline.2021.05.629.

36. Mohammed Ali Shaik, Dhanraj Verma, P. Praveen, K. Ranganath, and Bonthala Prabhanjan Yadav, "RNN based prediction of spatiotemporal data mining," *IOP Conference Series: Materials Science and Engineering*, vol. 981, 2020, p. 022027, https://doiorg/101088/1757-899X/981/2/022027.

37. P. Praveen, and B. Rama, "An efficient smart search using R Tree on spatial data," *Journal of Advanced Research in Dynamical and Control Systems*, no. 4, 2017, ISSN:1943–023x.

38. P. Praveen, and B. Rama, "A novel approach to improve the performance of divisive clustering-BST," in: Satapathy S., Bhateja V., Raju K., and Janakiramaiah B. (eds) *Data Engineering and Intelligent Computing. Advances in Intelligent Systems and Computing*, vol. 542. Springer, Singapore, 2018.

14

The Role of Block Chain in Fog Computing

Tanupriya Choudhury

School of Computer Science
University of Petroleum and Energy Studies
Dehradun, India

Rohini A

Department of Artificial Intelligence & Data Science
Miracle Educational Society Group of Institutions
Vizianagaram, Andhra Pradesh, India

CONTENTS

14.1 Introduction: Background and Driving

The block chain in fog computing applications can change the wonders of the driven technologies to operate the decentralized framework. It aims to process faster to the end-nodes. This framework has supported enhancing security, lessening energy consumption and safety. To integrate block chain in fog computing, the distributed trust management criteria have been proposed along with security and reliability. In this approach, the study has given the roles of security management mechanism and analysis of block chain in fog computing integration. By using key-management techniques the study has discussed and clarified the vision of the integration of block chain in fog computing. The integration of block chain in Fog computing bring towards the directions of future research directions.

DOI: 10.1201/9781003188230-14

The block chain [1] [2] is the way to arrange the list of records in the centralized structure. Each list is a block; it contains a timestamp and transaction data in the chain. Get the data in the blocks using hashing techniques [3]. The role of block chain [4] [5] in fog computing can be used in four scenarios [6] [7] [8]:

- When extensive storage and decreased access are required
- When more services are needed in a large area with different demographics
- When computational processing is subjected to use block chain in fog computing
- When IoT devices have used the applications for fog computing [9]

The block chain (BC) based fog computing (FC) gives service to a specific vendor of a decentralized storage system [10]. The network nodes are contributing their space to store the data and demand the space for each node. For strengthening security, encrypted data and cipher text are distributed to the nodes to hide the location.

The encrypted location of information (LoI) has been maintained by the block chain as metadata [19]. The data are stored and managed securely. The access permission has been given by the data owners. This mechanism is said to be factual decentralized storage. However, data sharing has been related to two cases: (1) the architecture is not related to traditional data sharing; and (2) encrypted data sharing needs compatible protocols for block chain key management [11].

In the decentralized storage system, key-management (KM) and data sharing mechanisms have been compatible with BC-based FC. Proxy re-encryption is used to cipher text transformation for key-sharing under untrustworthy environments [12] [13]. BC-based FC decentralized storage system used for the specific node for the data has been encrypted as ciphertext to secure and strengthen the LoI.

14.2 Block Chain in Fog Computing

The block chain in fog computing applications is widely popular to bring the advanced technologies in artificial intelligence (AI) [20]. BC 4.0 and 3.0 will seek to innovate to improve the transparency, adaption, and integration with the AI. BC 3.0 has been used to fix the flaws in the earlier framework of block chain technology. Block chain in fog computing has used the AI techniques and algorithm. It's said to be BC 4.0. It innovates the ability to improve the data without affecting the mass adaption and transparency.

Characteristics of Block Chain in Fog Computing:

1. *Decentralization*—Functioning nodes in the block chain need maintenance. Each node has the same prominence; nodes will not affect the entire operating system. There is no centralized functional management in the block chain.

2. *Dependence*—According to the protocols of BC, dependence nodes were established, and the reliance between the links and collaborated and interaction can be accomplished.

3. *Privacy*—The block chain users are corresponding the transaction by the public key address without illuminating the real identities.

4. *Tamper resistant*—Entire blocks in the chain have been verified at a certain time by the higher security of the resistance in the system.

5. *Traceability*—Each transaction on the structure is cryptographically related to adjacent blocks. So the transactions are traceable.

14.3 Security Analysis

FC is lighter, faster, and more energy efficient in the distributed network. Smart devices act as a node in fog computing. The challenging study in the era BC 4.0 is how to incorporate the BC framework in FC. By the traditional block chain security analysis, crypto currency mining has not been restricted in the fog computing edges [14]. It provides cross-platform support for several BC framework operating systems.

The framework of security analysis is described in detail here:

1. Data storage—While uploading the data, the data has encrypted before upload, so the hackers can't hack the data in the stored files.
2. Interfere—To interfere the encrypted files with the precipitate of chaos coding in order to decrypt the data without obtaining an appropriate chaos code.
3. Theft prevention—The encrypted files are calculated by using the repeated hash values. It is required for decryption. According to the rule of hashing, consider the obtained values are corrupted by the hacker. If the owner can't retrieve the file means, the key management mechanism has been supported to ensure the source file and the user data security in all LoI.
4. Data privacy—The authorized owner makes the access policy for storing the data in block chain. The relevant data and requirements are encrypted by chaos coding. The end-users are required to request access from the owner for the data access.

14.4 Security Mechanism

The problem under BC has primarily been based on the storage structure. The data sharing techniques were based on the cloud service providers in the centralized mechanism. The chain of records were authorized by the owners and allowed the sharing process of the service vendors. The user's untrustworthy mechanism cannot be carried in the structure. Scott and Ellis [15] has discussed their support of encryption before communication and decrypted the receipt. Further, if facts are united in the encrypted shape, the authorized owner should decrypt the data keys to others; the security of the authorized user's information is untrusted or needs key management techniques to encrypt each block of records in the structure with the unique key.

Encryption was used to secure the recoded files in a BC-based cloud storage. Those record chains are listed in the meta-data so that owners' file statistics can be analyzed. For security, a decryption key and the LoI are shared with each authorized user. The data that will be shared will be encrypted and stored in the cloud [16]. While retrieving the file to download, request permission from the authorized owner, decrypt, re-encrypt and re-upload.

To addresses the difficulties of the sharing method, proxy encryption was chosen, and a cypher textual data mechanism was used for transformation.

14.5 Security Mechanism

The security of the meta key model has been analyzed in the section. It proves naturally from attack of collusion and proxy encryption development.

14.5.1 Meta Key Model

In the context of the meta key model, two series are discussed and shown in Figure 14.1. First stage is indistinctly of cipher text LoI. The hackers do not determine the cipher text file owner and could not find the target by the mechanism of decryption key management [17]. Eventually, the second series discussed is the security layer.

14.5.1.1 Series 1. Cipher-Text LoI Security

1) Formulating process. 'A' pretender 'C' selects the (L) location = l from 'n' in probable of nodes. 'A' hides the file cipher text, pretender 'C, into' l'.

2) The Hacker 'A' unable to read the file cipher. 'A' thinks (L) in the target cipher text of Information is 10 for his Target Cipher Text by his own.

3) If l = 10, shows, 'A' hacks the 'C' information. The 'A' has defined the event probability P (l=10)-1, where 'P' refers to attacker's cipher text LoI Security.

14.5.1.2 Series 2. Security of Cipher Text LoI

The possibility of attacker 'A' is ignorable. The 'D' has requested to N1 in the meta-key. The original nodes were stored in the cipher text 'C', and to encrypt again 'C' as 'C$^{l'}$. The proxy has sent 'C$^{l'}$ to M2 and read M2 from C^l. In this situation, the 'L' of M2 has been revealed 'D' and M1.

We have a corollary:

14.5.1.3 Corollary 1

C for D and M2, C$^{l'}$ for M2 are both Cipher Text LoI.

Proof: It states that both D and M2 has no LoI of C, so they are Cipher Text LoI. M2 knows C$^{l'}$ comes from M1; it does not know the information of 'D'. Besides, C and C^l are indistinguishable to M2, if the cipher-text has not been read. C^l is the Cipher Text of LoI to M2.

14.5.2 The Collision Attack

In effect of class 'C' and 'C$^{l'}$ for a single node has been proved in Corollary 1. Wilkson et al., proposed the approach of collision attack in the block chain based decentralized

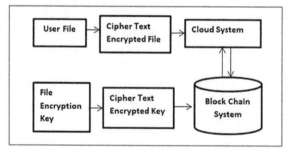

FIGURE 14.1
Key management for block chain-based fog computing.

storage. This study has analyzed the additional nodes and the combined benefits of the unique identities of LoI. Inbetween the malware nodes, if collision happens, the decryption key has been calculated by the expertise of nodes. The decryption key has been calculated by the expertise of R, C, C^l and D decryption keys. Accordingly, R knows the proxy; C collides with D, who is alert of C^l and S. It is susceptible to nodes being shown.

Series 3: The dyads of nodes are associated with prompt nodes. The possibilities are higher than the potential nodes; it has to reach collision. The level of ability to reach the states has followed the following rules:

Rule 1: For delegate D, proxy m1, sharing nodes m2, who can be malicious, they're no longer associates in a different context of the class.

Proof: The Attack of collision between D+m2 and m1 + m2.

14.5.2.1 Corollary 1

C and C^l have belonged to the class of m2. It associates all the nodes. Each C and C^l are class to n2. n2 has no facts to its conspirators. For this reason, the aggregate of D+m2 and m1 + m2 aren't prompted. For m1+D, they can screen statistics of C and C^l to every other, m1 regarded to A, to get the chance for probability of 'D'. There is distinction between to verify the request to follow two questions: "Does 'n1' conserve 'c', to select by way of 'A'?", "Are you the delegate 'D' chosen by 'A'? The attacker of a class sport has equal to the collusion. For this reason, they are now not inspired co-conspirators.

In meta key the proxy function has divided in to m1 and m2, M1 has re-encrypted C with the use of R and sends C^l to m2 and 'D' gets 'C$^{l'}$ from m2. As a result, m1 controls 'C', 'C$^{l'}$' and 'R', while 'D' holds S. Besides LoI of m2 has revealed to m1 and, 'D' through 'A'. Table 14.1 shows how the nodes are precipitated and how the information has been shared in the context.

14.5.3 Roles and Reviews of the Block Chain

TABLE 14.1

Review of Block Chain Technology

Year	Technology	Method	Application
1991–2008	Cryptographically encrypted block chain Crypto currency—Bitcoin	TamperProof Digital form of payment	Used timestamps to track the transactions
2009–2011	Bitcoin	Online purchase	Can enhance digital trust
2012–2014	Bitcoin code base Etherum	Peer-to-peer networking system	Digital marketing
2015–2017	Etherum	Smart contracts	Hyper ledger—modular architecture of the block chain; plugs in any kind of feature and uses it
2018	Cryptocurrencies	Highly volatile	Enterprise communities
2019	Security tokens	Security issues	Legal backups
2020	A great year for block chain technology	Bank digital currencies	Demand for block chain-based skills and tutorial at all-time high

TABLE 14.2

Nodes and Location of Information

Node	Information
D	S, M2
M1	R, C, Cl, M2
M2	Cl

The m2 has revealed to 'D' and m1; m2 can provide neither 'C' for 'D' nor 's' for m1. Therefore, best collusion among m1 and 'D' must be discussed: m1 doesn't realize something about 's' held by way of 'D', nor does 'A' know something about 'C' held by m1. The collusion facts are not exchanged in the in the level of anonymity.

Rule 2: The strategy of proxy encryption has not occurred in the collision, the hardness of collusion delegates the deduction of rule. The brute force algorithm has been applied and verified in the class recreation techniques of meta-key management. It naturally loosens the structure of the Attack of Collision.

14.5.4 Reliability of Data

The reliability of the data chain has been assured in the BC-based FC. The reliability of LoI has used the cipher-text for the proxy encryption and decryption. For authentication of information, hashing has applied to make completeness of nodes in the structure. If any replication has occurred, the node has requested the dependent nodes for re-ensure. Failed nodes are re-encoded and the data has been transferred, proxy encrypted, and ensures all the nodes. The sufficient data has been shared with the requested nodes.

14.6 Block Chain in Fog Computing Challenges

Standardization—Many possibilities are deployed in the BC-based FC systems. This study approaches the integration of BC-based FC looking towards successful integration.

Privacy—To enable the locations certainly enhanced the anonymity and security. These techniques have been adopted in the deployment of BC. The approach of decentralization has been proposed in the integration; it leads to increased security levels and decreased privacy.

Latency—BC-based FC has been beneficial for the different LoI to increase the latency. The energy consumption of BC is not recommended in the time-sensitive environments.

Energy consumption—It is the critical factor to deploy BC-based FC. The proposed study has approached the Brute Force algorithm to challenge the consumption of energy.

Trust—The integrity of BC-based FC implies and integrates a proportion of effort to become a reality. Otherwise, it is not trusted.

Mobility—Healthcare domains are required to solve challenges of mobile adaptive movements of clients. BC in FC smart edges was affected in the role of privacy and latency [18].

14.7 Conclusion

BC was introduced in the year 2009, and in the year 2013 FC was introduced. Several efforts have integrated the two technologies. This study has approached the data-sharing mechanism using meta-key in which nodes LoI has encrypted their data under block chain-based fog computing. Information has been encrypted by owners' public key, which inhibits the process of key management in block chain. Encryption data has been stored in their resolute storage edges, and re-encryption techniques are used for securing shared data in the distrusted environment. Security analysis of this mechanism exposes traffic-free encryption among the nodes with its specified meta-key architecture.

References

1. N. G. Nhu, et al., *Blockchain Applications in IoT Ecosystem*, 2021, Springer. https://doi.org/10.1007/978-3-030-65691-1
2. S. Rawat, et al., "Block chain platforms and smart contracts", in *Blockchain Applications in IoT Ecosystem*, Cham: Springer, 2021, pp. 65–76, https://doi.org/10.1007/978-3-030-65691-1_5
3. Satoshi Nakamoto, "Bitcoin: A peer-to-peer electronic cash system", Cryptography Mailing list at https://metzdowd.com, 2008.
4. P. Maheshwari, et al., "Blockchain technology for hospitality industry", in *European, Mediterranean, and Middle Eastern Conference on Information Systems*. Cham: Springer, 2020, pp. 99–112, https://doi.org/10.1007/978-3-030-63396-7_7
5. A. Sah, et al., "Intelligent mobile edge computing: A deep learning based approach", in *International Conference on Advances in Computing and Data Sciences*, Singapore: Springer, 2020, pp. 107–116. https://doi.org/10.1007/978-981-15-6634-9_112.
6. T. M. Fernández-Caramés, P. Fraga-Lamas, "Towards next-generation teaching, learning, and context-aware applications for higher education: A review on blockchain, IoT, fog and edge computing enabled smart campuses and universities", *Applied Sciences*, vol. 9, no. 21, p. 4479, 2019.
7. R. Iqbal, T. A. Butt, M. Afzaal, K. Salah, "Trust management in social Internet of vehicles: Factors, challenges, blockchain, and fog solutions", *International Journal of Distributed Sensor Networks*, vol. 15, no. 1, 2019, Art. no. 1550147719825820.
8. T. M. Fernández-Caramés, P. Fraga-Lamas, "Towards next generation teaching, learning, and context-aware applications for higher education: A review on blockchain, IoT, fog and edge computing enabled smart campuses and universities", *Applied Sciences*, vol. 9, no. 21, p. 4479, 2019.
9. N. Tariq, M. Asim, F. Al-Obeidat, M. Zubair Farooqi, T. Baker, M. Hammoudeh, I. Ghafir, "The security of big data in fog-enabled IoT applications including blockchain: A survey", *Sensors*, vol. 19, no. 8, p. 1788, 2019.

10. S. Wilkison, J. Lowry, "MetaDisk: Blockchain-based decentralized file storage application", 2014, http://metadisk.org/metadisk.pdf.
11. M. Blaze, G. Bleumer, M. Strauss, "Divertible protocols and atomic proxy cryptography", *Lecture Notes in Computer Science*, vol. 1403, pp. 127–144, 1998.
12. G. Ateniese et al., "Improved proxy re-encryption schemes with applications to secure distributed storage", *Acm Transactions on Information & System Security*, vol. 9, no. 1, pp. 1–30, 2006.
13. G. Taban, A. A. Crdenas, V. D. Gligoret, "Towards a secure and interoperable DRM architecture", *Proceedings of the ACM Workshop on Digital Rights Management 2006*, New York: ACM, 2006, pp. 69–78.
14. G. George, S. Sankaranarayanan, "Light weight cryptographic solutions for fog based blockchain", *2019 International Conference on Smart Structures and Systems (ICSSS)*, 2019, pp. 1–5. doi: 10.1109/ICSSS.2019.8882870, IEEE.
15. Scott R. Ellis, "A cryptography primer", in *Computer and Information Security Handbook* (Third Edition), 2013, pp. 35–58. O'Reilly.
16. R. B. Uriarte, R. DeNicola, "Blockchain-based decentralized cloud/fog solutions: Challenges, opportunities, and standards", *IEEE Communications Standards Magazine*, vol. 2, no. 3, pp. 22–28, 2018.
17. L. Ibraimi et al., "A type-and-identity-based proxy re-encryption scheme and its application in healthcare", in *SDMc 08*, Heidelberg: Springer, 2008, pp. 185–198.
18. M. A. Bouras, Q. Lu, F. Zhang, Y. Wan, T. Zhang, H. Ning, "Distributed ledger technology for eHealth identity privacy: State of the art and future perspective", *Sensors*, vol. 20, no. 2, p. 483, 2020.
19. Stephen Leibel et al., "A review on blockchain technology and blockchain projects fostering open science", *Frontier Blockchain*, vol. 2, p. 16, 2019. https://doi.org/10.3389/fbloc.2019.00016.2019.
20. G. Zyskind, O. Nathan, A. Pentland, "Enigma: Decentralized computation platform with guaranteed privacy", *Computer Science*, 2015.

15

Fog Computing Framework: Mitigating Latency in Supply Chain Management

Rahul Gupta

Amity Business School
Amity University
Noida, India

Ajay Singh

ABES Engineering College
Ghaziabad, India

CONTENTS

15.1 Introduction

Unprecedented growth in international trade has led to the complex multi-echelon supply chains moving enormous quantities of materials across the world. Manufacturers, distributors, warehouses, and retailers process/supply tons of material with terabytes of information. This information is regarding the origin, supplier, intermediaries, buyers, finances, taxes, foreign exchange, and another complex sets of procedures for smooth handling of material and customer expectations. Handling this enormous data with safety and security is a challenging task for organizations.

Cloud computing has evolved from the distributed, parallel grid and supports scalability on virtual/physical allocation, flexible prices, and services. Virtualized resources like operating systems, hardware platforms, storage devices, and networking resources are made available due to the virtualization characteristic of cloud computing. Virtualization supports cloud resources to be available in virtual machines (VM). VM is the environment

DOI: 10.1201/9781003188230-15

to install and run an operating system, matching physical environment, where software can be copied and shared among host servers. Virtualization supports elasticity, on-demand resource allocation, load balancing, and economies through cloud computing. With numerous advantages and widespread utility, the cloud suffers from limited connectivity with end devices, latency-sensitive applications, by Mourandian et al. (2018). Martino (2014) explained that cloud applicants consist of multiple components available with multiple clouds. Inter-cloud communication increases latency due to overhead issues. In the absence of a cloud data center, processing may be done locally.

Technology like Internet of Things (IoT) operationalizes these issues and generates enormous data. These avalanches of data created by IoT are important and tumultuous for prediction, and its analytical functioning was impeccably fingered by cloud computing. Fog computing structure antagonizes these disruptions, with cloud framework and its prevailing accompaniment functionality, based on the placement of small clouds at the immediacy of the data source. Fog computing structure is gaining its acceptance in generating quality data and smart selections.

Fog computing/networking (or fogging) is a program that supports an extended version of existing architecture, supporting computing applications, services, and data for processing that is streamed form the edge through the cloud. Fog advantages are low latency, processing at the edge on a specific location, i.e., fog nodes. In case cloud computing is unable to support, then, in that case, IoT and fog are promising technologies. However, fog computing is beyond IoT computing and embraces content provisioning for communication.

Primarily, networking is controlled by switches and gateways, whereas fog computing creates the configuration and management over the Internet as a backbone, embedded within the LTE network. Fog computing framework illuminates the computing infrastructure with hierarchical computing facilities at server nodes. These nodes organize the services and applications for storing and processing content to support the users. Being conceptually distinct, *fog* and *edge* are used interchangeably, with intelligence and processing abilities to the proximity. The architectural difference among them is their computing ability and its intelligence. Information is transmitted from the same source or physical asset like a relay, sensor, etc., and these devices physically work like an electrical circuit or pump, sensing or switching the commission around. Fog is architectural computing with a pool of resources. Tasks are processed at fog nodes without any interference from a third party. Process collaboration is done with advanced communication, computational flexibility, storage capacity, and additional services in tiered surroundings for rising clients, devices, or users. Issues related to bandwidth, latency, and reliability are getting solutions from fog computing. Fog computing finds its application in transportation, warehousing, logistics, smart cities, healthcare, surveillance, agriculture, military, and many more industries.

15.1.1 Fog Computing Characteristics

Conceptually fog was initiated by Cisco (2014), for supporting cloud to the latency-sensitive, geographically distributed, service applications in the network. *Fog* as a nomenclature is taken from *cloud*, a platform providing storage services, processing, and connectivity among the data center and its users.

Fog capabilities have cognition, agility, security, efficiency, and latency (OpenFog 2017). Mukherjee et al. (2018) determined that fog computing helps geographic distribution, real-time application, ability to process several nodes, wireless access, end device mobility, low latency, awareness of location, and heterogeneity. Various geo-distributed devices like routers, switches, devices used by users, and access terminals are available at the end of network. They are managed in a dispersed manner. Fog computing avoids download/upload data from/to the core network and uses nearby accessible edge devices. Few resources from edge devices are released to support demand from devices in proximity. If a certain task is not possible to process at an edge device, is sent to a core cloud resource.

15.1.2 Fog Definition

Computing is appreciated by various definitions. Vaquero and Rodero-Merino (2014) said fog presents an idea for empowering cooperation and networking among heterogeneous (autonomous, wireless), ubiquitous, and centralized devices—also, among networks and devices for processing and storage requests, in the absence of a third party. A consortium, OpenFog (2017), defines it as an architecture distributing computing services, control, storage, and networking joining along continuum: "A system-level horizontal architecture that distributes resources and services of computing, storage, control and networking anywhere along the continuum from cloud to Things."

IBM (2016) in a report said these computings are considered the same as other computing, but instead of founding channels for cloud utilization and storage, they enable resources and processes at the edge of the cloud. Naha et al. (2018) discussed the technology as a disseminated technology, processed at nonvirtualized/virtualized end or edge devices. Fog computing supports through the cloud for non-latency-aware processes and storing user data for the long term. Definitions discussed here consider processing and storing capacity as fog devices and classify cloud computing in a fog environment.

15.1.3 Fog Computing Architecture

Sarkar et al. (2018) offer a three-tier hierarchical structure: end device, sensor nodes coupled with Internet of Things, and terminal nodes as smart devices as first layer. Computing is performed at the second layer with nodes such as switches, routers, and gateways sharing storage and other resources. The last layer is used for cloud computing, having a cloud data center, offering enough storage, and computing resources. Aazam and Huh (2016) also suggested layered structure, with the following layers: preprocessing, security, virtual monitoring, physical storage, and transportation.

15.1.4 Cloud and Fog Computing Differences

Both are interdependent for computational and storage resources. However, they differ in their computing paradigms. Fog, being a resource-constant device, extends computational and storage support, communication supported by cloud computing near devices. Fog computing is a promising solution for resource-constant devices, whereas cloud computing is high-latency and delinquent in real-time interactions. However, cloud computing offers highly reliable service provisions. Table 15.1 shows the comparison of Fog Computing and Cloud Computing.

Focus on cloud computing is on overall resource optimization, whereas fog computing embraces local resources and management, and enhances overall system efficiency. The success rate is comparatively low due to decentralized management and wireless connectivity. Fog and cloud both contribute to performance enhancement. Some other similar computing paradigms technologies are not exclusively dependent on cloud resources, like mobile cloud computing (MCC), mobile-edge computing (MEC), and edge computing (EC).

TABLE 15.1

Comparison of Fog Computing and Cloud Computing

Parameters	Cloud	Fog
Managerial practices	Centrally managed	Centralized and decentralized
Size	Very large cloud data centers	Numerous small nodes
Latency	High	Low
Resource allocation	Globally	Local
Control	Wireless and fixed both	Generally wireless
Movement	Less	More
Computation capacity	Very high	Low
Mobility	Low	High
Expansion	Lower	Higher
Application type	Non-latency-aware	Latency-aware
Failures	Known chance	Unknown chance
Deployment costs	High	Low

15.2 Fog Computing Applications

Technologies are getting upgraded to support Industry 4.0, and all processes from source to supply are performing better, utilizing intelligent technologies without extra manpower. IoT, drones, and robotics are replacing humans supports. Performance in warehousing, logistics, and supply chain gets enhanced by using technologies.

15.2.1 Warehouse Management

Lin and Yang (2018) described intelligent operations for suppliers' trucks with cargo moving by mobile robots, through RFID gates (supply quantity is auto-confirmed). Robots may shift the material to warehouse by an optimum route plan by avoiding any possibility of collision. They can extract the inventories with RFID tags as per order and transfer to a conveyer for picking. RFID keeps track to confirm the quantity to be shipped and where the uploading on the carrying trucks will be performed by robots.

Big warehouses with large areas to operationalize face latency in communication, among IoT sensors, and clouds. Fog applications are the key for connecting numerous IoT devices in centralized cloud computing. The task is completed efficiently and flexibly by relying on local fog resources. IoT devices reduce power consumption by 40 percent, according to Sakar and Misra (2016).

Cloud offers access to both virtual/physical resources in various models, like Infrastructural (IaaS) Platform (PaaS) Software (SaaS). As a service, it serves as a gateway connecting unsuited services. Fog computing devices transmit information to the cloud through gateways once collected from edges. Edge devices are connected to physical locations. Data are stored and processed temporarily, pass gritty decisions to devices, and communicate with the cloud for analysis and long-term storage.

15.2.2 Supply Chain Management

Value is generated in products and services through various supply chain activities from sourcing of material by guanine suppliers to supply points. Globalization of business activities has added massive data processing from geographically distributed endpoints. Centralized storing and processing are not an optimal solution due to complications in operations, motion applications constraints in equipment, manpower limitations, and various other operating issues in the supply chain. All these issues propagate severe challenges while handling enormous data, however, comparative organizations find cost-saving and revenue opportunities with IoT big data analytics. Analytics support users in sensing what's important for value generation and instantly capture the right values instead of juggling in the flood of data. Analytics engage with customers to enhance new product features, new product development, and open new revenue streams. The remote cloud center may delay the processing for latency-sensitive applications (situation ruins if the critical value exceeds the parameter). Manufacturers use analytics in improving quality and predicting failures and improving responsiveness by enhanced collaborations among complex supply chain partners. Today retail store operate in competitive market, their customer's expectation have increased many folds, they wish to be served 24×7, at a location of their choice and return facility for their purchase. The real-time allocation of merchandise to and from any location is necessary. Networking and computation resources require suitable architecture to split among local sites (temporary storage/processing) and the cloud (for further analysis and storage). Fog computing serves as supply chain support paradigm, according to Musa and Vidyasankar (2017).

15.2.3 Fog Computing Framework Supports Three Levels

0 Level—Data is produced at this level, with the support of RFID readers. Generated information is related to various environmental parameters like sensors, temperature, pressure (external/internal), humidity, and light exposure, etc.

1 Level is the controlling and monitoring layer. Sensors give the readings, which are analyzed through control logic. These encompass alarms, generating events, and may trigger workflows through the intervention of humans or machines. Smart/active readers and trucks are supported by mobile fog nodes as fog devices. These are installed in the fields, on equipment, and in display units in retail. Smart readers store and forward data at a certain interval in case of poor connectivity. This helps and supports intelligence within the reader to provide notifications and alerts in case of failure. Fog node aggregate sensor readings are filtered and kept in a momentary buffer. This layer acts as the first processing hub/stage. Vehicles are fitted with RFID tags which serves as a mobile fog nodes, these tags carry readers, onboard decision support unit (ODSU), and event notification unit (ENU).

Vehicles carry RFID tags as mobile fog nodes, with readers, onboard decision support unit (ODSU) and event notification unit (ENU). OSDU gets sieved dimensions through readers for comparing it with critical values of observed parameters. In case the value exceeds, an alarm is triggered by OSDU and automatic adjustments and corrective measures are performed. After corrective measure, ENU is triggered, which alerts the warehouse/distribution manager.

2 Level is a cloud data center; at this layer the history of supply chain operations is analyzed and stored. The optimal route and quantity of supply to be delivered are determined at this layer.

15.2.4 Application to Support Drone Delivery

Streaming IoT big data offers an important opportunity, and advantages show extrapolative progress as a five-dimension target through smart devices of users in smart industrial development.

1. Time taken for an aerial drone passes a message to the cloud in 8 milliseconds, and during a round trip message, the drone travels roughly 12 feet. Lapsed time may result in a safety threat. Fog-computed drones support autonomous awareness, analysis, and sub-millisecond response for diverse climatical conditions.

2. Drones rely on satellite links for communication to travel to remote areas for delivery and thereby make them cost-prohibitive. However, fog-computing drones access regional fog nodes for diverse climatical conditions and airspace. Fog eliminates reliance on satellite links and ensures remote communication and delivery via new routes.

3. Cooperative behavior can be observed with pre-programmed multiple drones, like supporting oversized packages. Preprograming and cooperative behavior of devices have their limitations. Fog-computing nodes are self-conscious, self-organizing, peer-aware and serve with dynamic community behavior. Individual autonomy of drones is maintained even while working cooperatively.

4. Autonomy is one of the architectural pillars for fog computing, encompassing situational analysis and sub-millisecond response in dynamic situations. Otherwise, cloud connectivity or limited bottom support infrastructure cannot retort erratically in the absence of real-time instructions.

   Mobile fog computing nodes supports onboard intelligence and drone's autonomy.

5. Drone fleets are vital for precious deliveries. Fog computing and its multi-tenancy properties enable drone fleet behavior. Fog computing application software on a drone can be owned by multiple shareholders on a time-sharing basis. Inherent variability in multi-tenancy is handled by fog computing multitenancy. For example, one party may prefer its data in strict privacy, while another may need selective sharing.

Fog computing commands a key role in managing complex supply chains efficiently. Fog orchestrates numerous hand-offs with the chain while authorizing a central cloud to concentrate on historical analytics to determine an optimized supply chain.

15.3 Issues in Fog Computing

Various applications found a wide adoption for fog computing. Like other technologies, fog computing also faces few challenges. Due to many connecting devices, levels in fog layers may face latency issues. So, fog-computing architecture must have a fixed number of tiers. Decisions are based on the requirements of the task available at each level, on the number of sensors, and reliability and capability of fog instruments. Fog computing is heterogeneous and dynamic; resource allocation is a challenge in fog. Fog devices perform their computing on available resources, hence the precision of resources needs to be taken care of.

Software and hardware failure, users' activity, bandwidth, or power source may lead to fog failure. Being decentralized, devices are mobile and prone to failure. For time-sensitive applications, seamless uninterrupted connectivity is required. Different devices follow different protocols; hence a standard communication protocol is essential to operate and communicate with all types of fog devices.

15.4 Conclusion

Fog is an emerging computing paradigm, extensively researched, supporting latency-sensitive applications without traffic congestion, minimum bandwidth, with handsome energy savings. Communication, computation, and storage service get shifted to the edge from the center of the network. We discussed key features and compared fog with cloud, showing that fog is complementary to cloud technology and supports virtualization. A few parallel computing paradigms are also discussed and compared with fog computing. Fog computing applications are discussed in warehousing management, with a fog framework to support the drone delivery, for efficient supply chain management. In warehousing, application of fog computing improves energy efficiency, mitigates latency, subsides cost, and enhances mobility. Additionally, fog supports advanced automation in manufacturing. Fog computation supports improving product quality, availability through production efficiency, prompt decision-making, and condition monitoring. Nevertheless, fog computing offers great potential and wide technological adoption, but fog computing still is an emergent architype. A few challenges with reference to future research are also discussed.

References

Aazam, M., Huh, E. N. (2016). Fog Computing: The Cloud-IoT/IoE Middleware Paradigm, *IEEE Potentials*, 35 (3), 40–44.

Cisco (2014). *Cisco Delivers Vision of Fog Computing to Accelerate Value from Billions of Connected Devices* [Online]. Available: https://newsroom.cisco.com/press-release_content?type_webcontent&articleId=1334100 www.mirrorreview.com/how-fog-computing-can-uplift-the-supply-chain-management-system/

IBM (2016). *What Is Fog Computing?* [Online]. Available: www.ibm.com/blogs/cloud-computing/2014/08/fog-computing/

Lin, C.-C., Yang, J.-W. (2018). Cost-efficient Deployment of Fog Computing Systems at Logistics Centers in Industry 4.0. *IEEE Transactions on Industrial Informatics*, 14 (10), 4603–4611.

Martino, B. D. (2014). Applications Portability and Services Interoperability among Multiple Clouds. *IEEE Cloud Computing*, 1 (1), 74–77.

Mouradian, C., Naboulsi, D., Yangui, S., Glitho, R. H., Morrow, M. J., Polakos, P. A. (2018). A Comprehensive Survey on Fog Computing: State-of-the-art and Research Challenges. *IEEE Communications Surveys & Tutorials*, 20 (1), 416–464.

Mukherjee, M., Shu, L., Wang, D. (2018). Survey of Fog Computing: Fundamental, Network Applications, and Research Challenges. *IEEE Communications Surveys & Tutorials*, 22 (3), 1826–1857.

Musa, Z., Vidyasankar, K. (2017). A Fog Computing Framework for Blackberry Supply Chain Management. *Procedia Computer Science*, 113, 178–185.

Naha, R. K., Garg, S., Georgakopoulos, D., Jayaraman, P. P., Gao, L., Xiang, Y., Ranjan, R. (2018). Fog Computing: Survey of Trends, Architectures, Requirements and Research Directions. *IEEE Access*, 6, 47980–48009.

OpenFog Consortium (2017). *The 8 Pillars of the OpenFog Reference Architecture* [Online]. Available: www.openfogconsortium.org/ra/

Sarkar, S., Chatterjee, S., Misra, S. (2018). Assessment of the Suitability of Fog Computing in the Context of Internet of Thing. *IEEE Transactions on Cloud Computing*, 6 (1), 46–59.

Sakar, S., Misra, S. (2016). Theoretical Modelling of Fog Computing: A Green Computing Paradigm to Support IoT Applications. *IET Networks*, 5 (2), 23–29.

Vaquero, L. M., Rodero-Merino, L. (2014). Finding Your Way in the Fog: Towards a Comprehensive Definition of Fog Computing. *Computer Communication Review*, 44 (5), 27–32.

Index

Note: Page numbers in *italics* indicate a figure and page numbers in **bold** indicate a table on the corresponding page.